HIGH PERFORMANCE COMPUTING

HIGH
PERFORMANCE
COMPUTING

Problem Solving With Parallel
And Vector Architectures

EDITOR

Gary W. Sabot

Sabot Associates, Inc.

Addison-Wesley Publishing Company

Reading, Massachusetts • Menlo Park, California • New York
Don Mills, Ontario • Wokingham, England • Amsterdam • Bonn
Sydney • Singapore • Tokyo • Madrid • San Juan • Milan • Paris

The cover is a three-dimensional perspective view of an incipient tornado simulated using the adaptive grid refinement option of the Advanced Regional Prediction System (ARPS). The ARPS is a scalable-parallel simulation model being developed as a prototype for operational storm-scale numerical prediction in the United States. Only the innermost grid of the four-grid system is shown. Regions of intense rotation about the vertical axis (yellow) are depicted by an isosurface of vertical vorticity, while the storm-relative streamlines are shown in black. Horizontal cross sections through the simulation at the ground and 2 km above the ground are also shown, the colors indicating temperature deviation relative to the environment. Cold air is shown in blues and greens and warm air in reds and yellows. (Photo courtesy of Dr. Ming Xue, Center for Analysis and Prediction of Storms, University of Oklahoma.)

 This book was acquired, developed, and produced by
Manning Publications Co., 3 Lewis Street, Greenwich, CT 06830
Managing Editor: Lee E. Fitzpatrick

Library of Congress Cataloging-in-Publication Data
Sabot, Gary, 1963–
High performance computing : problem solving with parallel and vector
architectures / Gary Sabot
    p. cm.
Includes bibliographical references (p.) and index.
ISBN 0-201-59830-2
1. Electronic digital computers--Programming. 2. FORTRAN
(Computer program language) I. Title.
QA76.5.S215 1995
502'.85'5133--dc20   94-19262
                               CIP

The programs and applications presented in this book have been included for their instructional value. They have been tested with care but are not guaranteed for any particular purpose. The publisher does not offer any warranties or representations, nor does it accept any liabilities with respect to the programs or applications.

Many of the designations used by manufacturers and sellers to distinguish their products are claimed as trademarks. Where those designations appear in this book, and Addison-Wesley was aware of a trademark claim, the designations have been printed in initial caps or all caps.

1 2 3 4 5 6 7 8 9 10 MA 9998979695

Contents

Preface

The purpose of this book is to show by example how to create efficient programs that solve scientific problems on high performance computers. The book is structured as a group of case studies in a variety of problem domains, written by experts in those domains. The process of mapping or transforming abstract problems into concrete solutions that execute rapidly on high performance hardware can seem a mysterious and arcane art; the case studies help dispel some of the mystery. The spectrum of target machines covered ranges from SIMD and MIMD massively parallel machines, through vector machines and networks of workstations, down to desktop workstations.

Each case study chapter describes how to choose and develop appropriate algorithms for solving problems, and then evaluate the resulting implementations. By example, the chapters demonstrate the spectrum of possible parallel solutions and how a programmer can change naive solutions into more efficient ones. Although most chapters center around a single application area, their focus is on demonstrating techniques useful to readers from other application areas rather than on application-specific details. The various application domains were chosen for their general applicability; each chapter presents fundamental techniques.

The chapters emphasize different aspects of the problems encountered in mapping scientific problems onto parallel machines. For example, multiple algorithms or data layouts are evaluated in the context of a single target machine in some of the case studies, while others concentrate on producing a single Fortran 90 code that runs efficiently on multiple architectures. However, all of the chapters have been written according to a single basic outline which covers a set of important core issues, including:

- Introduction
- Application
- Target machine
- Data representation
- Algorithm
- Effects of architecture
- Optimization, tuning, and tradeoffs

Although this book focuses on parallelism, it also applies to a number of important architectures that are not massively parallel, including vector, superscalar, and superpipelined computers and networks of workstations. Several chapters make the initially surprising argument that a parallel description of an algorithm is often the best one for a broad class of architectures, including many not normally thought of as parallel. One reason for this is that a parallel program is easily optimized and vectorized by conventional compiler technology for common processor features, such as overlapped or pipelined functional units.

This book is targeted at a variety of readers—with backgrounds ranging from computer science to physics to financial analysis—who have in common the need to solve a large computational problem on a high performance machine. The chapters of this book are directed to those readers familiar with the computing issues involved in scientific problems, but with little expertise in parallel computing. To understand the programming examples, it is best to have a reading familiarity with Fortran 77 or C. Any book that contains high performance computing examples is almost by definition out of date before it appears, because the field is moving so rapidly. This book presents general concepts and techniques as much as possible, and uses programming examples simply to make the explanations more concrete.

The information presented in this book is important to users of high performance machines. Without it, a scientist struggles to reinvent techniques for achieving high performance that are already known. For example, simple techniques for handling boundary conditions on SIMD or vector machines can double the speed of a finite difference code. Given that high performance machines are expensive and are purchased for their speed, such information is of great value. More indirectly, the information in this book can be valuable to someone evaluating the possible purchase of a high performance computer.

In order to get this information today, scientists often need to work one on one with an expert who has previously solved a similar problem. Many of the same problems and solutions are encountered repeatedly by new users of high performance machines, and by the developers of each new machine. This book gathers together some of the pioneering users of high performance computers and encapsulates their experiences for the reader.

Acknowledgments

My work at Thinking Machines Corporation introduced me to a community of scientists who seek to apply the fastest computers available to a wide variety of important problems. This book would not have been possible had I not been immersed in this fascinating environment, which brought me into contact with many of the people who contributed the chapters that follow.

GARY W. SABOT

About the Editor

Gary W. Sabot received the A.B. and S.M. degrees in Computer Science from Harvard University in 1985, and the Ph.D. degree in Computer Science from Harvard University in 1988. He is the author of the book *The Paralation Model: Architecture-Independent Parallel Programming* (MIT Press, 1988) and has won the Gordon Bell Prize for compiler parallelization. Until the spring of 1994, Dr. Sabot was a Senior Scientist at Thinking Machines Corporation. He is currently performing proprietary consulting work for a number of investment management firms.

Contributors

Guy E. Blelloch
Carnegie Mellon University
Pittsburgh, PA

Connected Components Algorithms

Jack Dongarra
University of Tennessee
Knoxville, TN

Libraries for Linear Algebra

Kelvin K. Droegemeier
University of Oklahoma
Norman, OK

*Weather Prediction: A Scalable
Storm-Scale Model*

Edward W. Felten
Princeton University
Princeton, NJ

Dynamic Tree Searching

John Greiner
Carnegie Mellon University
Pittsburgh, PA

Connected Components Algorithms

Kenneth Johnson
Florida State University
Tallahassee, FL

*Weather Prediction: A Scalable
Storm-Scale Model*

Neng-Tan Lin
Syracuse University
Syracuse, NY

*Weather Prediction: A Scalable
Storm-Scale Model*

Kim Mills
Syracuse University
Syracuse, NY

*Weather Prediction: A Scalable
Storm-Scale Model*

Matthew O'Keefe
University of Minnesota
Minneapolis, MN

*Weather Prediction: A Scalable
Storm-Scale Model*

Steve W. Otto
Oregon Graduate Institute
Beaverton, OR

Dynamic Tree Searching

Allen C. Robinson
Sandia National Laboratories
Albuquerque, NM

Block Grid Application

Gary W. Sabot
Sabot Associates, Inc.
Cambridge, MA

*Introduction; Weather Prediction:
A Scalable Storm-Scale Model*

Aaron Sawdey
University of Minnesota
Minneapolis, MN

*Weather Prediction: A Scalable
Storm-Scale Model*

Courtenay T. Vaughan
Sandia National Laboratories
Albuquerque, NM

Block Grid Application

David Walker
Oak Ridge National Laboratory
Oak Ridge, TN

Libraries for Linear Algebra

Skef Wholey
Sun Microsystems Computer Co.
Chelmsford, MA

*Weather Prediction: A Scalable
Storm-Scale Model; Scalable
Programming in Fortran*

Ming Xue
University of Oklahoma
Norman, OK

*Weather Prediction: A Scalable
Storm-Scale Model*

Stavros A. Zenios
University of Cyprus
Nicosia, Cyprus

*Mathematical Programming and
Modeling*

1

Structured Grid Application

GARY W. SABOT

Contents

Other case study chapters of this book treat a real application in depth, covering multiple approaches, multiple target machines, and the issues that actually arose during implementation. This introductory case study is much less ambitious. It describes a few simple algorithms centered around uniform, structured cartesian grids, and uses them as a vehicle for introducing issues that are covered in greater depth in later chapters. Fortran code is provided for all of the algorithms described. Uniform, structured grids were among the first to be used with high performance computers because of their simplicity, so they are ideal for this purpose.

Grids of many kind and levels of complexity are useful in important applications such as climate or seismic modeling. Later chapters discuss nonuniform and unstructured grids, which address some of the practical shortcomings of simple structured grids.

1.1 Target Machine and Language

This introductory case study maps its structured grid problem onto the data parallel computational model represented by a high-level language, Fortran 90, and relies on compilers to map that onto several different target machines. A key feature of Fortran 90 for high performance computing is that it adds array operations to Fortran 77. Fortran 90 also adds many other features, and most vendors will likely not have full implementations of all of these features for years to come.

Fortunately, subsets of Fortran 90 that include the array features have been implemented on most high performance target machines. These subsets have various names, such as Connection Machine Fortran, High Performance Fortran, Fortran-D, Cray Fortran, etc.[1-4] As many of the later chapters demonstrate, it is possible to write a single program that can work with several compilers in spite of the differences between dialects. In addition, translators such as KAP[†] and NAG[‡] are available that can transform Fortran 90 array syntax into Fortran 77 or C, making Fortran 90 a very portable base for high performance programming.[§]

Fortran 90 Array Features

Much as later chapters describe their target machines, this chapter describes the array features of Fortran 90. The most important feature of Fortran 90 array syntax is that it

---

[†] See the "KAP User's Guide," Kuck and Associates, Urbana-Champaign, IL, 1988.

[‡] F90 Development Group, NAG Ltd., Oxford, U.K. (44.865.511245). U.S. telephone number: 708-971-2337.

[§] Generating a useful translation in the other direction, producing Fortran 90 from Fortran 77 input, is a more difficult proposition, and is discussed in Chapter 8.

STRUCTURED GRID APPLICATION   Chapter 1

$$
a_{i,j} = b_{i,j} + 2 * c_{i,j}
$$

$$
\begin{bmatrix}
a_{1,1} & a_{1,2} & a_{1,3} & \cdots & a_{1,m} \\
a_{2,1} & a_{2,2} & a_{2,3} & \cdots & a_{2,m} \\
a_{3,1} & a_{3,2} & a_{3,3} & \cdots & a_{3,m} \\
a_{4,1} & a_{4,2} & a_{4,3} & \cdots & a_{4,m} \\
\vdots & \vdots & \vdots & \ddots & \vdots \\
a_{n,1} & a_{n,2} & a_{n,3} & \cdots & a_{n,m}
\end{bmatrix}
=
\begin{bmatrix}
b_{1,1} & b_{1,2} & b_{1,3} & \cdots & b_{1,m} \\
b_{2,1} & b_{2,2} & b_{2,3} & \cdots & b_{2,m} \\
b_{3,1} & b_{3,2} & b_{3,3} & \cdots & b_{3,m} \\
b_{4,1} & b_{4,2} & b_{4,3} & \cdots & b_{4,m} \\
\vdots & \vdots & \vdots & \ddots & \vdots \\
b_{n,1} & b_{n,2} & b_{n,3} & \cdots & b_{n,m}
\end{bmatrix}
+ 2 *
\begin{bmatrix}
c_{1,1} & c_{1,2} & c_{1,3} & \cdots & c_{1,m} \\
c_{2,1} & c_{2,2} & c_{2,3} & \cdots & c_{2,m} \\
c_{3,1} & c_{3,2} & c_{3,3} & \cdots & c_{3,m} \\
c_{4,1} & c_{4,2} & c_{4,3} & \cdots & c_{4,m} \\
\vdots & \vdots & \vdots & \ddots & \vdots \\
c_{n,1} & c_{n,2} & c_{n,3} & \cdots & c_{n,m}
\end{bmatrix}
$$

Figure 1.1 Two ways of showing how the Fortran 90 array statement a = b + 2 * c gets executed.

allows whole arrays to be treated as uniform objects. For example, if an array s is dimensioned to be $10 \times 20 \times 30$, one could multiply each element by 3.14 with a simple array statement:

```
s = s * 3.14
```

Similarly, if two arrays have the same dimensions, one can combine them in expressions. So, given three $n \times m$ arrays named a, b, and c, the statement:

```
a = b + 2 * c
```

will double the elements of c, add them to corresponding elements of b, and store the result into the corresponding elements of a. This is illustrated in Figure 1.1.

Array syntax is extremely useful for describing parallel algorithms. Elemental (or elementwise) operations on whole arrays can be mapped efficiently onto parallel or vector hardware, even by a nonoptimizing compiler. For example, on a massively parallel machine, each processor might be responsible for computing a square subset of the elemental operations. A group of elements on an individual processor might be collected into a vector that can be operated on by multiple functional units (the processor might be superpipelined or superscalar).

Fortran 90 also contains various transformational operations which move data between different grid points. For example, one might want to shift the elements of a two-dimensional grid d positions to the right. There are several ways to do this; one is with eoshift (end-off shift):

```
d_shifted = eoshift(d, shift=1, dim=2)
```

If eoshift is shifting to the right, it must insert new values to fill in the left edge. By default, eoshift fills with zeros. Alternatively, one can specify values to use for filling, or one can use cshift (circular shift), which would rotate values that fall off one side and put them back on the other side.

- Array assignments involving entire arrays or array sections:
  - if A and B are conformable (same shape) arrays of any rank, the statement A = B assigns each element of B to the corresponding element of A.
  - `A(2:N+1) = B(1:N)` assigns the first N elements of the one-dimensional array B to A in positions from 2 to N+1.
  - `A(2:N+1) = B(1:N:-1)` assigns the same elements in reverse order.
- Arithmetic operations on arrays and array sections:
  - B+C indicates an elementwise addition of the arrays B and C.
  - `A(2*N:2:-2) * B(3:N+2)` calls for multiplication of the described subsections of A and B. In this case, it would produce a one-dimensional array of length N+1 containing, in sequence, the values `A(2*N)*B(3)`, `A(2*N-2)*B(4)`, ..., `A(2)*B(N+2)`.
  - relational operations such as `A .EQ. B` are allowed, and return arrays of booleans.
- Masked array assignments. For example, `WHERE(B .NE. 0) B = A/B` assigns the quotient of A and B to the nonzero elements of B.
- Array intrinsic functions:
  - elemental array functions, such as SIN, which extend scalar operations to elementwise operations on arrays.
  - transformational functions, such as CSHIFT (circular shift) and EOSHIFT (end-off shift).
  - array reduction functions, such as ALL, ANY, COUNT, MAXVAL, MINVAL, PRODUCT, and SUM. Each of these functions has two forms: one reduces an entire array to single scalar value, and the other reduces the array along a single dimension and returns an array of rank one less than its argument.
  - array construction functions, such as RESHAPE and SPREAD.
- Vector-valued subscripts: A vector integer expression is used to specify an array section. For example, if V is a one-dimensional array with elements 3, 4, 22, and 6 then

  `A(V)` evaluates to `[A(3), A(4), A(22), A(6)]`

  When used on the right-hand side of an assignment statement, a vector-valued subscript performs a gather operation. On the left-hand side, it acts like a scatter.
- FORALL: a parallel version of a DOLOOP in which all the iterations can run in parallel.

Figure 1.2   Overview of CM Fortran array features.

Fortran 90 has many other array features, including array sections and vector-valued subscripts; various other dialects have additional features, such as directives to control array layout. Most of the array capabilities of Fortran 90 are summarized in Figure 1.2.

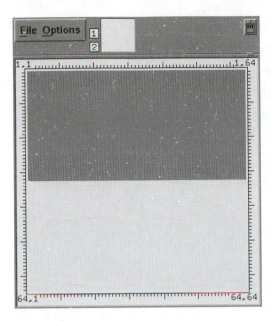

Figure 1.3   Input to simulation: a disk whose initial state is hot on one half and cool on the other. The disk is embedded in a plane with the same temperature, and so it is not yet visible. The disk will change temperature as the simulation runs, while the plane will not.

1.2 Data Representation

A k-dimensional space can be subdivided using a k-dimensional grid, and measurement samples in the space can be captured in the form of a k-dimensional array of numbers. The measurements in one such array might represent the temperature or pressure at evenly spaced grid points. While it is easy to imagine that computations on the grid are an end in themselves when one is simply dealing with the mathematics (as we do in this chapter), in the end the grid is only a representation of some computation, simulation, or process in the original space.

The computation in this chapter is a simulation of a circular disk embedded in a two-dimensional grid. The disk has a fixed temperature of 100° applied to one edge and a fixed temperature of 0° applied to its opposite edge. In addition, all points in the half of the disk with the hot edge start out with temperature of 100°; the other points have a temperature of 0°. The goal of the simulation is to determine the final temperature at each point in the interior of the disk. Not surprisingly, we end up with a temperature gradient across the disk. The initial and final conditions are shown in Figures 1.3 and 1.4, respectively. Later, we will complicate matters by adding a high-frequency "checkering" to the input. Visually, you might expect the checkering to appear as a fine checkerboard superimposed on the original data. However, the variation is very low in amplitude

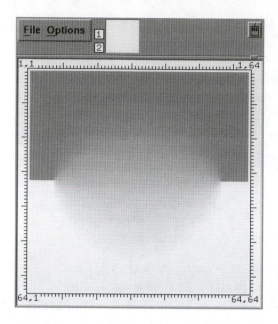

Figure 1.4   **Output from simulation: a smooth temperature gradient across the disk.**

(only 1° of difference), so it would be difficult to see it in print; a figure with the checkering would look identical to Figure 1.3.

1.3 Algorithm

The computation we will do in this space is based on Laplace's equation as applied to a two-dimensional grid. The equation is:

$$\left(\frac{\partial^2}{\partial x^2} + \frac{\partial^2}{\partial y^2}\right) A(x,y) = 0$$

One possible discretization for this continuous equation is:

$$A_{i+1,j} + A_{i-1,j} + A_{i,j+1} + A_{i,j-1} - 4A_{i,j} = 0$$

or equivalently:

$$A_{i,j} = 0.25 * (A_{i+1,j} + A_{i-1,j} + A_{i,j+1} + A_{i,j-1})$$

This equation states that in the final solution any point $A_{i,j}$ is equal to the average of its neighbors. We can iteratively apply the equation to an input grid, producing a new grid. Each element of this new grid will be equal to the average of its four neighbors' values in the input grid. If we repeat the process, it can be shown that the solution will eventually converge to satisfy the equation (as we will see later, initial data that contains high-frequency variations can delay convergence). Figure 1.5 shows one way to implement this solver in Fortran 90. Figure 1.6 shows the support routines that it calls. The array operations in the subroutine make it clear to a compiler that operations along the two dimensions of the data can be accomplished in parallel. This subroutine was called under the Prism[5] program development environment to produce the images in Figures 1.3 and 1.4.

1.4 Effects of Architecture

Much as a serial loop describes individual operations and a serial order in which to perform them, Fortran 90 array syntax describes array operations and an order in which to perform them. This is a close match to vector or SIMD hardware, which only allow a single operation to proceed at any one time, albeit on multiple data items.

The algorithm discussed in this chapter has built-in synchronization in that each iteration must fully complete and update A before the next iteration can begin. Beyond that, a compiler applied to this program is free to implement the kernel statement, which contains four cshifts, three additions, and one multiplication, as efficiently as it can. Some machines will be able to overlap computation with communication, or multiplications with additions. It is up to the compiler to do that; the algorithm and the code do not inhibit that kind of compiler optimization with extraneous synchronization.

When the algorithm to be implemented has inherent synchronicity, Fortran 90 can be a good match for MIMD hardware. However, if it does not, Fortran 90 forces the programmer to introduce notational synchronization that a compiler may not be able to recognize as unnecessary. Chapter 5 discusses an application that would be difficult to implement efficiently in Fortran 90 due to its inherent lack of synchronization.

```
      subroutine grid_f90_branch_code(size)
      include 'grid.h'
      real a(size, size)
      logical interior(size, size)
      integer i, j, iter
      call init_grid_f90_branch_code(a,interior,size)
      do iter=1, num_iterations
         where (interior)
            a = .25 * (cshift(a, dim=1, shift=1) +
     $                 cshift(a, dim=1, shift=-1) +
     $                 cshift(a, dim=2, shift=1) +
     $                 cshift(a, dim=2, shift=-1))
         endwhere
      enddo
      call display_results(a,size,iter)
      end
```

Figure 1.5 **Iterative solver implemented in Fortran 90.**

1.5 Optimization, Tuning, and Tradeoffs

Boundary Conditions

In the real world being modeled by our grid, there are no boundaries; space is infinite. Computer memory, however, is not infinite, so the area of interest in our simulation has edges, and the computation of grid edge values must be handled differently than for interior values. In general, there are two approaches to handling this difference: one can branch the code, or one can branch the data.[6] An initial implementation will often branch the code because doing so is conceptually simple. The where statement in Figure 1.5 performed code branching.

```
        subroutine init_grid_f90_branch_code(a,interior,size)
        include 'grid.h'
        real a(size, size)
        logical interior(size, size)
        integer i,j,halfsize,limitsize
        integer xcoord(size, size)
        integer ycoord(size, size)
        halfsize = (1 + size)/2
        limitsize = .8 * halfsize
        forall(i=1:size,j=1:size) xcoord(i,j) = i
        forall(i=1:size,j=1:size) ycoord(i,j) = j
        interior = .true.
        where ((((xcoord-halfsize)**2 + (ycoord-halfsize)**2)
     $         .ge. limitsize**2)
           interior = .false.
        endwhere
        a = 0
        where (xcoord.gt.halfsize) a = 100
C global variable to control whether initial data should
C include high-frequency checkering
        if (hifreq) then
           where (interior .and. (mod(xcoord,2).eq.mod(ycoord,2)))
              a = a + 1
           endwhere
        endif
        end

The include file 'Grid.h' contains:
        implicit none
        integer num_iterations
        parameter (num_iterations=3000)
        real epsilon
        parameter (epsilon=.1)
        integer size
        logical hifreq
        common/global/ hifreq
```

Figure 1.6   Support for iterative solver implemented in Fortran 90.

In contrast to conventional code branching, the example in Figure 1.7 branches the data rather than the code. The main difference is that the logical value of `interior` is translated into two integers, `inside` and `outside`. Since they are numbers, these new variables can be treated arithmetically rather than logically. The basic idea is to perform the same computations (code) for all grid points at all times, regardless of whether they are interior or boundary cells. The conditional branch statements (`if/where`) that were in the kernel equation have been eliminated.

The task of optimizing a high performance program often boils down to finding the place where a program spends most of its time, and then trying to remove code. Most of the time in Figure 1.7 will be spent inside the main loop, calculating the next generation of the grid. Figure 1.8 shows a version of this code containing two hand

```
      subroutine grid_f90_branch_data(size)
      include 'grid.h'
      real a(size, size)
      real inside(size,size)
      real outside(size,size)
      integer i, j, iter
      call init_grid_f90_branch_data(a,inside,outside,size)
      do iter=1, num_iterations
         a = outside * a +
$           inside * .25 * (cshift(a, dim=1, shift=1) +
$                           cshift(a, dim=1, shift=-1) +
$                           cshift(a, dim=2, shift=1) +
$                           cshift(a, dim=2, shift=-1))
      enddo
      call display_results(a,size,iter)
      end

      subroutine init_grid_f90_branch_data(a,inside,outside,size)
      include 'grid.h'
      real a(size, size)
      real inside(size,size)
      real outside(size,size)
      logical interior(size, size)
C First call earlier init routine, since most of the required setup
C for data branching is the same.
      call init_grid_f90_branch_code(a,interior,size)
      inside = 0
      outside = 0
      where (interior)
          inside = 1
      elsewhere
          outside = 1
      endwhere
      end
```

Figure 1.7   Fortran 90 version using data branching to implement boundary conditions.

1.5 OPTIMIZATION, TUNING, AND TRADEOFFS

```
      subroutine grid_f90_branch_data2(size)
      include 'grid.h'
      real a(size, size)
      real inside(size,size)
      real outside(size,size)
      integer i, j, iter
      call init_grid_f90_branch_data2(a,inside,outside,size)
      do iter=1, num_iterations
        a = outside +
     $        inside * (cshift(a, dim=1, shift=1) +
     $                  cshift(a, dim=1, shift=-1) +
     $                  cshift(a, dim=2, shift=1) +
     $                  cshift(a, dim=2, shift=-1))
      enddo
      call display_results(a,size,iter)
      end

      subroutine init_grid_f90_branch_data2(a,inside,outside,size)
      include 'grid.h'
      real a(size, size)
      real inside(size,size)
      real outside(size,size)
      logical interior(size, size)
      call init_grid_f90_branch_code(a,interior,size)
      inside = 0
      outside = 0
      where (interior)
         inside = .25
      elsewhere
         outside = a
      endwhere
      end
```

Figure 1.8   More efficient version of data branching code.

optimizations: two pieces of code (the multiplication by 0.25 and the multiplication
by a) have been moved out of the inner loop and into the initialization/precalculation
routine.

Comparing this hand-optimized data branching code, we find that we still have four
cshifts and three additions in the kernel, but now we have two multiplications rather
than one. Why would we prefer to branch the data rather than the code? The main
reason is that that conditional branch code can force implementation by control flow
statements, which can be expensive on high performance machines. Compilers have
difficulty predicting the outcome of conditional branches, and such branches often force
the compiler to generate conservative, inefficient code. For example, on a pipelined
workstation, it can force pipelines to be emptied and waste cycles. On a SIMD machine
(depending on the compiler) it may idle a large fraction of the machine. For example,
all processors containing interior grid points might idle while exterior points are processed. Clearly, border handling is an important issue in tuning parallel code. It can take

```
      do iter=1, num_iterations
         do j=1, size
            do i=1, size
               if (interior(i,j)) then
                  a(i,j) =
$                       .25 * (a(i+1,j) + a(i-1,j) +
$                               a(i,j+1) + a(i,j-1))
               endif
            enddo
         enddo
      enddo
```

Figure 1.9   Fortran 77 code branching kernel, as executed on the Cray C90.

up a disproportionately large part of execution time, especially for small data sets or those with many dimensions.

Converting code branching to data branching can improve execution time on a variety of platforms and target languages. The code we have just seen was timed on several target machines, with grid sizes ranging between 128 and 512, with the highest level of compiler optimization available. Since the grid is only two-dimensional, one would expect border handling to be even more critical in the three- and four-dimensional codes that are more often used in practice.

The code was timed on a vector machine, a SIMD machine, and a MIMD machine. On one vector head of a Cray C90, the data branching version was found to consistently be more than 40 percent faster than the code branching version. (Timings were taken on array sizes between 16×16 and 512×512.) Because the Cray does not yet have a Fortran 90 compiler, Fortran 77 versions of the two codes were generated, using IFs instead of WHEREs, DO loops instead of array syntax, and so on. The Fortran 77 kernels are shown in Figures 1.9 and 1.10.

On the SIMD CM-2, data branching improved run time over code branching by 13 to 18 percent for the various array sizes, and the additional hand data branching optimization took off an additional 5 to 8 percent. The gains on the MIMD CM-5

```
      do iter=1, num_iterations
         do j=1, size
            do i=1, size
               a(i,j) =
$                    outside(i,j) * a(i,j) +
$                    inside(i,j) * (a(i+1,j) + a(i-1,j) +
$                                    a(i,j+1) + a(i,j-1))
            enddo
         enddo
      enddo
```

Figure 1.10   Fortran 77 data branching kernel, as executed on the Cray C90.

1.5 OPTIMIZATION, TUNING, AND TRADEOFFS

```
        subroutine grid_f90_check(size)
        include 'grid.h'
        real a(size, size),new_a(size,size)
        real inside(size, size)
        real outside(size, size)
        integer i, j, iter
        call init_grid_f90_branch_data(a,inside,outside,size)
        do iter=1, num_iterations
          new_a = outside * a +
$                inside * .25 * (cshift(a, dim=1, shift=1) +
$                                cshift(a, dim=1, shift=-1) +
$                                cshift(a, dim=2, shift=1) +
$                                cshift(a, dim=2, shift=-1))
          if (all(abs(a-new_a).lt.epsilon)) exit
          a = new_a
        enddo
        call display_results(a,size,iter)
        end
```

Figure 1.11   Fortran 90 version that checks for convergence.

(which was equipped with vector units) were more modest; the best gain was about 6 percent.

The code we have been working with has only two types of grid points, interior and border. A more realistic code might have several different types of points.[†] Each new type of point that needs special handling will require branching. If one is branching the data, one simply introduces a new coefficient (like inside or outside) and initializes it once. The coefficient can then be used repeatedly in a fast, condition-free kernel update expression. More complex kernels will tend to favor data branching more than the simple ones in this chapter, because there is more opportunity for hand optimization.

This section demonstrates that the somewhat unfamiliar technique of branching the data is useful for speeding up programs on several kinds of target machines. While the boundary conditions in actual applications are usually more complicated that those in the examples above, the principles remain the same and the performance gains impressive.[7, 8]

Other Optimizations

There is very little fat left in the inner loop for us to remove. To demonstrate further optimization, the application will have to become more complicated. We will add a convergence test, and then work to optimize the resulting code. Optimizations tend to obscure intent as they improve code speed; to make the code clearer, the multiplication by 0.25 will be moved back into the inner loop.

[†] The code can be generalized, such as by introducing periodic (wraparound) boundary conditions, varying the weights of the neighbors, using more than four neighbors, or even neighbors from several time steps back; the data branching technique can be applied to many such changes.

```
subroutine grid_f90_check_unfold(size)
include 'grid.h'
real even_a(size, size),odd_a(size,size)
real inside(size, size)
real outside(size, size)
integer i, j, iter
call init_grid_f90_branch_data(odd_a,inside,outside,size)
do iter=1, num_iterations
    even_a = outside * odd_a +
$           inside * .25 * (cshift(odd_a, dim=1, shift=1) +
$                           cshift(odd_a, dim=1, shift=-1) +
$                           cshift(odd_a, dim=2, shift=1) +
$                           cshift(odd_a, dim=2, shift=-1))
    odd_a = outside * even_a +
$           inside * .25 * (cshift(even_a, dim=1, shift=1) +
$                           cshift(even_a, dim=1, shift=-1) +
$                           cshift(even_a, dim=2, shift=1) +
$                           cshift(even_a, dim=2, shift=-1))
    if (all(abs(odd_a-even_a).lt.epsilon)) exit
enddo
call display_results(odd_a,size,iter)
end
```

Figure 1.12 **Fortran 90 version that checks for convergence and also unfolds even/odd loop iterations.**

Convergence test In the earlier examples, the program ran for a fixed number of iterations. Depending on the input data, it might be necessary to continue iterating for an unknown number of iterations until the output array settles down and converges; the fixed number of iterations has to be set to a number large enough to reach convergence. The code from Figure 1.5 has been rewritten in Figure 1.11 so that it now tests to see if the output has settled down, and stops earlier, right after convergence is reached.

The additional code used to implement the test comes in two parts: a copy of the array a into old_a, and then the test itself, which first compares old_a to a elementwise, then checks to see if all of the differences are less than the threshold for stopping, epsilon. If they are, it means that a is basically the same as old_a. Because adding the inexpensive test allows the program to terminate long before iteration 3000 (the value of num_iterations), putting in this check is a kind of optimization in itself. In fact, it terminates after 122 iterations, a significant improvement. We now optimize the code in two *more* additional ways.

The first optimization involves copying from a to old_a. While the statement appears innocuous enough, it is actually calling for a large amount of data movement: a large block of data must be read from a and written to old_a. This unnecessary work can be eliminated by unfolding two iterations of the loop and alternating computations between the two, as shown in Figure 1.12. The iterations of the resulting program have two phases, even and then odd.

The codes in Figures 1.11 and 1.12 were timed on the CM-2 and CM-5. The unfolded code does twice as much work in each iteration, so terminates in half as many iterations (61 iterations rather than 122, for the array sizes tested). As one would expect, each iteration is slightly less than twice as expensive, so there is an overall improvment in run time. The improvement on the CM-2 was 22 to 23 percent, while the improvement on the CM-5 ranged between 22 and 28 percent. The biggest improvements occur for larger array sizes, because startup overhead (which is not affected by this optimization) is proportionally smaller for large arrays.

Figure 1.11 did the convergence test after every complete pass over the grid, while the code in Figure 1.12 does it only after every odd step. The latter is better, because the array operations in the test, especially the `all` reduction (which is likely to require interprocessor communication), are expensive. It is acceptable because after convergence is reached performing an extra pass over the grid will no longer change anything. Clearly, another optimization would be to perform the test for convergence even less often, perhaps every 10 or 100 iterations, in order to better amortize the cost of the test. This could be done by checking that `iter` is a multiple of say 100 before doing the convergence test.

Methods of iteration The basic kernel loop in our application has computed a completely new array and then stored the array back into a. This iteration method, called the point–Jacobi method, requires many iterations to converge when compared to other techniques (and is therefore rarely used in practice). For example, the natural iteration method on a serial machine is to compute the value of a single point and then store that back into the array before computing the value of its neighbor (therefore, the neighbor will use the most up-to-date value when calculating its own next value). This method, called Gauss–Seidel, converges rapidly but is inherently serial, since it requires each point to be stored before its neighbor can be computed.

Red–black Gauss–Seidel is a similar iteration method but is more amenable to parallelization. Imagine that a checkerboard with red and black squares is superimposed on the grid. First, all of the red squares update themselves and store their updated values. When that is done, all the black squares do likewise. Since the four neighbors of a square are always of the opposite color there is no interference, and all squares of a given color can be done in parallel. Like our unfolded convergence checker from Figure 1.12, Gauss–Seidel is a two-phase process. We combine the two optimizations to produce the four-phase program in Figures 1.13 and 1.14.

The Gauss–Seidel code is the most complex in this chapter. Each iteration does more than twice as much work as the iterations in code in Figure 1.12. When it is run on the input we have used so far, Gauss–Seidel takes the same number of iterations to terminate, 61; so its overall run time is a bit more than twice that of the original unfolded code. However, it turns out that in practice Gauss–Seidel can converge much faster than the point–Jacobi codes. In particular, this is true for our example when the data is initialized with the variable `hifreq` set to true, so that a high-frequency variation is inserted into the initial data by `init_grid_f90_branch_code`. This high-frequency

```
      subroutine grid_f90_check_gauss_seidel(size)
      include 'grid.h'
      real even_a(size, size),odd_a(size,size)
      real inside_red(size, size)
      real inside_black(size, size)
      real outside(size, size)
      integer i, j, iter
      call init_grid_f90_gauss_seidel(odd_a,inside_red,inside_black,
     $     outside,size)
      do iter=1, num_iterations
C Do black, then red
         even_a = (outside + inside_red) * odd_a +
     $            inside_black*.25 * (cshift(odd_a, dim=1, shift=1) +
     $                                cshift(odd_a, dim=1, shift=-1) +
     $                                cshift(odd_a, dim=2, shift=1) +
     $                                cshift(odd_a, dim=2, shift=-1))
         even_a = (outside + inside_black) * even_a +
     $            inside_red * .25 * (cshift(even_a, dim=1, shift=1) +
     $                                cshift(even_a, dim=1, shift=-1) +
     $                                cshift(even_a, dim=2, shift=1) +
     $                                cshift(even_a, dim=2, shift=-1))
C Again do black, then red, as part of unfolding
         odd_a = (outside + inside_red) * even_a +
     $            inside_black*.25 * (cshift(even_a, dim=1, shift=1) +
     $                                cshift(even_a, dim=1, shift=-1) +
     $                                cshift(even_a, dim=2, shift=1) +
     $                                cshift(even_a, dim=2, shift=-1))
         odd_a = (outside + inside_black) * odd_a +
     $            inside_red * .25 * (cshift(odd_a, dim=1, shift=1) +
     $                                cshift(odd_a, dim=1, shift=-1) +
     $                                cshift(odd_a, dim=2, shift=1) +
     $                                cshift(odd_a, dim=2, shift=-1))
         if (all(abs(odd_a-even_a).lt.epsilon)) exit
      enddo
      call display_results(odd_a,size,iter)
      end
```

Figure 1.13   **Gauss–Seidel version that checks for convergence and also unfolds even/odd loop iterations.**

data has no effect on the number of iterations it takes Gauss–Seidel to converge, but it prevents the other algorithms we have seen from converging at all (so they all run to the num_iterations limit, 3000). The reason point–Jacobi does not converge is that averaging all cells with their old neighbors simply shifts the high-frequency variation a bit without eliminating it, but red–black Gauss–Seidel averaging quickly dampens it out.

It is not surprising that changing the underlying iteration method and adding a termination check makes the biggest improvement of all, while reducing the expense of operations that occur in the inner kernel leads to more modest gains. Clearly, a knowledge of one's application and the properties of appropriate algorithms can be crucial in

```
      subroutine init_grid_f90_gauss_seidel(a,inside_red,inside_black,
     $      outside,size)
      include 'grid.h'
      real a(size, size)
      real inside_black(size,size)
      real inside_red(size,size)
      real outside(size,size)
      logical interior(size, size)
      integer xcoord(size, size)
      integer ycoord(size, size)
      integer i,j
C do regular initialization
      call init_grid_f90_branch_code(a,interior,size)
C now set up the red and black arrays
      inside_red = 0
      inside_black = 0
      outside = 0
      where (.not.interior)
         outside = 1
      endwhere
      forall(i=1:size,j=1:size) xcoord(i,j) = i
      forall(i=1:size,j=1:size) ycoord(i,j) = j
      where (interior .and. (mod(xcoord,2).eq.mod(ycoord,2)))
         inside_red = 1
      endwhere
      where (interior .and. (mod(xcoord,2).ne.mod(ycoord,2)))
         inside_black = 1
      endwhere
10    format (16F7.1)
30    format (16F7.1)
      end
```

Figure 1.14   Initialization routine for Gauss–Seidel.

writing high performance code. Unwinding loops and tuning kernels is useful, but only if the algorithm one is tuning is appropriate for the data to which it will be applied.

Overhead of subroutine calls   Using subroutine calls to divide a program into functional modules improves abstraction and code maintainability, but it also adds overhead that might not be acceptable in a high performance kernel. One reason is the work involved in the call: register context must be saved and restored, arguments must be passed, etc. Another reason is that the call is a branch and has many of the performance problems that we encountered earlier with conditional branches. In general, introducing a procedure will often reduce the opportunity for compiler optimizations to be applied. Since most compilers do not do interprocedural analysis or subroutine inlining, the fact that the branching caused by a subroutine call seems easier to predict than conditional code is not necessarily useful.

For the reasons above, the examples in this chapter, like most high performance codes, remove computations that can be thought of as "precalculation," such as initialization,

into subroutines which can then be called once. However, the number of subrou[...]
in the kernel of the program, the main loop which repeatedly applies the gri[...]
equation, and in the update equation itself, is carefully kept to a minimum. The [...]
is that subroutine call overhead can be expensive in an inner loop. This not to sa[...]
calls in a kernel are never useful; perhaps the call is being made to a more efficient lib[...]
routine written in machine language. In that case, the call overhead is likely to be cove[...]
by the efficiency of the called routine. For example, on the Connection Machine a stenc[...]
library is available that can perform the same four-point (four neighbors) update that
our code performs. Because it does a better job of overlapping simultaneous communication with multiple neighbors than the CM Fortran compiler does with multiple
eoshifts, it may make sense to call a subroutine in that optimized library rather than
using several eoshifts.

Of course, calling an optimized, machine-specific routine reduces portability. Where
modularization is necessary for code portability, conditional compilation or conditional
file inclusion can be used. This is demonstrated in some of the later chapters.

Nonuniform and Unstructured Grids

An important shortcoming of uniform structured grids is that attention cannot be focused on areas of interest. There is a single factor that controls accuracy: the fineness of
the grid, which is determined by the number of points in the grid. A regular grid
containing 64 times as many points requires at least 64 times as much computational
work, even though the increased accuracy might only be needed in one small area of the
grid. In contrast, nonuniform and unstructured grids allow computational power to be
focused more accurately just where it is needed.

One way to create a nonuniform grid is to stretch and shrink the grid as required,
much as if it were a piece of rubber wrapped around the object to be simulated. The
stretching and shrinking might happen once when a grid is set up, or it might happen repeatedly to match changing conditions. The result is a nonuniform structured
grid. It is structured because it can still be addressed with cartesian coordinates, although a local coordinate transform is needed to move between cartesian space and the
stretched space of the rubber grid. Alternatively, one could take several different resolution grids and "glue" them together, producing an irregular, unstructured grid. More
radically, one can imagine tearing up links that bind a grid together, allowing the individual grid points, where all the work takes place, to roam freely to where they are
needed most!

Nonuniform and unstructured grid algorithms are more complicated than regular
grid algorithms. Old issues like border handling must be revisited, and new issues such
as load balancing must be dealt with. Grid points might have trouble determining how
much area their neighbor is currently covering, let alone finding out about torn off grid
points that have roamed into the neighborhood! But depending on the target architecture, a nonuniform or unstructured grid algorithm will often outperform a uniform
structured grid algorithm.

References

Fortran Reference Manual. Thinking Machines Corporation, Cambridge, A, 1993.

High Performance Fortran Language Specification, ver. 1.0 draft. High Performance Fortran Forum, Rice University, Houston, Jan. 1993. Available by anonymous FTP from titan.cs.rice.edu in the directory public/HPFF/draft.

3 G. Fox, S. Hiranandani, K. Kennedy, C. Koelbel, U. Kremer, C.-W. Tseng, and M.-Y. Wu. *Fortran-D Language Specification*. Publ. no. COMP TR90-141, Rice University, Houston, April 1991.

4 D. M. Pase, T. MacDonald, and A. Meltzer. *MPP Fortran Programming Model*. Cray Research, Inc., Eagan, MN, August 1992.

5 Prism User's Guide, ver. 1.2. Thinking Machines Corporation, Cambridge, MA, March 1993.

6 J. Bailey. *Implementing Fine-Grained Scientific Algorithms on the Connection Machine Supercomputer*. Publ. no. TR-169, Thinking Machines Corporation, Cambridge, MA, 1990, p. 15.

7 E. S. Oran, J. P. Boris, R. O. Whaley, and E. F. Brown. "Exploring Fluid Dynamics on a Connection Machine," *Supercomputing Review*. May, 1990.

8 C. Li, E. S. Oran, and J. P. Boris. "A Uniform Algorithm for Boundary and Interior Regions and Its Application to Compressible Flow Simulations." Submitted to *SIAM J.*

2

Block Grid Application

ALLEN C. ROBINSON and
COURTENAY T. VAUGHAN

Contents

This chapter describes a different approach to handling structured grids. The focus is on making efficient use of target hardware in the face of the numerous problems that were touched on in Chapter 1. Thus, this chapter explains how and why the authors have addressed key issues such as handling of irregular data, performance tuning, and code portability.

2.1 Introduction

Physical systems that change over time are often modeled using computational techniques. For example, how does the stress on a structural element of a car change during an impact? Exactly how does a laminar flow transition to turbulence? How quickly does a sudden heat source on the boundary of a component adversely affect its function? What are the time-dependent cratering and thermodynamic characteristics of a meteor impact? Each of these examples involves a physical system that changes over time but whose evolution is defined by equations which are essentially spatially localized. To model a very complicated system, the computational scientist must keep track of state information to evolve the system. The large amount of spatial information required leads the computational scientist to believe that there must be a way to solve this time evolution problem by dividing the problem into smaller regions so that different computers solve separate subproblems concurrently. After all, these physical systems evolve very nicely without significant long-range effects, so the computational simulation should proceed effectively if decomposed onto many processing elements. This is the essential proposition of parallelization in computational physics: physics that, in some sense, is intrinsically parallel can be simulated using parallel computational techniques.

In this chapter we discuss a particular three-dimensional block structured grid application in which the form of the time integration is explicit. That is, the equations, in one dimension, have the form

$$u_i^{n+1} - f(u_{i-I}^n, \ldots, u_i^n, \ldots, u_{i+I}^n) = 0 \tag{2.1}$$

where i represents a discrete spatial coordinate, I is a small integer, and n represents a discrete time. This application will be treated as a prototype for similar applications. To resolve disparate length scales for some of our problems, we are interested in extremely fine spatial resolution for our simulations. This fine spatial resolution requires large amounts of memory and processing speed in order to integrate our simulations for many time steps. The fact that we have a large database to map to a large distributed-memory machine makes parallel processing appealing. Such a correspondence between problem size and machine characteristics is always necessary in order to use a parallel architecture successfully.

We will discuss our technique for load balancing grid decomposition—how boundary conditions are handled relative to interprocessor communication, how much memory is

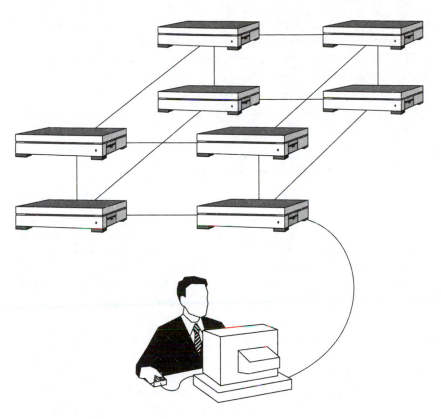

Figure 2.1   The generic MIMD message-passing parallel computer.

actually available on a parallel machine, and our techniques for writing portable code. In addition, we will discuss how to obtain useful point and field information from a parallel machine.

We are primarily interested in various MIMD message-passing systems. These machines can be described simply as a collection of computers that communicate using messages. (A message is a set of bytes transferred from one computer to another computer.) We have chosen to use this very general model of a parallel machine since we wish to be able to move our simulations to a wide variety of current and future machines without being tied to a particular parallel language. Figure 2.1 illustrates the common characteristics of a message-passing parallel computer. First, each processor or node on the system is roughly equivalent to a single workstation-class machine. The machines are connected by a communication network. A hypercube network is illustrated, although mesh, tree, ring, and other network topologies are also possible. For our purposes, the total computational work is shared by subdividing the computational space among the processors on the network. For example, the spatial decomposition of a $50 \times 50 \times 50$ mesh is most effectively accomplished by dividing the cube into eight equal subcubes of size $25 \times 25 \times 25$. Finally, the user of the parallel machine generally sits essentially at the end of a single serial communication line so that whatever information resides in the parallel machine (which may have up to several thousand processors) must be filtered in some reasonable way to obtain a minimal usable subset of information at the terminal. We use several serial languages in our software system: C, C++, and Fortran in conjunction with the SPMD style of parallel programming. This means that a separate copy of the same simulation code runs on each node while the corresponding spatial information for each node is different.

2.2 PCTH: A Shock-Wave Physics Simulation Code

The application code PCTH, which we will describe, is being developed at Sandia National Laboratories to assist in the modeling of various high energy events, such as those occurring due to high velocity impact or explosive detonation. Possible applications include the detailed analysis of space shield protective capabilities, explosives manufacturing processes, analysis of shaped charge effects in oil well perforation, and conventional weapons. The PCTH (parallel CTH) code is based on the CTH code used by Sandia and other government contractors for some time.[1] PCTH is being developed for production use and at the same time new ground is being explored in terms of next-generation hardware and software technology. The PCTH code is intended to be extended over some years all the while maintaining a close relationship with other shock-wave physics development projects at Sandia. Code and algorithm sharing currently occurs between three different development projects at Sandia which include the CTH, PCTH, and RHALE shock physics codes. More information about the PCTH and RHALE projects, especially with respect to the use of C++, may be found in References 2–6.

The type of calculation which may performed with these solid dynamic simulation codes is shown in Figure 2.2. A copper ball is shown hitting a steel plate at 4.52 km/s. The figure illustrates the complexity found in the algorithms for the CTH and PCTH codes, which include initial definition of possibly complex objects, modeling of the dynamic shock-wave behavior of interacting fluids and/or solids, the tracking of interfaces on the grid, and the necessity for graphical output.

2.3 PCTH Target Machines

The PCTH code is intended to be run on any distributed memory, MIMD message-passing system. For example, a major portion of the original development of the code was on the nCUBE/2™ at Sandia. This machine has 1024 nodes connected with a hypercube topology. Each node has 4 MB of memory which must be shared among the node's operating system, message-passing buffers, application executable, and user data. We have also used a 64-node Intel/860™ hypercube and are currently working with Sandia's Intel Paragon™, which has 1840 nodes connected as a flat mesh. Another important parallel supercomputer which is just beginning to demonstrate feasibility is the workstation network. In the future, we intend to explore using PCTH on a workstation network. Versions of PCTH have also been run successfully in message-passing

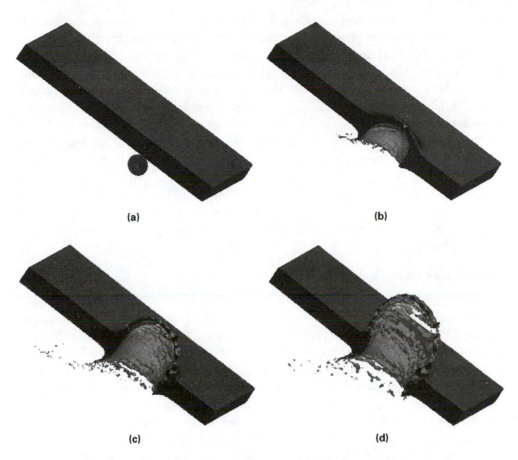

(a)

(b)

(c)

(d)

Figure 2.2　PCTH simulation sequence of a ¼-in. diameter copper ball striking a 5.6 mm steel plate at 4.52 km/s and a 30° impact angle. Simulation times shown are (*a*) 0.0 μs, (*b*) 4.0 μs, (*c*) 8.0 μs, and (*d*) 11.6 μs.

mode on a multiprocessor shared-memory Cray Y-MP™. Thus the MIMD message-passing paradigm can be utilized on shared-memory multiprocessor systems as well as distributed-memory machines. The wide variety of intended machines for PCTH, the uncertain nature of the future of parallel languages, and the code development schedule were significant factors in our choice to develop PCTH as a SPMD code.

2.4　Data Distribution and Representation

The simulation space for PCTH is specified by a set of "mesh regions." Each mesh region is a three-dimensional cartesian block. As input, the user specifies each mesh region as well as the boundary conditions on each face. Boundary conditions include transmitting and symmetric boundaries as well as so-called neighbor boundaries. The neighbor boundary condition is used to specify an adjacency relationship between mesh regions.

Periodic boundary conditions may also be defined in this way. Given the number of mesh regions and the number of cells requested in each cartesian direction, as well as the number of computational nodes or processors available, we developed an algorithm to subdivide the mesh regions rationally. This algorithm attempts to minimize the surface-to-volume ratio of the subregions. Each subregion is called a hydroblock or block. Generally, on a homogeneous MIMD machine, one block is placed on a single CPU and corresponds essentially to a single executable module. Our algorithm will be described in detail here because it represents one pragmatic way to subdivide a set of mesh regions into equally sized blocks and might be found useful to developers in many application areas as they begin to develop software for parallel MIMD machines. The algorithm can also be extended in a limited way for parallel machines having nodes of different memory sizes. For noncartesian grids, more sophisticated subdivision strategies may be employed.[7] Adaptive mesh algorithms on cartesian grids will require more sophisticated strategies.[8]

A Subdivision Strategy for Multiple Mesh Regions

To utilize any parallel machine, the user's data must be decomposed across the machine. Parallel languages provide for this decomposition somewhat automatically. For example, Thinking Machines Corporation provides three different parallel languages, CM Fortran, C* and *LISP. CM Fortran may have the largest following among scientific programmers. Recently, standardization efforts have proposed the High Performance Fortran standard, which is an extension of the ANSI/ISO Fortran 90 definition. However, even with these parallel languages, applications will be most efficient if users, knowing their own data and algorithms, ensure that sufficient data locality is maintained to avoid large amounts of communication and strive to minimize communications. Generally, the program developer must pay attention to specifying something about data layout to the parallel language and/or adjusting data location in parallel arrays based on another algorithm in order to minimize communication. In PCTH, we do not require a parallel language, as we implement our own static mesh decomposition based on a description of a set of mesh regions and the number of nodes (computers) available to work on the problem.

To set up problems for PCTH, one may in the simplest case specify a single rectilinear region of space (a box) which contains all of the objects of interest. In order to do parallel processing, this mesh region must be divided into blocks so that each processor has a block of cells to work on. These blocks are also rectilinear regions which combine to fill the mesh region. On any surface where two mesh regions meet, the interface contains the entire face of both mesh regions. This way, the four vertices of each face meet, and the number of processors in each direction on the face must be the same. This allows messages to be easily exchanged across the boundary. A single mesh region is easily divided by specifying the number of processors in the x, y, and z directions such that the product of these numbers is the total number of processors. Once a number of processors is assigned in each coordinate direction, the number of cells in that direction is chosen so that each block has about the same number of cells. This is easily done

Figure 2.3   One mesh region (*a*) versus several mesh regions (*b*).

by dividing the number of cells in a given direction by the number of processors in that direction. If there is a remainder r, then r subregions are assigned one additional cell each.

However, this method of using one rectilinear region of space for all problems can result in inefficiencies because the region might include space which is not essential to the calculation. In order to save space, PCTH can operate in a domain having an arbitrary number of mesh regions. Figure 2.3 shows a two-dimensional penetrator on the left hitting a plate on the right. Figure 2.3*a* shows the problem as one large mesh region while Figure 2.3*b* shows the same problem as four smaller mesh regions with a savings of one-third of the size of the problem.

These arbitrary mesh regions must meet like the blocks in the one-mesh region case. When this problem is put on a parallel machine, each of the mesh regions has to be divided into blocks such that the total number of blocks equals the number of processors. In addition, blocks at the boundary of mesh regions must match with neighboring blocks. This is accomplished by dividing adjacent mesh regions into the same number of blocks in each adjacent direction. Figure 2.4 illustrates the problem domain of Figure 2.3 divided into cells with dashed lines. The wide solid lines are the divisions between the mesh regions; the thin solid lines divide the problem into groups of cells, which are called blocks. Mesh region 2 requires a finer resolution than the other three regions and is, therefore, subdivided into more blocks. In this example, the domain has been divided into 10 blocks for execution on 10 processors, with each processor having 20 cells. Notice that the number of cells across each boundary, whether between mesh regions or blocks, is constant and that mesh regions 1, 2, and 3 are divided into the same number of blocks in the horizontal direction.

The mesh decomposition problem reduces to dividing the mesh regions into blocks such that each block is properly connected, the number of blocks is less than or equal to the number of available processors, and each block has about the same number of cells. The last objective is accomplished by producing a mapping that minimizes the maximum number of cells that any processor can have. If two solutions are equal in this regard, then the one that has the smaller surface area in cells on the face of the block is chosen since that will minimize the amount of information that has to be communicated to neighboring processors.

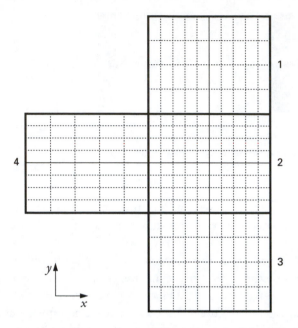

Figure 2.4   Four mesh regions divided into 10 blocks of 20 cells each.

Any two adjacent mesh regions must have identical subdivisions on their common face. This requirement for subdivision consistency leads to the construction of mesh region sets. Each mesh region is in exactly one mesh region set for each coordinate direction. To construct the mesh region sets the following algorithm is performed:

1 If all directions have been processed, then quit. Otherwise, select a direction for subsequent work.

2 If all mesh regions are in a mesh region set for the current direction, then go to 1. Otherwise, select a mesh region for subsequent work that is not in any mesh region set associated with the current direction.

3 Create a new set containing the selected mesh region.

4 Add to the set any mesh regions which are neighbors in the coordinate direction to the current set members.

5 Go to 4 until every coordinate direction neighbor of every mesh region in the set is included in the set.

6 Go to 2.

The mesh regions are now grouped into sets. Each mesh region is in one set for each direction. This reduces the problem to that of determining the number of subdivisions for each set. In the three-dimensional case, each mesh region is in three sets. In the two dimensional example in Figure 2.4, each mesh region is in two sets. Mesh regions 1, 2, and 3 will each be divided into the same number of blocks in the x direction. Therefore, they are put into a set. Mesh region 4 is the single member of another x-direction set. Likewise, mesh regions 2 and 4 will be divided into the same number of blocks in the y direction and are thus put into the same set. Mesh regions 1 and 3 are the single members of two y-direction sets. To summarize, the problem in Figure 2.4 can be divided into five sets: two in the x direction (one with mesh regions 1, 2, and 3 and one with mesh region 4) and three in the y direction (one for mesh region 1, one for mesh regions 2 and 4, and one for mesh region 3). The decomposition problem is reduced to finding the five variables representing the number of subdivisions for each set.

The problem of determining a division of mesh regions into blocks is solved by a recursive search. A number of subdivisions for set 1 is selected from a list of allowable subdivisions. Given this number, the set of allowable subdivision numbers for set 2 is calculated and one of these is selected, and so on. The algorithm proceeds until all sets have been examined. The allowable range of subdivision numbers for a particular set can be calculated by using the subdivision numbers from the previous sets and the total number of blocks desired, and by noting that all future sets will have at least one subdivision. The total number of blocks for all mesh regions not contained in the current set is calculated and subtracted from the total number of desired blocks. This number is divided by the total number of blocks for all mesh regions that contain the current set, assuming that the number of blocks in the current set is one. This gives an upper bound on the number of subdivisions for this set. As each set is assigned a number of subdivisions, the maximum number of cells per block in the direction associated with the set is the least integer greater than or equal to the number of cells divided by the number of subdivisions. At least one block in the mesh region will have this number of cells in the set direction. For the last set, the maximum number of cells in a block is computed and compared to the current best arrangement. It is obvious that if an exhaustive search is done, the result will be a solution which has the smallest maximum number of cells per processor. Such a search can be somewhat slow in some cases. However, the search can be optimized by the use of counting arguments which quickly eliminate portions of the search while giving the optimal answer rapidly.

The lighter solid lines in Figure 2.4 show an optimal division of the problem onto 10 processors. Each of the processors has 20 cells. The set for the x direction, which contains blocks 1, 2, and 3, has been divided into two processors; the set for the x direction, which contains block 4 was divided into one processor; the sets for the y direction for blocks 1 and 3 were each divided into one processor; and the set for the y direction which contains blocks 2 and 4 has been divided into two processors.

Once all possibilities have been tested and the best configuration has been found, the number of blocks in the three directions is determined by looking at the number of blocks for the set for those directions. Once the program has this information, it can divide the mesh regions into blocks and assign each of these blocks to a processor. The above algorithm can also be extended for nodes with different memory capacities using appropriate weightings. This permits additional flexibility in choosing block widths in one of the mesh directions.

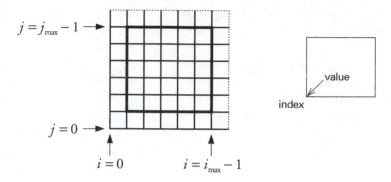

$j = j_{max} - 1$ →

$j = 0$ →

$i = 0$

$i = i_{max} - 1$

value

index

Figure 2.5 Cell-centered fields. The single rows and columns of cells exterior to the heavy dark box are "ghost" cells.

Data Members in Each Block

The simulation data for each block are associated with a separate executable. For convenience and order, most of the PCTH data are located in a single nested C++ class hierarchy. This might roughly correspond to a nested set of C structures or a set of common blocks in Fortran 77. In any case, the executable which contains the block information must reside as a separate process or thread of control. On a machine like the nCUBE/2 there is only one executable on each node. Since we organize our work with C++ classes, we tend to think of the "hydroblock" or "block" as controlling the calculation by calling class methods rather than main(). Thus the terms hydroblock, block, node, and executable are used somewhat interchangeably. We shall use "block" for conciseness. Thus each block is a separate program which runs essentially oblivious to the state of the other blocks until synchronization with other blocks is required. Within the block structure, which is created in main(), there are a number of entities which comprise a simulation state on each node.

Some examples of data structures contained in the block (remember that we have equated this with a separate thread of control) are cell-centered fields like energy and pressure and face-centered fields like velocity components. Fields correspond to an array in Fortran. Currently, exactly one extra boundary cell, termed a ghost cell, is allowed around the exterior of the simulation field structure that belongs to a given block. A face-centered field has an extra cell in the direction perpendicular to its faces but contains only the face edges on the boundary. In the code we think in terms of operations on a cell-centered field, such as averages or differences in a given direction, which return a face-centered field. A cell-centered field with correct boundary values can undergo a single cell stencil operation and obtain a fully correct face-centered field (see Figures 2.5 and 2.6). However, if this face-centered field undergoes an additional operation to a cell-centered field in the face direction, then this requires that cell boundary values be supplied before the cell-centered edge values can be used again. These boundary values are supplied either by communication with another block or by setting a real boundary

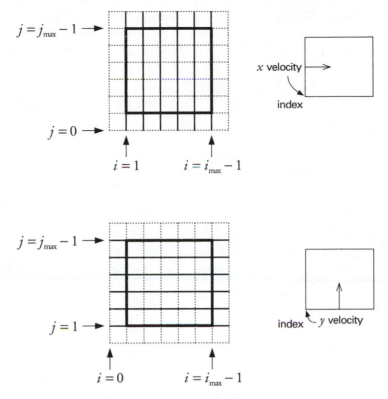

Figure 2.6   Face-centered fields.

condition. Although we implement many such operations in C++ using operator over-loading, the concept can just as easily be implemented using C or Fortran arrays. The formality of a C++ structure for fields presents the look of a vector or data-parallel language and provides some consistency checking. Nothing we do in our code really requires C++; it is only used to help manage complexity and improve clarity. The concept of "loss of boundary information," implying a boundary communication or a boundary update, is key.

The foregoing discussion can be clarified using a very simple example. Suppose we have a one-dimensional operator which takes neighboring values to obtain new values. For example, suppose the equation is

$$u_i^{n+1} = u_i^n + \alpha(u_{i-1}^n - 2u_i^n + u_{i+1}^n) \tag{2.2}$$

where $i = 0, \ldots, N$. Note that the difference equation can only be performed for $i = 1, \ldots, N-1$ and that u_0^{n+1} and u_N^{n+1} are undefined for any future operation of this type. These values must then be defined in one of two ways. They can be specified by the user code if they are actually true boundaries for the complete mesh, or they must be

provided by a neighboring block via a message. Some simple code for such an update in
C is given as

```
void update( double * u)
{
#ifdef NCUBE
    int mes_type = BOUNDARY_UPDATE;
    int r;
    int l_neighbor;
    int r_neighbor;
    if(have_right_neighbor())
        nwrite(&u[N-1], sizeof(double), right_neighbor(), mes_type, &r);
    if(have_left_neighbor())
        nwrite(&u[1], sizeof(double), left_neighbor(), mes_type, &r);
    if(!have_right_neighbor())
        u[N]=boundary_value;
    if(!have_left_neighbor())
        u[0]=boundary_value;
    if(have_left_neighbor())
        return_length = nread(&u[0], sizeof(double), l_neighbor, &mes_type, &r);
    if(have_right_neighbor())
        return_length = nread(&u[0], sizeof(double), r_neighbor, &mes_type, &r);
#elif INTEL
    ...other similar code...
#elif PVM3
    ...other similar code...
#endif
}
```

Note that the update is hidden in a separate boundary routine and is not directly in
the main body of the code. Also observe that all the message sends are done before
actually filling in any boundary values. This helps to overlap communication and avoid
idle time in the `nread` subroutines while waiting for messages to appear in the message
queue. Such a wait state is called a "blocked read."

The face-centered field idea can be nominally illustrated by breaking up the previous
equation into two steps.

$$\nu_i^n = u_i^n - u_{i-1}^n \tag{2.3}$$

$$u_i^{n+1} = u_i^n + \alpha(\nu_{i+1}^n - \nu_i^n) \tag{2.4}$$

Equation 2.3 is a single difference operation which yields $N-1$ values. The values in
two or three dimensions would be oriented in the difference direction. No communication updates are necessary at this point, although it is conceivable that a face-centered
boundary condition may be desired. The next equation performs another difference
operation on the face-centered values. The cell-centered boundary values resulting from
Equation 2.4 must be updated before they can be used in further difference operations.

We now discuss our choice of a single layer of ghost cells. This single layer provides an available buffer for each field for use in boundary computations and updates.
Having no ghost cells would minimize storage but maximize communications, while a

multiple-cell boundary treatment with sufficient ghost cells to complete a full cycle without communication would be extravagant in the use of memory for our application. The single boundary cell is in fact consistent with the original CTH implementation.

The block structure also contains other "simulation" scope data variables such as time step information, algorithm options, and diagnostics objects. Another important structure is our material object, which contains specific material state arrays and material modeling information such as pointers to equation-of-state objects which provide material-specific evaluation routines.

2.5 PCTH Algorithm

PCTH solves explicit finite difference or finite volume equations representing the principles of conservation of mass, momentum, and energy for solid and/or gaseous objects interacting at high velocities and/or pressures. The solid material response is fluid-like in many cases. These conservation equations must be augmented as well by including constitutive models which provide a description of the relationship between density, energy, and pressure, for example, as well as models to describe the deviatoric stress response of solids. The algorithm is in two parts: a Lagrangian part, which computes the motion of the material, and an Eulerian part, which computes the state of the material at the coordinate locations of the fixed mesh. The details of the PCTH algorithms are not appropriate for this chapter and would only tend to obscure the general ideas we wish to convey. We shall discuss two general ideas in this chapter: multidimensional boundary updates and the tracer particle algorithm.

Multidimensional Boundary Update Algorithm

From a logical point of view, various portions of the PCTH algorithm can be treated as a map which changes cell state variables based on information in neighboring cells. Whenever an operation invalidates a plane of ghost cells, it must be updated in one of two ways. Either the information must be obtained from a neighboring block (e.g., the boundary is a "neighbor" boundary) and communications are required, or the boundary is a "real" boundary and must be updated from local information. Depending on the particular boundary condition, different values might be required and must be available. Such local information is ignored in the update code if the boundary must be updated by communication. To repeat, there is logically no apparent difference in our highest level code between a boundary update request on a cell-centered field which is supplied by communication and a boundary update request which is supplied from a true boundary condition. This implies that each "block" or "node" is viewed as an independent entity that evolves itself forward in time. This is illustrated in Figure 2.7. A useful trick becomes apparent in order to update "corner" cells: one updates the complete ghost plane in each of the three directions consecutively rather than each specific section individually. Notice how all the corner ghost cells are, in fact, correctly set in Figure 2.7 after an update first in the x direction and then in the y direction. This concept is

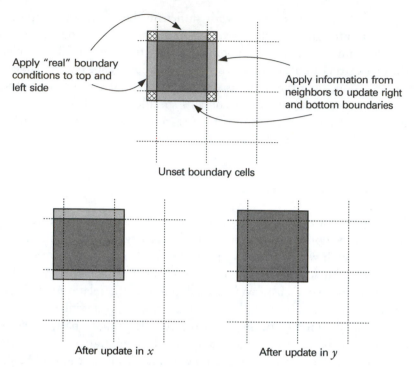

Apply "real" boundary conditions to top and left side

Apply information from neighbors to update right and bottom boundaries

Unset boundary cells

After update in x

After update in y

Figure 2.7 **Updating consecutively in coordinate directions leads to correct boundary information in corner ghost cells.**

important because it reduces the number of "neighbors" of a given block from 26 to 6 in three dimensions and from 8 to 4 in two dimensions.

Note that only a final result from an extensive set of operations may need to be updated on the boundary. If several cell-centered fields have stencils applied to them in various directions and the final result is a single cell-centered field, it may not be necessary to update all of the intermediate results. Only the final cell-centered field is required to be correct through a boundary update call.

Although each node operates independently on its own data, the PCTH algorithm requires that the time step be synchronized among all the blocks in the problem. This entails a call to a global minimization routine in the time step control routine. Global algorithms are described in Section 2.6.

Tracer Particles

Another important algorithm is the tracer particle algorithm. A tracer particle is a diagnostic point in the flow which may or may not move with the fluid. Each node computes and writes out point values for the particles in its block. Eulerian tracer particles are fixed in space. Lagrangian tracer particles move with the fluid, and their location must be integrated forward in time as the simulation proceeds. Such tracer diagnostics are critical to gaining meaningful physical information about the results of the calculation. When a tracer is discovered to no longer be in a given block, then it must be sent to a neighboring block.

One algorithm to solve this problem for each block or node is as follows:

1. Update tracer particle positions of all tracer particles.
2. If any tracer has left the block, then invalidate it (set a flag or delete the structure) after sending its information to the neighbor in the direction of one of the invalid coordinates.
3. Enter a polling loop to receive any incoming tracers.
4. Globally sum the number of tracers. Go to 3 until all tracers are accounted for.
5. If no tracers were exchanged, then go to 6. Otherwise, go to 2 to catch corner crossing tracers.
6. Done. All tracers reside on the correct block for the next time step and/or output request.

This algorithm is easy to understand and is effective. The global sum code is described in Section 2.6.

The PCTH coding is meant to be totally deterministic and independent of the number of nodes used to compute a given problem. The only variation from this design goal is in the output of global summations of mass, momentum, and energy. These summations differ slightly for different numbers of nodes due to round-off errors inherent in the different summation orders.

2.6 Using Different Machines

Any program written for a MIMD machine must be able to do certain operations such as sending information to another processor. Some programs, such as PCTH, use the individual processor numbers to determine which part of the global data each processor operates on. All MIMD machines have library calls which allow the program to do operations such as determine processor number and the total number of processors, send a message to another processor, and receive a message from another processor. Most MIMD parallel programs can be written with these basic operations and some knowledge of the architecture of the machine. Some machines also come with routines to allow users to perform basic operations such as efficiently calculating a global sum. The user in this case need not determine what communication pattern between processors is best for the particular architecture and need not code an appropriate algorithm using standard read and write message protocols. Fortunately, a standard message-passing interface is likely to be available in the near future on many machines. The emerging MPI (message-passing interface) standard has the support of a number of institutions, and the portability problem should become less of an issue as soon as implementations become widely available.[9]

As an example of these message-passing libraries, the nCUBE/2 uses the routine npid() to return the processor number while the Intel machines use the function call mynode(). To receive a message from another processor, the nCUBE/2 uses the function call nread() while the Intel Gamma™ uses the call crecv(). The arguments to some of these functions vary among machines, but the calls allow the same functionality. For example, the nread call for the nCUBE/2 allows the programmer to specify both the type of message to be received and the processor to receive the message from, while the crecv call for the Intel Gamma only allows messages to be selected by type. When a processor receives a message on the nCUBE/2, the processor number and message type arguments to the nread() call are set to reflect the processor number that sent the message and the message type of that message. This is useful when the processor is receiving a message of any type or from any processor. On the Intel Gamma, to get the same information the program uses the call infonode() to determine the processor that sent the last message received or infotype() to determine the type of that message. Different machines from the same vendor may have different or extra functionality. For example, the Intel Paragon, which uses a two-dimensional mesh, has most of the function calls of the Intel Gamma, which uses a hypercube. The Intel Paragon, however, has an extended crecv() call, crecvx(), which allows the program to specify which processor to receive a message from.

In order to run the same program on different machines, conditional compilation using the C pre-processor selects different code for the different machines. Since PCTH was written in C++ in an object-oriented manner, the number of routines which need to be changed to accommodate a new message-passing protocol when moving to a new machine is small (fewer than ten). In some cases, other changes may have to be made for PCTH to compile on various machines. A well-designed code in C or Fortran would also have very few places where changes would have to be made. An alternative approach would be to define our own message-passing interface and place all the compile time-dependent message-passing code in a subroutine library. In any case, it is generally easy with appropriate code design to port MIMD code to different parallel MIMD systems.

Below is an example of a routine which uses the C pre-processor #ifdef statement to select a message-passing protocol. The routine does a global sum, where each processor has a floating-point number that must be summed across the processors. For the nCUBE/2, which is a hypercube, an exchange across each dimension of the hypercube is done, summing the number that a processor has with the one it gets from its neighbor in each dimension. After the end of $\log_2$ of the number of processor steps, each processor has the global sum. If the program has been compiled to run on either the Intel Gamma or the Intel Paragon, we call the library function gdsum(), which efficiently returns the sum. The algorithm it uses is based on the topology and is presumed to be highly optimized. On a single processor system such as a workstation, the routine simply returns the value that it was passed. In this way, the program calls this routine whether it is on a single-processor system or a parallel machine, and the routine returns the correct value.

```
double global_sum(double value)
{
#ifdef NCUBE
    unsigned int myself = node_number();
    unsigned int while_counter = number_of_nodes();
    int message_type = SUM_OVER_ALL_NODES;
    double other_value;
    int return_length;
    int reserved;
    while (while_counter >>= 1)
    {
        int neighbor = myself ^ while_counter;
        nwrite(&value, sizeof(double), neighbor, message_type, &reserved);
        return_length = nread(&other_value, sizeof(double), &neighbor,
            &message_type, &reserved);
        value+=other_value;
    }
#endif
#ifdef INTEL
    double other_value;
    long length = 1;

    gdsum(&value, length, &other_value);
#endif
    return value;
}
```

In this way, code can be structured to be easily ported to another MIMD machine. The algorithms modeling the physics remain the same, and all we have to do is add the machine-specific interfaces to the PCTH routines where any given communication function is performed. In this way, we could also add support for any other standard message-passing library, such as PVM, by allowing it to be one of the options.[10]

2.7 Optimization, Tuning, and Tradeoffs

Effect of Number of Nodes

Table 2.1 shows performance results for PCTH on the nCUBE/2. These results are for a two material problem which was run for 50 time steps. In the table, size is the total size of the problem. For each run, each processor has a $14 \times 14 \times 14$ cell block of the total problem. Time/cycle is the wallclock time in seconds it takes to compute one time step. The scaled speedup is the ratio of an estimate for the wallclock time the problem would take on one node to the wallclock time for the problem on multiple processors. Since none of the problems except for the first will fit on one processor, the time for one processor to run the larger problem is estimated by taking the time for the one-processor run and multiplying it by the number of processors, since the size of the problem is proportional to the number of processors. The parallel efficiency is the scaled speedup divided by the number of processors.

Note that the parallel efficiency in Table 2.1 remains above 98.5%. This means that the problem is scaling well as long as the problem size increases with the number of

# Nodes	Size	Time/Cycle	Scaled Speedup	Parallel Efficiency, %
1	$14 \times 14 \times 14$	47.9	1.0	100
2	$28 \times 14 \times 14$	48.1	1.97	98.5
4	$28 \times 28 \times 14$	48.2	3.97	99.3
8	$28 \times 28 \times 28$	48.5	7.90	98.7
16	$56 \times 28 \times 28$	48.5	15.78	98.7
32	$56 \times 56 \times 28$	48.5	31.6	98.8
64	$56 \times 56 \times 56$	48.5	63.2	98.8
128	$112 \times 56 \times 56$	48.5	126.3	98.7
256	$112 \times 112 \times 56$	48.5	252.4	98.6
512	$112 \times 112 \times 112$	48.5	505.6	98.7
1024	$224 \times 112 \times 112$	48.3	1011	98.8

Table 2.1   Timings on the nCUBE/2™.

nodes so that the same size subproblem exists on each node. Since most of the communication between processors is done with at most six other processors, it is reasonable to expect that more nodes could be used efficiently for a correspondingly larger problem. From this table, it appears that communication takes at most 1.5% of the execution time for PCTH for these large problems.

These results are for an optimized version of the code in which the base level vector operation libraries contain specially tuned assembly language code. Table 2.2 shows the results of running the same problem without using the assembly code libraries. The assembly libraries speed the code up by about 47% in the one-processor case. Note that in Table 2.2, the parallel efficiencies are slightly better than the efficiencies in Table 2.1. The explanation for this is that the amount of communication is constant in similar rows in both of the tables, but the time for computation is larger in Table 2.2; thus, the percentage of the time spent in communication is smaller, leading to better efficiency numbers. Better parallel efficiency does not necessarily imply faster run times.

In reality, when the code is run in production mode, we use tracer particles and dump files for visualization. Table 2.3 shows timings for a problem when these features are turned on. These results were obtained while running the $224 \times 112 \times 112$ problem on the whole machine. In this case, 16 tracer particles were used with output every cycle. This increases the run time by about 1% over the base run time. For the timings with visualization turned on, we dumped visualization results for 20 time steps in a 100 time step run. This increases the time for the cycles in which we dump the visualization information by about 484% for an overall run time increase of about a factor of 2. The reason for this extreme performance degradation is that the visualization files are dumped to the front end of the nCUBE/2, which means a serialization of a large number

# Nodes	Size	Time/Cycle	Scaled Speedup	Parallel Efficiency, %
1	$14 \times 14 \times 14$	90.8	1.0	100
2	$28 \times 14 \times 14$	91.0	1.99	99.7
4	$28 \times 28 \times 14$	91.3	3.98	99.5
8	$28 \times 28 \times 28$	91.4	7.95	99.3
16	$56 \times 28 \times 28$	91.5	15.88	99.2
32	$56 \times 56 \times 28$	91.5	31.75	99.2
64	$56 \times 56 \times 56$	91.6	63.4	99.1
128	$112 \times 56 \times 56$	91.8	126.6	98.9
256	$112 \times 112 \times 56$	91.8	253.1	98.9
512	$112 \times 112 \times 112$	91.9	506.2	98.9
1024	$224 \times 112 \times 112$	91.9	1013	98.9

Table 2.2 **Timings on the nCUBE/2™ without assembly libraries.**

of parallel data. The link between the nCUBE/2 and the front end is also slower than the interprocessor communication speed. Thus, the user of PCTH must be painfully aware of the cost associated with a dump of a graphical post-processing file.

Memory Considerations for MIMD Machines

The general programer is perhaps unaware that massively parallel MIMD message-passing machines have four major sources of memory usage. Memory is occupied by the operating system, system message-passing buffers, application program space, and data. Part of user data, which is generally insignificant on most serial machines, is the space for the ghost or boundary cells, because this memory is usually a small fraction of the overall memory. However, with a MIMD spatial decomposition it is not necessarily a very small fraction. A specification of the total memory alone when compared against a shared memory space application may not characterize memory needs well at all. For

Tracers	Visualization	Average Time/Cycle
off	off	48.5
on	off	49.0
off	on	95.3
on	on	95.9

Table 2.3 **Timings for a 224 × 112 × 112 problem on 1024 nodes of the nCUBE/2™.**

2.7 OPTIMIZATION, TUNING, AND TRADEOFFS

many projects with only a few thousand lines of code, the size of the executable is not a consideration. However, with codes such as PCTH the executable size is very significant since it is replicated on every node. The "creeping featurism" found in production codes as they are continually updated with new capabilities can affect performance due to larger executable sizes. The following represents an approximate memory usage constraint equation in bytes for double-precision codes with cubic meshes such as PCTH:

$$T \geq O + B + E + 8N(w + 2G)^D \qquad (2.5)$$

where T is the total memory on each node, O is the memory used by the operating system, B is the space required by the system for message buffers, E is the size of the executable of a SPMD code, N is the number of permanent and temporary memory blocks needed by the user, w is the length of one side of the memory block, G is the width of the ghost cell planes, and D is the dimensionality of the problem (1, 2, or 3). How much memory is really usable by the application? The memory efficiency can be expressed as the total available user memory divided by the total memory on the machine:

$$e = \frac{8NW^D}{T} \qquad (2.6)$$

where W is defined implicitly by

$$T = O + B + E + 8N(W + 2G)^D \qquad (2.7)$$

Equation 2.6 is valid for any number of nodes. However, the implications can be impressive. This is easily seen in the case of the nCUBE/2, where only 4 MB of memory/node are available on Sandia's machine. The PCTH executable image (text and static data) take up over 1 MB, so it is easy to see that the memory efficiency is less than 75% for PCTH. This implies that no more than 3 GB of the full 4 GB of memory on Sandia's nCUBE/2 is really usable for our application data. Even the G ($G = 1$ for PCTH) term can be significant. It turns out that the O term is small on the nCUBE/2 and the B term is user adjustable. For many applications, the E term may also be negligible. The potential buyer of any MIMD machine should be aware of such memory traps and should use the true useful memory in evaluating capability and cost. For example, a hypothetical node operating system which required 4 MB/node and a message-passing buffering scheme which required another 1 MB/node would result in an overall user memory efficiency of less than 63% for the PCTH application on a 16 MB/node system! In summary, a fixed, significant percentage of the whole machine memory can be occupied by the operating system and user code, and a significant fraction can be tied up in ghost cells. A node memory size which works well for small test codes may be a real constraint for a large production code due to the fact that the very largest desired problems may not be able to be run at all, and worse, the surface/volume ratio may be too large (granularity too small) for good message-passing efficiency. On a SIMD machine, the O term would be relatively small. A SIMD implementation may not have the ghost cell terms, but more communication overhead may be incurred during stencil operations and a speed penalty may be incurred.

Database Generation

The original PCTH research work moved only the computational kernel of code to the nodes of the nCUBE/2 machine and the Connection Machine. done for simplicity in order to determine if parallel machines could be used for t. computationally intensive portions of the simulation algorithm. The complete production software suite entails close to 200,000 lines of Fortran 77, so it made r sense to try to do everything at once. This is probably typical of many projects develo ing production software for parallel machines using previously developed code as a base In the initial research work, all of the code used by CTH to set up a restart database was left to run on a workstation-class front-end machine: a host program distributed infor- mation using both broadcast and serial sends. Many current massively parallel machines operate with workstation-class front-ends, and this typically leaves a large bandwidth mismatch between the capability of the massively parallel hardware and the capability of the front-end machine. This annoying mismatch for two-dimensional computations was seen to be disastrous for moving into three-dimensional computations. The conclu- sion is that any of the pre- or post-processing computations and restart capabilities which somehow scale with the size of the problem should be considered for migration to the massively parallel hardware in order to move—in any sense—into a "production" mode. On the pre-processing end, a full "restart" database for PCTH is not now required to run a problem (as is still true for CTH). Essentially all of the information required to begin a calculation is contained in a small text file and an encoded volume fraction file. The volume fraction file avoids the storage of zeroes by indexing nonzero regions and encodes runs of repeated values (in particular, the value 1) by a repeat count scheme. The information in the input text files is broadcast to all the computational nodes using a log- arithmic broadcast scheme. The nodes then decide what to do with this information based on their individual node numbers. Much of the text file information is common to all of the processors, while each block decides which portion of which mesh region it should own and thus which portion of the volume fraction file to use. A logarithmic fan scheme may sound difficult but is rather simple. One way to code such an input fan follows:

```
void broadcast_from_node_zero(char * value, int length)
{
#ifdef NCUBE
   int myself = node_number();
   int bit = 1;
   int message_type = BROADCAST_FROM_NODE_ZERO;
   int r;
   int return_length;
   while(bit <number_of_nodes()) {
      int neighbor = myself ^ bit;
      if(neighbor<number_of_nodes()) {
         if(bit > myself )
            nwrite(value, length, neighbor, message_type, &r);
         else if((bit<<1)>myself)
            return_length = nread(&value, length, &neighbor, &message_type, &r);
      }
      bit<<=1;
```

```
  c INTEL
    ong message_type = BROADCAST_FROM_NODE_ZERO;
    if (node_number() == 0)
        csend(message_type, value, length, -1, 0);
    else
        crecv(message_type, value, length);
  #endif
    return;
  }
```

In the case of the nCUBE/2 the broadcast algorithm has been written with sends and receives, while in the case of Intel machines, the functionality is already available in a library routine. A diagram of the broadcast tree for the above coding is given in Figure 2.8. Note that the number of communications levels required for all the nodes to receive a given piece of information is only $\log_2$ of the number of nodes. For 1024 nodes, this means that only 10 communications time intervals are required for all the nodes to receive the relevant information.

The volume fraction generator was written using an object-oriented solid modeling toolkit. This generator uses geometric information to avoid unnecessary volume fraction calculations and uses a modular arithmetic technique on the mesh-region cells to divide the computational work among the nodes. With this simple scheme, it is sufficient to use only 32 or 64 nodes of the nCUBE/2 to get acceptable speed for mesh sizes on the order of 100 cubed, even though the speedup efficiency can be poor. Calculated values are output by each node in an encoded format to avoid redundant zeroes and ones. This problem is illustrative of a very important concept. It is wallclock time that matters, not speedup. The application of an embarrassingly parallel brute-force algorithm to this problem proved disastrous. A good algorithm which has poor parallel speedup may still beat a poor algorithm with a well-balanced work load by orders of magnitude in real wallclock time.[11] The volume fraction algorithm generates file information which is broadcast using a logarithmic fan to all the nodes to start a PCTH run. Each node collects the information it needs during the broadcast operation. In summary, the PCTH database to start a calculation has been minimized and very large problems can

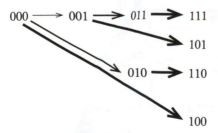

Figure 2.8   Broadcast logarithmic tree for eight nodes. Successively thicker lines represent bit values of 1, 2, and 4, respectively.

be set in motion with a very small database. We suspect that many developers will have to develop similarly innovative techniques to deal with the generation of large databases on massively parallel machines.

Restart Capability

When calculations run for many hours, it is highly desirable to be able to restart calculations from a previously saved state. If restart information is requested, only the minimal set of information required to restore the current state is stored. Each block in the simulation writes its own separate restart file to an appropriate, separate disk file (preferably on a parallel disk system, if such is available). Although this may seem like a serious limitation, a given problem usually is fairly well matched to the number of nodes on a given machine so that, in general, the same number of nodes will be used to continue a calculation as are used to start the calculation. Thus, as yet, a more general restart capability has not been developed which would allow restart of a calculation where the calculation was mapped to a different number of nodes.

Serial Output

It is apparent that graphical capabilities are required to gain understanding from very large databases residing in the memory of a parallel machine. This large amount of available information must be filtered in some way. In PCTH, filtering includes a compressed plot file format in which double-precision numbers are scaled to 16-bit integers and then run-length encoded. The user can also exactly specify which information is desired in order to minimize the number of output data. This information, as well as tracer particle information, is collected and written from one of the nodes. This output, which is sent to a serial workstation, must undergo serialization at some point. Currently, we do this at run time by having one of the nodes write the file output (it is common, and indeed true in the case of PCTH, that node zero is this designated node). The designated node opens the file, and the rest of the nodes send information, as requested, to this node for output to the file. This is essentially the SPMD model. There is only one program, but a given node performs different actions based upon its own node number.

In the future, production software may have separate MIMD programs residing on a much smaller number of nodes to be utilized for asynchronous input/output subtasks which are essentially downsizing and/or serializing algorithms. Collecting visualization data and tracer particle data and writing a serial file while the rest of the computation proceeds is a good example of a useful software system optimization. The results of Section 2.7 (in the subsection "Effect of Number of Nodes") on the effect of large serialized output illustrates the importance of achieving a balance between the capability of the parallel hardware and the ability to receive and analyze data from the machine. In addition to the post-processing capability mentioned above, we also have a frame buffer capability from the nCUBE/2 to output two-dimensional slices to a raster image. This improves output bandwidth, but only to those physical locations where graphics hardware is available.

2.8 Conclusion

The PCTH development project evolved from a system in which major portions of the original software resided on the front-end machine, with only the computational kernel on the nodes, to its current state as a SPMD code, in which there is no front-end code and one node initiates a broadcast of all input information. Each node operates as a separate program that makes decisions and interacts with the collection of nodes based solely on the knowledge of its own node number and the total number of nodes involved in the computation. The current code uses, with good results, a static spatial decomposition technique to subdivide the computational work.

Acknowledgments

We would like to acknowledge the contributions of the many staff members at Sandia National Laboratories who have provided support to the PCTH effort, including all those participating in the CTH, PCTH and RHALE development. This work was performed at Sandia National Laboratories and was supported by the U.S. Department of Energy under contract number DE-AC04-76DP00789.

References

1 J. M. McGlaun, S. L. Thompson, and M. G. Elrick. "CTH: A Three-Dimensional Shock Wave Physics Code," *Int. J. Impact Engng.* **10**, 351, 1990.

2 A. C. Robinson, A. L. Ames, H. E. Fang, D. Pavlakos, C. T. Vaughan, and P. Campbell. "Massively Parallel Computing, C++ and Hydrocode Algorithms," *Computing in Civil Engineering Proceedings.* 8th Conference in conjunction with A/E/C Systems '92, TCCP/ ASCE, Dallas, June 7–9, 1992.

3 H. E. Fang, A. C. Robinson, and K. Cho. "Hydrocode Development on the Connection Machine," *Proceedings.* 5th SIAM Conference on Parallel Processing for Scientific Computing, SIAM, 1992.

4 A. C. Robinson, C. T. Vaughan, H. E. Fang, C. F. Diegert, and K. Cho. "Hydrocode Development on the nCUBE and the Connection Machine Hypercubes," *Shock Compressions of Condensed Matter–1991.* North-Holland, Amsterdam, 1992.

5 K. G. Budge, J. S. Peery, and A. C. Robinson. "High-Performance Scientific Computing Using C++," *Proceedings.* 1992 USENIX C++ Technical Conference, Portland, OR, August 10–14, 1992.

6 A. C. Robinson. "New Approaches for Developing High-Performance Solid-Dynamic Simulation Systems," *Computing Systems in Engineering.* **3**, 477, 1992.

7 B. Hendrickson and R. Leland. "Multidimensional Spectral Load Balancing." Report SAND93-0074, Sandia National Laboratories, Albuquerque, NM, 1993.

8   C. Ozturan, B. Szymanski, and J. E. Flaherty. "Adaptive Methods and Rectangular Partitioning Problem," *Proceedings*. IEEE Scalable High Performance Computing Conference, Williamsburg, VA, 1992.

9   "MPI: A Message-Passing Interface Standard," final report version 1.0. Message Passing Interface Forum, University of Tennessee, Knoxville, May 5, 1994.

10   A. Geist et al. "PVM User's Guide and Reference Manual." Report ORNL/TM-12187, Oak Ridge National Laboratory, Oak Ridge, TN, 1994.

11   A. L. Ames, A. C. Robinson, and T. L. Edwards. "VFGEN: A Parallel Volume Fraction Generator for Hydrocodes," *Proceedings*, 1st Annual Object-Oriented Numerics Conference, Sunriver, OR. Rogue Wave Software, Inc., Corvallis, OR, 1993.

3

Weather Prediction: A Scalable Storm-Scale Model

KELVIN K. DROEGEMEIER, MING XUE,
KENNETH JOHNSON, MATTHEW O'KEEFE,
AARON SAWDEY, GARY W. SABOT,
SKEF WHOLEY, KIM MILLS, and NENG-TAN LIN

Contents

In this chapter, the authors describe a weather model application, the Advanced Regional Prediction System (ARPS), that has been designed from the start to run on a wide range of parallel machines. The development cycle of a large code like the ARPS is worth examining because of the issues and tradeoffs it addresses. All applications encounter tradeoffs such as efficiency versus portability, but the ARPS encounters them in a magnified and clarified form. The authors discuss how the ARPS was ported to a wide variety of architectures, and they describe the resulting performance measurements and optimization work.

3.1 Introduction

We describe the development and implementation of a new three-dimensional atmospheric model designed for the operational prediction of thunderstorms and related weather. This application, known as the Advanced Regional Prediction System (ARPS), is the first full-physics, general-purpose mesoscale atmospheric model developed specifically for broad classes of scalable-parallel architectures. It has been carefully and professionally written and completely documented, including an external user's guide. Because of its coding style and the societal relevance of its objectives, the ARPS has been welcomed into the computer science community as a framework for developing and testing compilers, translation tools, and automated differentiation techniques. The ARPS was one of five finalists for the 1993 Gordon Bell Prize in High Performance Computing.[1]

Unique to the ARPS is the use of structured finite difference operators which, being the discrete analogs of partial derivatives, preserve the formal structure in the code of the governing equations of fluid dynamics, making the code more readable and easier to learn and modify. The finite difference operators also expose the parallelism inherent in but typically masked by the solution algorithms, making the code naturally scalable for general classes of parallel machines. This operator-based solution methodology is applicable to any finite difference, finite volume, or finite element code, and has been shown to reduce development and debugging time substantially relative to more conventional methodologies.

We have evaluated the ARPS on several parallel architectures, and in this chapter we compare and contrast our experiences using four separate approaches:

1 Explicit message passing using a portable communications library, Parallel Virtual Machine (PVM), on a networked cluster of IBM RISC (reduced instruction set computer) System 6000™ workstations (Section 3.6).

2 A data-parallel approach in which serial Fortran 77 is translated into Connection Machine Fortran (CMF) on the CM-200™ and CM-5™ using the Fortran-P translator (Section 3.7).

3 A data-parallel approach in which serial Fortran 77 is translated into Connection Machine Fortran (CMF) on the CM-5 using the Thinking Machines CMAX™ translator (Section 3.8).

4 Explicit message passing applied to the original Fortran 77 ARPS on the CM-5 and Intel Delta™, representing the first step toward a port using Fortran-D/High Performance Fortran (Section 3.9).

Each approach uses a domain decomposition rather than functional or task parallelism because the number of grid points in the three-dimensional domain far exceeds the number of functions.

Our results demonstrate that spatial domain decomposition on a workstation cluster yields significant improvements in performance compared to single-processor execution. As verified by our analytic performance model, interprocessor communication overhead is the greatest impediment to parallel speedup, suggesting enhanced scalability with the use of faster communication (both hardware and software).

The automatic translators both yielded marginal performance on the CM-5 (32 nodes of the CM-5 were roughly equal to a single Cray Y-MP™ processor). Nevertheless, we were encouraged by the ease with which the entire 65,000 line application was ported, and pleased with the speedup of 907 obtained on a 1024-node machine. Not only did the ARPS show remarkable scalability over large problem sizes and numbers of processors, but the large memory of the CM-5 allowed us to run our "ultimate" domain size of $1024 \times 1024 \times 32$ grid points on a dedicated 1024-node system at a speed about five times slower than real time.

Finally, the explicit message-passing approach used on the CM-5 and Intel Delta proved to be the most effective, achieving speeds some four times faster than attainable with the automated translators and no hand tuning.

3.2 Operational Numerical Weather Prediction: Past, Present, and Future

Beginning with the first numerical weather prediction (NWP) experiments conducted by John von Neumann and associates at Princeton's Institute for Advanced Study in the late 1940s and early 1950s,[2] the discipline of meteorology and, in particular, operational weather prediction, have helped drive the creation of high performance computers. Indeed, a vision for NWP was put forth in the early 1920s by L. F. Richardson,[3] including a strategy for distributing equally, among hundreds of (human) processors, the computational workload even though the digital computer was at least two decades away. Richardson's vision was remarkably futuristic and complete, down to the details of communication and synchronization among processors working in parallel. Although the tools associated with his vision have now become reality, our ability to utilize them effectively remains somewhat elusive.

Operational NWP is now conducted almost exclusively at the national or multinational level,[4] wherein a centralized facility collects and processes all relevant observational data, runs a suite of numerical models ranging in scale from regional to global, and generates and disseminates forecasts and related products, often targeted to specific needs such as aviation. Because the associated models use grid point spacings (or equivalent grid point spacings in the case of spectral models) on the order of several tens to hundreds of kilometers, depending upon the aerial extent of the domain, they are unable to represent explicitly individual thunderstorms or storm complexes. The desire to predict such events with a lead time of a few hours is obvious, as thunderstorms and their related weather are principally responsible for flash floods, damaging surface winds, hail, tornadoes, and low-level turbulence that poses a threat to aircraft.

To attack the storm-scale prediction problem in a focused manner, the National Science Foundation established in 1988 the Center for Analysis and Prediction of Storms (CAPS) at the University of Oklahoma. Its mission is to demonstrate the practicability of numerical storm-scale prediction, nominally to result in a prototype for *regional* forecast capability that would augment present-day centralized NWP.

The ability of CAPS to accomplish its mission depends critically upon the effective use of high performance computing and communications systems. Because thunderstorms have relatively short lifetimes (a few hours) compared to larger-scale weather systems (a few days), their associated numerical forecasts must be generated and disseminated to the public very quickly (50 to 100 times faster than the weather evolves) to be of practical value. This poses an extreme computational challenge since the required domain for storm prediction is nominally 1000×1000 km horizontally and 20 km vertically, with horizontal and vertical grid spacings of 1 km and 0.5 km, respectively (i.e., $1000 \times 1000 \times 40$ grid points per three-dimensional computational array). Considering the pre-forecast data assimilation procedure, which involves running the prediction model before the actual forecast to arrive at an appropriate set of initial conditions, along with the fact that not one but several forecasts will likely be made during each prediction cycle in order to evaluate forecast variability,[5, 6] it becomes clear that computers having sustained teraflop performance, gigabyte capacity memories, and parallel input/output will be needed if operational storm-scale prediction is to be successful. Such capability can be achieved only through the use of hundreds to thousands of processors; thus, the development of a new model suited for such architectures is a principal goal of the CAPS effort.

3.3 MPP Research at the Center for Analysis and Prediction of Storms (CAPS)

Background

CAPS is developing techniques for the practical prediction of weather phenomena on scales ranging from a few kilometers and tens of minutes (individual thunderstorms) to hundreds of kilometers and several hours (storm complexes and mesoscale systems). More specifically, depending upon the specific type of event in question, the location (to within a few miles) and intensity of new thunderstorms and their associated severe weather (hail, strong winds, heavy rain) are believed predictable three hours in advance, and the detailed evolution of existing storms foreseeable for up to six hours.[7, 8] Initial operational tests are now underway[9, 10] and will continue and expand into the next century.

The principal goal of CAPS-supported research in parallel processing is to attain problem sizes and model execution rates with the ARPS appropriate for storm-scale NWP. To achieve this rather ambitious goal, several approaches to parallelism are being investigated, ranging from the use of large, loosely coupled networks of stand-alone workstations to shared-memory scalar–vector computers to distributed-memory parallel and massively parallel processors (MPP). As a complete application developed with modern software engineering strategies, the ARPS serves as a unique testbed for MPP compilers and translation tools, and has fostered important communication and collaborative studies among meteorologists, computer scientists, and electrical engineers throughout the world. Experiences gained through this type of interaction have led to improvements in MPP tools, and will hopefully drive the creation of new tools appropriate for broad classes of real application codes.

3.4 The Advanced Regional Prediction System (ARPS)

We overview in this section the development philosophy and constraints of the ARPS, describe its physical and dynamical frameworks, and discuss generally applicable coding constructs that have been devised to promote flexibility, scalability, and readability of this and similar large production codes. Those unfamiliar with meteorological modeling may wish to skim the "Dynamic framework" and "Numerical framework" sections in "An Overview of the ARPS" and proceed directly to "Operator-based solution technique."

Development Philosophy

After an extensive survey of existing hydrostatic and nonhydrostatic models that might serve as platforms for achieving its scientific goals, CAPS chose to develop an entirely new code for five principal reasons.

First, most widely used simulation models were initially developed by a few individuals for a specific research problem or set of problems and have since undergone considerable modification, thus reflecting the disparate programming styles of each contributor. Such codes tend to be poorly documented internally and lack user manuals and flow diagrams that facilitate usage. Consequently, they require substantial investments of time to learn—up to several months in some instances, particularly for students and in classroom applications—and are difficult to modify for the rapid investigation of new ideas.

Second, such codes were mostly developed on single-processor scalar or scalar–vector computers, and in many cases require substantial retooling for, or are virtually impossible to convert for use on, current parallel and massively parallel machines. For example, in order to perform three-dimensional simulations on early generation supercomputers with limited core memory (e.g., order 1 megaword), many codes used slice-wise two-dimensional stencils that involved extensive input/output (either to regular disk or solid-state storage devices). In many cases, adapting such codes for *efficient* execution on MPP machines is no less a task than writing an entirely new code.

Third, sophisticated numerical models tend to be the most complex and difficult to learn and use, though the most attractive from a scientific viewpoint. Consequently, many such codes inhibit the investigation of new ideas by virtue of their completeness. CAPS sought to develop software engineering practices and algorithmic structures that facilitate rapid changes to model physics and numerical solution algorithms without adverse effects on scalability and vectorization. Further, the constructs used in the ARPS express the structure of the underlying physical problem directly in the language most familiar to the scientist-user (i.e., the partial differential equations of fluid dynamics), thus making the code more readable and reducing substantially the learning time in many cases.

Fourth, the quality of a numerical forecast depends greatly upon the model's initial conditions; for small-scale meteorology, obtaining a complete set of initial data is a major challenge because the principal observing instrument, the Doppler radar, provides only one wind component (parallel to the beam) and a measure of rainfall intensity over the volume being scanned. From a time history of these two quantities, all other variables must be inferred (e.g., the cross-beam and vertical wind components, temperature, pressure, water vapor, etc.). One method of parameter retrieval, based on control theory, involves repeated integrations of the forward-in-time prediction model and its associated backward-in-time adjoint. The creation of the adjoint code (which is a transformation of the forward discrete model), particularly an efficient one, is tedious and prone to error, and can be greatly simplified by a careful design of the forward model. Further, care in developing the forward model also facilitates the use of automated differentiation techniques for obtaining the adjoint.[11, 12] Because most storm-scale codes in use today were developed before the emergence of the adjoint assimilation strategy, they are suited for neither manual nor automated adjoint development.

Finally, for the purposes of storm-scale NWP, many processes such as cloud microphysics, land surface interactions, and surface-layer and subgrid-scale turbulence must be represented credibly. Long- and short-wave radiation can also affect significantly storm morphology, particularly initiation processes. By developing a completely new model, advances in each of these areas made during the past several decades can be incorporated into an overall balanced physics package.

Based on the above considerations, we list below the principal design characteristics and constraints of the ARPS model system:

- modular code structure for the sequential introduction of improved physics and numerical solution algorithms

- scalable code structure to accommodate broad classes of parallel architectures and the MIMD, SIMD, and SPMD programming models

- extensive internal and external documentation, including tutorials, and the use of modular discrete differencing operators to facilitate learning, use, and modification

- coupling to an interactive visualization system that also permits window/menu control of model execution and examination of model results during model execution

- use of prevailing Fortran standard constructs to ensure maximum portability

- ability to handle multiple-scale phenomena through the use of adaptive mesh refinement

- ability to accommodate WSR-88D Doppler radar data through various assimilation strategies

- rapidly optimizable for any chosen computer system

- ability to serve as an operational test bed for storm-scale NWP without substantial retooling.

An Overview of the ARPS

Dynamic framework The ARPS is a general nonhydrostatic, compressible atmospheric prediction model designed for storm- and meso-scale phenomena with an emphasis on deep convection. The governing dynamics center around prognostic equations for momentum, thermodynamic energy (potential temperature), mass (pressure), and water substance (water vapor, cloud water, rainwater, cloud ice, snow and hail), supplemented by the equation of state and various representations for sub-grid scale turbulence. These prognostic equations are cast in curvilinear coordinates that are horizontally orthogonal and can be stretched vertically. The computational grid can be defined either numerically or analytically, and the governing equations in the curvilinear system are a direct transformation from the cartesian system in conservative form. For the versions of the ARPS reported on here (3.0 and 3.1), microphysical processes are represented by the Kessler warm rain parameterization, and the ice phase is neglected. Unresolvable motions are parameterized using the Smagorinsky/Lilly first-order closure scheme[13, 14]; a 1.5-order turbulent kinetic energy–based parameterization, as well as the Germano[15–17] dynamic closure scheme, are now available.

Several options exist for the lateral boundaries, including "open" or wave-radiating, rigid, periodic, zero-gradient, and externally specified conditions (e.g., as might be provided by a larger-scale model). At the upper and lower boundaries, rigid, periodic, and zero-gradient conditions are available. The upper boundary radiation condition is simulated using Rayleigh damping. In order to represent multiscale phenomena, the ARPS contains an adaptive mesh refinement capability,[18] in which subgrids of successively finer spatial resolution can be introduced at arbitrary locations and orientations within the model base grid.[19]

Version 4 of the ARPS, formally released in February, 1995, has the following additional features:

- global terrain database and configuration software with 30 min terrain for most of the U.S. and 1° terrain for the world

- one-dimensional, two-dimensional, and three-dimensional cartesian geometries

- three-phase ice microphysics

- surface energy and moisture budgets with USDA surface characteristics data and associated pre-processing software

- stability-dependent surface fluxes

- two-layer soil model

- forward-variational data assimilation system designed for use with spherical coordinate Doppler radar and other data

- automated domain translation and storm-tracking capability

- solution validation suite

- multiple data formats for history and restart dumps

- ARPSplot post-processing and graphics package

- ARPStools diagnostic analysis package that includes time-dependent trajectories, statistics, and other features.

A complete description of the ARPS equation system and numerical framework can be found in the ARPS Version 4.0 User's Guide.[20]

Numerical framework The continuous equations for the ARPS are discretized on the staggered Arakawa C-grid, and are solved using standard second- or fourth-order finite difference techniques.[20] The migration towards high-order upstream-biased advection schemes for momentum, and monotonic schemes for scalars, is planned immediately after the release of version 4.0. For most of the second-order spatial differencing, only nearest-neighbor communications are involved. For higher-order schemes, more grid points are required and thus the communication overhead increases. In such cases, the differencing operations can be broken down into steps involving only nearest neighbor operations. For example, the fourth-order difference operator $\delta_{xxxx}\Phi$ can be written as $\delta_{xx}(\delta_{xx}\Phi)$, where $\delta_{xx}\Phi$ is defined as $(\Phi_{i+1} - 2\Phi_i + \Phi_{i-1})/(\Delta x)^2$. The operator $\delta_{xxxx}\Phi$ is calculated by applying the discrete differencing operator δ_{xx} twice. In the ARPS, such operations are easily achieved using the operator-based strategy discussed in the next subsection, "Operator-based solution technique."

The ARPS time-integration scheme uses the mode-splitting approach of Klemp and Wilhelmson[21] (see also Skamarock and Klemp[22]), in which the fast (slow) acoustic (gravitational and advective) wave modes are integrated using relatively small (large) time steps as dictated by linear stability. This approach preserves the hyperbolic character of the governing equations and thus renders a fully prognostic model (i.e., all equations are time-marching). The alternative is an anelastic system,[23] in which the acoustic modes do not appear explicitly and a three-dimensional elliptic equation has to be solved for the pressure. Because the elliptic equation is a global boundary-value problem, it is not readily amenable to solution on MPP systems.

In versions of the ARPS subsequent to 3.3, an implicit algorithm[21] is used to handle the vertical acoustic waves, thereby allowing for a much bigger small time step size when the horizontal grid scale is much larger than the vertical grid scale. Such is often the case for mesoscale applications, though not necessarily so for individual convective storms. Because a tridiagonal equation (resulting from the three-dimensional elliptic equation) must be solved in the vertical direction, the overall model solution algorithm can no longer be entirely local; as a result, domain decomposition in the vertical direction is no longer straightforward, and the most efficient MPP strategy is to maintain all time levels for each column of the three-dimensional model arrays on a single processor (see Sections 3.6 and 3.7). Some physical processes, such as radiation, must be computed along directions oblique to the model grid, adding to the complexity of a domain decomposition strategy. Fortunately, most applications require horizontal domain sizes much greater than the vertical, making a two-dimensional x–y domain decomposition (see Figure 3.4d) the most natural choice.

Operator-based solution technique The essential elements or building blocks of finite difference, finite element, or finite volume models are basic discrete operators used for spatial and temporal differencing, array element–wise multiplication, grid point averaging, etc. These operations represent a level of very fine granularity that can be exploited for a particular computer architecture. Unfortunately, most computer languages do not preserve this fine-grained structure when the original differential equations are cast in discrete form, *even if the code is highly modular*. With this in mind, a set of generalized discrete operators has been developed for use in the ARPS. By design, the operators preserve the formal algebraic structure of the hydrodynamic equations, producing a code that resembles the equations themselves rather than unwieldy expressions involving multiple increments to array subscripts. As fundamental units of discrete computation, the operators preserve the fine granularity inherent in hydrodynamics computations (e.g., multiplication of two dependent variables, single and multiple derivatives), giving the user an ability to distribute this granularity and associated parallelism in a manner most appropriate for the target computer architecture. The simplicity of the operators facilitates code maintainability, ease of modification, and ease of learning, and therefore greatly reduces the time required to develop and, most importantly, to debug and validate complex models.

To illustrate the value of the operator-based solution strategy, consider the four basic steps for solving the equations of hydrodynamics in either differential or integral form using grid point techniques. In the first step, the appropriate continuous equation or set of equations is prescribed, as shown in Equation 3.1 for a simple scalar conservation law

$$\frac{\partial T}{\partial t} = -\frac{\partial(uT)}{\partial x} - \frac{\partial(vT)}{\partial y} - \frac{\partial(wT)}{\partial z} \tag{3.1}$$

Here, T is a scalar, t is time, and u, v, and w are the velocity components in the x, y, and z directions, respectively. This equation possesses considerable parallel structure in that all terms on the right-hand side (RHS) are similar in form but different in direction. This is more evident if the RHS is written using summation notation

$$\frac{\partial T}{\partial t} = -\frac{\partial(u_i T)}{\partial x_i} \tag{3.2}$$

where a summation $i = 1,2,3$ is implied. In an explicit numerical scheme, and in some implicit schemes as well, the three element-wise matrix multiplications of u_i and T, as well as the subsequent differentiations, can be performed independently. Unfortunately, this parallelism is not exploited in most numerical codes, as shown below.

In the second step, the appropriate continuous equations are recast into discrete form, often through the use of differencing and averaging operators as a notational convenience, in a manner appropriate for a given computational mesh and solution method. Consider, for example, the centered operator notation used by Lilly[24]:

$$\overline{A(x)}^{nx} = \frac{A\left(x + \frac{1}{2}n\Delta x\right) + A\left(x - \frac{1}{2}n\Delta x\right)}{2} \tag{3.3}$$

$$\delta_{nx}A(x) = \frac{A\left(x + \frac{1}{2}n\Delta x\right) - A\left(x - \frac{1}{2}n\Delta x\right)}{n\Delta x} \tag{3.4}$$

where A is the dependent variable at an arbitrary location x (the independent variable), n is a positive integer, and Δx is the grid spacing. Equation 3.4 is the discrete representation of a continuous first derivative $\partial A/\partial x$, while Equation 3.3 represents an averaging operator that has no continuous counterpart. Other forms of these operators with varying definitions are widely used. As described below, Equations 3.3 and 3.4, along with other fundamental operators (e.g., one-sided spatial difference), may be used in combination to create a variety of higher-order expressions provided that certain commutative and associative properties, similar but not identical to those in the calculus, are obeyed.[25]

Applying Equations 3.3 and 3.4 to Equation 3.1 using second-order quadratically conservative spatial differences on the Arakawa C-grid, along with a second-order leapfrog time discretization, yields

$$\delta_{2t}T^n_{i,j,k} = -\delta_x(u\overline{T}^x)^n_{i,j,k} - \delta_y(v\overline{T}^y)^n_{i,j,k} - \delta_z(w\overline{T}^z)^n_{i,j,k} \tag{3.5}$$

where i, j, and k correspond to the x, y, and z directions, respectively (e.g., $x_i = i\Delta x$), n indicates the time level, and $t = n\Delta t$, where Δt is the time step. At this point, the full structure of the governing Equation 3.1 remains intact.

In the third step, Equation 3.5 is expanded using the rules given in Equations 3.3 and 3.4 to yield a set of linear algebraic equations:

$$\begin{aligned}
\frac{T^{n+1}_{i,j,k} - T^{n-1}_{i,j,k}}{2\Delta t} = &-\frac{1}{\Delta x}\left[u^n_{i,j,k}\frac{(T^n_{i+1,j,k} + T^n_{i,j,k})}{2} - u^n_{i-1,j,k}\frac{(T^n_{i,j,k} + T^n_{i-1,j,k})}{2}\right] \\
&-\frac{1}{\Delta y}\left[v^n_{i,j,k}\frac{(T^n_{i,j+1,k} + T^n_{i,j,k})}{2} - v^n_{i,j-1,k}\frac{(T^n_{i,j,k} + T^n_{i,j-1,k})}{2}\right] \\
&-\frac{1}{\Delta z}\left[w^n_{i,j,k}\frac{(T^n_{i,j,k+1} + T^n_{i,j,k})}{2} - w^n_{i,j,k-1}\frac{(T^n_{i,j,k} + T^n_{i,j,k-1})}{2}\right]
\end{aligned} \tag{3.6}$$

In the final step, these algebraic equations are cast in an appropriate computer language using subscripted arrays. For the example shown here, the code might be written in Fortran 77 as

```fortran
real u(nx,ny,nz),v(nx,ny,nz),w(nx,ny,nz),T(nx,ny,nz)
do k = 1,nz
   do j = 1,ny
      do i = 1,nx
         T(i,j,k,future) = T(i,j,k,past)
         -0.5*rdx*dt*(u(i,j,k,now)*(T(i+1,j,k,now)+T(i,j,k,now))
            -u(i-1,j,k,now)*(T(i,j,k,now)+T(i1,j,k,now)))
         -0.5*rdy*dt*(v(i,j,k,now)*(T(i,j+1,k,now)+T(i,j,k,now))
            -v(i,j-1,k,now)*(T(i,j,k,now)+T(i,j1,k,now)))
         -0.5*rdz*dt*(w(i,j,k,now)*(T(i,j,k+1,now)+T(i,j,k,now))
            -w(i,j,k-1,now)*(T(i,j,k,now)+T(i,j,k-1,now)))
      end do
   end do
end do
```
$$(3.7)$$

where future, now, and past are the time indices for levels $n + 1$, n, and $n - 1$; rdx = $1/\Delta x$, rdy = $1/\Delta y$, rdz = $1/\Delta z$; dt = Δt; and nx, ny, and nz are the number of grid-points in the three coordinate directions. In moving from Equation 3.5 to the Fortran code, much of the functional (i.e., mathematical operation) parallel structure has been lost. For example, it is no longer possible to compute independently, or to separate, the three products of the scalar T with the velocities u, v, and w. The same is true for the three differentiations. Furthermore, any resemblance to the governing equation (Equation 3.1) has been greatly diminished, and the code is inherently prone to transcription error due to the number of array index manipulations involved. Extension of this code to different or higher-order schemes, though perhaps straightforward in theory, is cumbersome and time consuming, presenting formidable challenges to users and greatly reducing the utility of the code.

The obvious solution to these problems is to *eliminate the operator expansion step (step 3) and use the operator constructs in the computer code itself.* Consider, therefore, a set of subroutines that perform the discrete operations shown in Equations 3.3 and 3.4. Each routine receives on input a dependent variable and perhaps information concerning its dimensionality and location within the grid, and returns on output a transformed variable according to the operation performed.

For example, let avgx(input-var,output_var) and difx(input_var,output_var) be the Fortran counterparts of Equations 3.3 and 3.4, respectively, for the x direction (similar routines are presumed to exist for the y and z directions), and let routine eemult(input1,input2,output) return as output the element-wise product of two input matrices input1 and input2. Assuming that the appropriate nested DO-loops are contained within each operator routine, and for clarity neglecting other arguments passed, the operator-based code for solving Equation 3.1 can be written as

```
real u(nx,ny,nz,3), v(nx,ny,nz,3), w(nx,ny,nz,3), T(nx,ny,nz,3)
real temp1(nx,ny,nz), temp2(nx,ny,nz),temp3(nx,ny,nz)

call avgx(T, temp1) ! temp1 contains T̄ˣ
call avgy(T, temp2) ! temp2 contains T̄ʸ
call avgz(T, temp3) ! temp3 contains T̄ᶻ

call eemult(u, temp1, temp1) ! second temp1 contains UT̄ˣ
call eemult(v, temp2, temp2) ! second temp2 contains VT̄ʸ
call eemult(w, temp3, temp3) ! second temp3 contains WT̄ᶻ

call difx(temp1, temp1) ! second temp1 contains δₓ(UT̄ˣ)
call dify(temp2, temp2) ! second temp2 contains δᵧ(VT̄ʸ)
call difz(temp3, temp3) ! second temp3 contains δᵤ(WT̄ᶻ)

do k = 1,nz
   do j = 1,ny
      do i = 1,nx
         T(i,j,k,future) = T(i,j,k,past) - 2.0*dt*(temp1(i,j,k)
                           +temp2(i,j,k) +temp3(i,j,k))
      end do
   end do
end do
```

$$(3.8)$$

Four important points are worth noting about this code relative to that described by Equation 3.7. First, the fundamental mathematical structure of the three types of operations (averaging, matrix multiplication, and differencing) is clearly evident. Second, it is clear that, although the *types* of operations must be performed sequentially for each pairing of variables (e.g., the matrix multiplication of u with the average of T cannot occur until the average of T is available), computations *within* each type (e.g., all averaging operations) can be done independently. Third, the code in Equation 3.8 bears more of a resemblance to the governing equation (Equation 3.1) and its discrete-operator representation (Equation 3.5) than does Equation 3.7 because Equation 3.8 is written in a manner analogous to the continuous problem using functionally similar constructs. As a result, once the operators are known to be correct and properly applied, *the code can be verified largely by inspection*, thereby facilitating debugging, maintenance, and correct usage. Implementing higher order or more complex numerical schemes, virtually all of which can be expressed using some form of operator notation, simply involves using other operators or different combinations thereof. Finally, the complexity of the array index manipulations, all of which are extremely basic and occur in the operator routines (each of which contains fewer than 10 lines of executable code), is hidden from the user. By redefining a particular operator, one can change literally hundreds of lines of code in a matter of minutes.

There are also several drawbacks to using the operators outlined above. First, temporary arrays are needed to store intermediate results or terms (e.g., output from the operator subroutines). However, this is not a major problem when the temporary storage is carefully managed and reused by different routines, as is the case with the ARPS. Only 8% of the total three-dimensional storage used in the ARPS is associated with the operators.

A limitation that deserves closer examination is the inefficiency associated with the calling or startup overhead of the operator subroutines. An application having only a few loops and a significant amount of work per loop is more efficient than a code that distributes small amounts of work among a larger number of loops. The latter occurs when fine-grained operator subroutines are used (Equation 3.7), as opposed to direct computation of an entire equation (Equation 3.8). This issue can be partly resolved by subroutine in-lining and loop fusion (i.e., combining loops), features that are available on some but not all compilers. In general, subroutine in-lining does not improve substantially the overall efficiency of the ARPS because subroutine calls seldom occur within loops that operate over the entire model domain. When Fortran 90 array syntax is used, as is the case in the Fortran-P and CMAX versions of our code (see Sections 3.7 and 3.8), simple operators are reduced to Fortran line statements, and in-lining was found to improve the overall application efficiency by as much as 15% on a CM-5.

Another way to reduce overhead associated with the operators is to express them in a meta-language that can be translated by a pre-processor, thereby eliminating the need for subroutine calls. This strategy, early instantiations of which have been tested at CAPS on shallow water models, uses the LEX and YACC tools to construct a pre-processor that parses and decodes operator notation within a Fortran program. To demonstrate, consider the previous example (see Equation 3.5) written using the revised operator notation:

```
real u(nx,ny),v(nx,ny),w(nx,ny),T(nx,ny)
do k = 1,nx
   do j = 1,ny
      do i = 1,nx
         T(i,j,future) = T(i,j,past) - 2.0*dt*(
.uex_on
         diffx(u*avex(T))-diffy(v*avey(T))-diffz (w*avez(T))        (3.9)
.uex_off
            )
      end do
   end do
end do
```

where the directives .uex_on and .uex_off surround the text to be expanded by the macro program. In this instance, the pre-processor passes directly into another program all code *not enclosed* within the .uex_on and .uex_off commands, and expands the code within the commands to yield the following:

```
real u(nx,ny,nz),v(nx,ny,nz),w(nx,ny,nz),T(nx,ny,nz)
do k = 1,nz
do j = 1,ny
do i = 1,nx
   T(i,j,k,future) = T(i,j,k,past) - 2.0*dt*(
&    *(((((u(i,j,k,now)*((T(i+1,j,k,now)+T(i,j,k,now))*0.5))-(
&    *u(i-1,j,k,now)*((T(i,j,k,now)+T(i-1,j,k,now))*0.5)))*rdx)*
&    *(-1.0))-(((v(i,j,k,now)*((T(i,j+1,k,now)+T(i,j,k,now))      (3.10)
&    **0.5))-(v(i,j-1,k,now)*((T(i,j,k,now)+T(i,j-1,k,now))*
&    *0.5)))*rdy)-(((w(i,j,k,now)*((T(i,j,k+1,now)+T(i,j,k,now))
&    **0.5))-(w(i,j,k-1,now)*((T(i,j,k,now)+T(i,j,k-1,now))*
&    *0.5)))*rdz))
```

```
end do
end do
end do
```

Since the user maintains the source code (Equation 3.9) rather than Equation 3.10, no compilation difficulties arise because many compilers today are sophisticated enough to reference the line numbers in Equation 3.9 when reporting error messages. The macro parser-decoder is completely machine independent and does not require LEX or YACC on the host computer.

The advantage to this implementation is that the code in Equation 3.9 is much easier to write and understand than code using the operator subroutines (see Equation 3.8). The principal drawback is that the macro generates the type of unreadable Fortran code structure that we seek to avoid (compare Equations 3.7 and 3.10), thus complicating the debugging process, especially when the parsed/converted code is passed to other translation tools such as CMAX and Fortran-P. Further, the use of the modified operators violates the desirable goal of a self-contained code written entirely in Fortran. Although CAPS has not yet decided to convert to the simpler operator scheme, we believe that when a complete operator library of such is built and validated, and the behavior of the operators documented (including messages showing the stencil size and thus defining the validity of translated equations near boundary points), the time required to develop and validate new hydrodynamic codes will be significantly reduced.

Other ARPS constructs and features Apart from the operator-based strategy described above, several other constructs or design considerations have been used to improve the readability and scalability of the ARPS.

As discussed below, Fortran-P, as well as certain message-passing strategies, use explicit spatial domain decomposition to obtain good performance on parallel machines. In most cases, extra code must be generated for handling the interchange of information common to neighboring subdomains. For a scalable code, the computations done on one subdomain are similar to those over the entire grid, and the same is true for the boundary points. In the ARPS, the multi-option boundary condition code is isolated from the interior code as much as possible, and is handled in individual subroutines. Given this design, external boundary conditions, such as those for nested or subdivided grids, arise naturally. The additional code for the subdomain boundaries can be easily generated when and where the true domain boundary conditions are set.

Additionally, EQUIVALENCE statements, especially those used for associating arrays, are strictly avoided. No array is passed among subroutines via COMMON blocks, and the IMPLICIT NONE construct is strictly enforced. These restrictions greatly facilitate code translation to MPPs, and are especially valuable for either manual or automated generation of a corresponding adjoint or derivative code. Subroutine arguments are listed according to their definition as input, output, or temporary variables, and all variables are clearly defined and declared, with the physical units for each provided. A standard subroutine template is used to ensure a uniform coding style, and the modification history of each subroutine is documented for ease of maintenance. Extensive internal comments that describe the formulations and algorithms are included, citing literature where appropriate. Capital letters are used to emphasize certain elements such as key-words, and constructs that are likely to become obsolete in future versions of Fortran are avoided. Only generally available tools are are used (e.g., makefiles), unless otherwise provided as part of the model system, to maintain maximum portability.

All data input/output channels used are dynamically allocated within a specified range, and only free channels are selected, thus eliminating possible conflicts with other coupled software (e.g., graphics libraries). A set of pre- and post-processing tools, built around the ARPS standard data formats, is available, including data extraction, in-put/output, 4-D visualization, and fluid flow diagnostics. A comprehensive user's guide is available with each formal release of the code, and an automated suite of tests, some involving analytic solutions to the nonlinear equations,[26] is used to validate each new version of code. The current formal release of the ARPS, version 4.0, contains 100,000 lines of Fortran 77 code, about 50% of which are comment lines.

Further Development of the ARPS

CAPS will continue to develop and evaluate the ARPS during the next several years, principally through modifications to the code computational and physical frameworks. Further, CAPS will emphasize continued testing of parallel processing strategies, and apply the model to storm-scale problems using real data.[27] Figure 3.1 presents a road map of the planned development activities, together with the target *sustained execution rates* for each version of the model.

Availability of the ARPS

The ARPS model and associated documentation are available via anonymous ftp from ftpcaps.uoknor.edu (Internet number 129.15.46.20, user anonymous). The compressed tar file of the current release can be found in pub/ARPS/arps_current.tar.Z, and the User's Guide[20] in PostScript format is in file arps40.docs.tar. CAPS asks that users register themselves (see Appendix C of the User's Guide) in order to receive periodic updates of information concerning the model. Questions and comments may be directed to arpsuser@uoknor.edu.

3.5 General ARPS Performance Statistics

Throughout its development and testing phases, the ARPS has been run on as many different types of computers as possible to ensure portability, to identify peculiarities associated with certain compilers and architectures, and to investigate various types of parallel implementation strategies. These include

- Cray Y-MP/C-90 (16 processors)
- Cray Y-MP8/64
- Cray-2/4-512
- CM-2
- CM-200 (32K nodes)

ARPS Development Cycle

1995 **ARPS 4** 100 Gflops	1996 **ARPS 5** 250 Gflops	1997 **ARPS 6** 500 Gflops	1998 **ARPS 7** 800 Gflops
4th-order numerics	High-order upwind numerics	Physics refinements	Fully integrated system
Adaptive gridding	Vegetation param	Numerics refinements	
Germano and 1.5-order TKE Turb	Multilevel soil model	Multiparameter radar retrieval and assimilation system	
Ice microphysics	Full-physics adjoint		
2-layer soil model	Cloud-radiation interaction	Full links to operational models	
Surface energy budget	2nd-generation forward variational assimilation and retrieval system	3rd-generation forward variational assimilation and retrieval system	
Terrain and vertical stretching			
OLAPS, Eta, and MAPS interface	Cumulus param scheme		
Base forward variational data assimilation and retrieval system			
Dry adjoint			

Figure 3.1   Development cycle of the Advanced Regional Prediction System (ARPS).

- CM-5 (512 and 1024 nodes)
- VAX 6000
- DECstation
- DEC Alpha Workstation
- IBM RISC System 6000 single workstations and clusters
- Alliant FX/80
- Convex C3
- Stardent GS2525
- IRIS 4D/70
- IBM 3090
- Apollo
- Sun SPARC-10.

ARPS 3.1 achieves a sustained rate of 180 megaflops on a single processor of a Cray Y-MP for a $64 \times 64 \times 32$ domain with full turbulence and microphysics (a supercell storm simulation). This equals approximately 100,000 grid-point updates per CPU second. The speeds of ARPS 3.1 on other selected systems, in terms of CPU time relative to that of a single processor Cray Y-MP, are as follows:

Computer System	Speed Relative to Cray Y-MP
Cray Y-MP	1.00
Convex C3	2.50
Alliant FX/80	11.00
VAX/VMS 6520 w/Vector	13.78
IBM RISC System 6000 Model 530H	16.44
Cray Y-MP/C-90 single processor	0.36
Cray Y-MP/C-90 (16 processors)	0.03

For operational weather prediction, the wallclock time required to complete a forecast is a much more meaningful measure of model performance than the megaflop rating. The nominal or "ultimate" domain size for operational storm-scale NWP is believed to be $1000 \times 1000 \times 32$ points with a 1 km horizontal and 0.5 km vertical grid spacing. For the prediction (of say 4 h duration) to be useful, the model must run some 50 to 100 times faster than the weather. Figure 3.2 shows a nomograph of the ratio of dedicated wallclock time (DWT) to model simulated time (ST) measured for ARPS 3.0. This ratio, when plotted against the memory use (or equivalently, domain size), allows one to project future hardware (code) requirements based on anticipated code (hardware) performance. When DWT/ST < 1, the model runs faster than the weather. Figure 3.2 shows that, for the ultimate domain size sought, a sustained performance of 1 teraflop will be required to predict the weather 100 times faster than it occurs, and this estimate is made without considering the time-consuming tasks of data ingest, quality control, assimilation, post-processing and dissemination. The total time required will likely more than double when more sophisticated physical processes and data assimilation are included. Further, in situations where one attempts to predict the reliability of a forecast by generating an ensemble of predictions at equivalent or coarser resolution (e.g., as suggested by Brooks et al.[5] and tested by Droegemeier and Levit[6]), with the initial state of each ensemble member differing slightly from that of the control, the need for sustained teraflop performance becomes even more compelling.

3.6 Application of the ARPS on Moderately Parallel Workstation Clusters

Some of the earliest parallel simulations with the ARPS were done on clusters of workstations. Such clusters have emerged as a powerful yet economical alternative to supercomputers for production-scale numerical experiments,[28] and are gaining popularity as an environment for developing parallel codes. We describe in this section our experiences using workstation clusters, including both functional and domain decomposition strategies for various fixed and scaled problem sizes.

Rationale for the Use of Computer Clusters

Computer clusters may be defined as systems of networked computers, each with its own memory, and may be composed of collections of heterogeneous or homogeneous

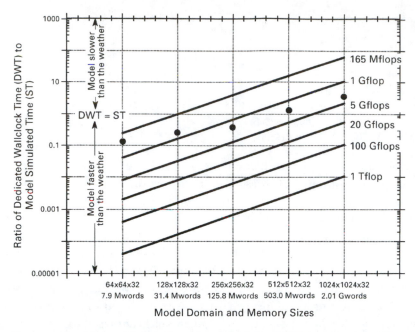

Figure 3.2 Nomograph of the ratio of dedicated wallclock time (DWT) to simulated time (ST) plotted against domain size for ARPS 3.0. The diagonal lines represent sustained model performance in megaflops, gigaflops, and teraflops. When DWT = ST, the ARPS is running as fast as the weather evolves. The bold dots indicate actual ARPS performance for each of the five domain sizes shown.

computers of various sizes and types. A common configuration is a network of stand-alone workstations, representing a cost-effective way to use the collective power of systems which would otherwise be used in single-processor mode. Many applications show significant parallel speedups on clusters, though overall performance is still well below that of more traditional vector supercomputers. One distinct advantage of clusters—though not obvious from speedup figures alone—is the availability of considerable memory. Networked execution allows for solving larger problems compared to single-processor execution, with relatively low overhead compared to the costs of memory paging on a single-processor system. Further, clusters can be used to develop applications for massively parallel processors having a distributed memory architecture. Message-passing libraries, such as the Parallel Virtual Machine (PVM) package,[29] that enable passing of data between processors, are available on MPPs as well as clusters.

In recent years, various versions of the ARPS have been ported to a networked cluster of workstations. The purpose was to conduct parallelization experiments to (1) determine the adaptability of the ARPS to this type of system; (2) quantify the parallel performance; and (3) detect and suggest corrections to performance-reducing bottlenecks in both the ARPS and the hardware. We used the host–node (also referred to as the master–slave) parallel programming model in which all processors execute the same instruction stream on data that have been partitioned (nearly equally) among all processors.

This is achieved for the ARPS by using a host machine that partitions and sends arrays of initial atmospheric data to as many as 16 node machines, whose task is to carry out the parallel computation on subdomains of the full model grid.

The principal lesson learned from this work is the effect on performance of network communication protocols and thus overall network speed. This was the overriding obstacle to higher performance in the results to be shown. From the standpoint of porting, there is a need for software tools to assist in problem decomposition and performance monitoring. Porting was found to be straightforward but error prone. Although these conclusions are drawn from porting an atmospheric model, they are likely to apply to any finite difference model being decomposed to run on a distributed system.

Implementation

Decomposition strategies Parallelism may be exploited at several levels in NWP models like the ARPS, as explained in detail by Kauranne.[30] These range from local parallelism involving loops within the code to global parallelism involving subroutines and tasks. The work here addresses the issue of parallelism at the global level by treating the ARPS as a coarse-grained application. Two general types of decompositions are possible: functional and spatial (also called domain).

Functional decomposition involves performing parallel calculations of the independent processes of a program on separate processors. In ARPS version 2.0, the time integrations of all prognostic equations were independent of one another; therefore, functional decomposition could be applied by solving each equation on a separate processor.[31] This decomposition potentially requires a large amount of communication among processors because each prognostic equation is a function of most or all of the other prognostic variables. Thus, the updated prognostic fields must be transferred from the processors they are being calculated on to all other processors needing them after each timestep. The effectiveness of functional decomposition also depends on the number of independent processes and the relative workload for each process. In a sophisticated atmospheric model, few processes are independent of the others. Programming techniques, such as the sharing of temporary work arrays among processors, often treat even independent processes as sequential. Such is the case for ARPS 3.0 and subsequent releases. Furthermore, computational load imbalances occur, resulting in poor concurrency because some processors remain idle waiting for others to catch up.

Domain decomposition involves assigning subdomains of the full computational grid to separate processors and solving all prognostic and/or diagnostic equations for that subdomain on that processor; no global information is required at any particular grid point[32] and interprocessor communications are required only at the boundaries of the subdomains. The inner border of a subdomain requires the outer border of the adjacent subdomain during a timestep because of spatial finite differences (Figure 3.3). The outer border data resident in the local memories of adjacent processors are supplied by passing messages between processors.

Even though all processors run the same code, domain decomposition is subject to load imbalances when the computational load is data dependent. This is most often true

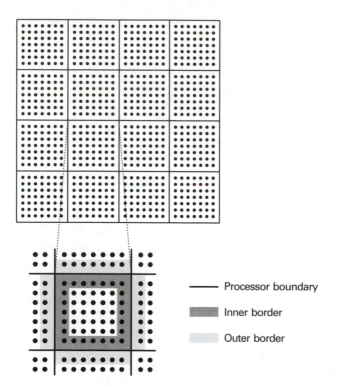

Figure 3.3 Spatial domain decomposition of the ARPS grid. Each square in the upper panel corresponds to a single processor with its own memory. The lower panel details a single processor. Grid points having a white background are updated without communication, while those in dark stippling require information from neighboring processors. To avoid communication in the latter, data from the outer border of neighboring processors (light stippling) are stored locally. (Adapted from Fox et al.[33])

for spatially intermittent physical processes such as condensation, radiation, and turbulence in atmospheric models. However, when these processes are written such that the calculations at all points are identical, independent of what is actually occurring (as is the case for microphysical processes in ARPS version 3.0 and beyond), the difference in work load due to data-dependent branching is often small relative to the total task, and in most cases this degradation in concurrency and parallel performance is inconsequential.

The choice of decomposition strategy depends on the target multiprocessor architecture and the type of application. For current distributed memory systems, domain decomposition is a more effective parallel processing approach for the ARPS, as described above and elaborated upon further below.

Several strategies exist within the domain decomposition paradigm for dividing the model into subdomains. Figure 3.4 shows possible decompositions for a three-dimensional grid. Assuming no other complicating factors, a logical strategy is to partition in a way that minimizes the surface area of each subdomain relative to its volume.[33] This

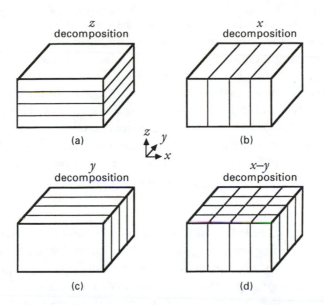

Figure 3.4 One- and two-dimensional domain decomposition strategies for a three-dimensional grid.[29]

keeps the computation-to-communication ratio high. The most natural decomposition from a coding standpoint is a one-dimensional decomposition in the z direction, that is, assigning a fixed number of consecutive x–y planes to each processor (Figure 3.4a). However, for most NWP grids, the computational domain is a parallelepiped with the least number of points in the z direction (i.e., the atmosphere is effectively confined in the vertical dimension, with the lateral extent chosen at the user's discretion). Further, one-dimensional decomposition in the z direction would be even less efficient if vertical integrations or sums, such as those involving column-wise physics or the hydrostatic relation, are central to the model solution process. In the newest version of the ARPS, a vertically implicit scheme has been applied to the acoustic modes, thereby coupling the calculations vertically (see "Numerical framework" in Section 3.4). This suggests that one-dimensional decompositions, with cuts made in either the x or y direction (Figures 3.4b and 3.4c), are better choices.

In two-dimensional decomposition, the computational domain is decomposed in two coordinate directions simultaneously (Figure 3.4d). The decision between a one- or two-dimensional formulation depends, in part, upon the characteristics of the communication network linking the processors. A one-dimensional decomposition will have longer but fewer messages than its two-dimensional counterpart, and thus may be more appropriate for a communication network having high message startup costs relative to transmission costs. A two-dimensional decomposition will transfer fewer data, at least for nearly square grids, despite a greater number of messages. Thus, for a nearly square grid, which is the most likely case for NWP problems, a two-dimensional decomposition may be the best choice when network transmission rates (hardware and software) are relatively slow.

In our implementation of domain decomposition, the same code that runs serially was used on each processor with some modifications, including changes to loop indices and array sizes as well as the addition of message-passing calls. The present code permits one- or two-dimensional decomposition in any of the coordinate directions.

Changes to the loop indices and array sizes were needed to account for the storage of the outer borders required by each subdomain. Consider a one-dimensional decomposition in the x direction (Figure 3.4b). For a computational domain of $N_x \times N_y \times N_z$ points, the N_x vertical planes are partitioned into P subdomains, each containing $[N_x/P] + 2$ contiguous y–z planes. The two extra y–z planes (or fake border zones) in each subdomain contain inner border data from adjacent subdomains. To accommodate these data, the dimensions of the arrays in the local memory of each processor are extended by 2 in the direction of the decomposition.

A scatter/gather routine was added to the program to accommodate the transfer of a processor's border data to its neighbors. Regardless of the type of decomposition, each processor has code that enables it to determine the identity of its adjacent processors. The gather routine collects a given processor's inner border data and sends them to the adjacent processors. This is done by filling a buffer array with an appropriate plane of data and sending the array as a single message. The scatter routine receives the messages from the adjacent processors and scatters those data to the current processor's outer border memory locations.

No explicit synchronization calls were added to the parallelized code. Synchronization occurs indirectly because of the message-passing. When a processor gets ahead of the calculations being done on adjacent processors, it has to wait until those processors complete their calculations and send border values to their neighbors.

Hardware The ARPS parallelization experiments were run on a cluster of IBM RISC System 6000 workstations connected via Ethernet. The host machine was a Model 530 with 128 megabytes of memory, while the node machines were identical Model 320Hs, each with 32 megabytes of memory. The machines were placed on a separate sub-net of the LAN to minimize network traffic unassociated with the parallelization experiments. All machines were run in a dedicated mode to eliminate competition for cycles by other processes. The host machine ran the initialization portion of the code and sent appropriate subdomains of the base state and prognostic fields to the nodes. The node machines did the timestepping for their associated subdomains.

Software Parallel processing generally requires special software; that is, a serial Fortran program usually will not run on a multiprocessor system without modification. It is generally easier to develop parallel software for shared-memory rather than distributed-memory machines, the principal reason being that software technology for the former is fairly well advanced, whereas compiler technology for distributed-memory MIMD systems is still in its infancy. For workstation clusters, problem decomposition requires communication among processors via message passing, which entails the insertion of subroutine calls in the source code. For the distributed-memory MIMD work reported here, several message-passing libraries were available. The PVM package[29] was selected. It supports process creation, message passing, and synchronization among processors through user interface primitives.

Results

Analytic performance models Two analytic performance models designed to predict elapsed wallclock time were developed to aid the analysis of the ARPS and to predict program performance resulting from system changes. One model describes the behavior of the sequential program, while the other describes the behavior of the parallel counterpart.

Consider first the sequential code performance model. The ARPS can be viewed as having two segments: an initialization portion and an iteration portion. The former reads data and initializes arrays, while the latter does the timestepping. The total sequential execution time, T_{seq}, can be expressed as

$$T_{seq} = T_{init} + T_{iter} \tag{3.11}$$

where T_{init} and T_{iter} are the execution times for the initialization and iteration portions, respectively.

The parallel code performance model builds upon the sequential model and must consider four issues not germane for sequential runs: nonparallelizable code, communication overhead, software overhead due to redundant decomposition calculations, and software overhead associated with creating and managing multiple processes. The initialization routines are the nonparallelizable portion of the code, and although parallelizable in principle, we chose to leave them serial in this exercise. Communication overhead results from the transfer of data to the outer borders of the subdomains from adjacent processors, while software overhead results from duplicated calculations of Jacobians on the outer borders of each subdomain (Figure 3.3). The Jacobian terms are needed for differencing and averaging in the direction of the decomposition (for the examples to be shown here, both horizontal differencing and averaging in the x direction). Overhead associated with creating and managing multiple processes was generally a small fraction of the total time and was neglected in the results to be shown.

The analytic performance model for the parallel code is derived assuming distributed-memory MIMD processing using P processors. Thus, there are P subdomains of size $N_x N_y N_z / P$.

The parallelized code's total execution time when run on P processors, T_P, consists of the computational time, T_{calc}, and the communication time, T_{comm}. When the computations and communications are not overlapped (as is the case for these experiments), the expression for total execution time is

$$T_P = T_{calc} + T_{comm} \tag{3.12}$$

Each of these terms has several components. The computational time, T_{calc}, includes the initialization component, T_{init}, and the iteration component, T_{iter}, from the sequential code. Also included is a redundant calculation time, T_{dup}, resulting from the parallelization of the ARPS. Thus, the computational time, T_{calc}, can be expressed as

$$T_{calc} = T_{init} + T_{iter}/P + T_{dup} \tag{3.13}$$

The total communication time, T_{comm}, relative to P processors consists of an initialization communication time, T_{base}, and an iterative communication time, T_{itcom}. Time T_{base} is required to send base state fields and initial values to each processor. Time T_{itcom} is required to send data to the outer borders of adjacent processors in the iterative part of the code. The expression for total communication time is thus

$$T_{comm} = T_{base} + T_{itcom} \tag{3.14}$$

The communication time required to transfer a packet of information from one processor to another depends on the startup time, the size of the message, and the transmission rate. The startup time is assumed to be independent of message size. For the decomposition used here, the quantity of data transferred between processors is a function of the data plane size and the number of prognostic fields. Also, the iterative communication time is a function of the number of communicating processes when using Ethernet.

Also when using Ethernet, as was done here, the communication time is not independent of the number of processors. As the number of processors increases, the transit time from sending to receiving processor also increases, as verified by experimentation.

Parallelization experiments Parallelization experiments were run for functional and domain decomposition strategies using the ARPS version 2.0 code. The functional decomposition experiments showed little speedup and, in some cases, a slowdown. As discussed earlier, this poor performance is due to the large messages that must be transferred to each processor during every timestep. Consequently, we abandoned this approach.

Parallelization experiments using one- and two-dimensional domain decomposition were done to examine fixed-size speedup and scaled speedup. For fixed-size problems, as the number of processors increases the amount of work done by each processor decreases while the amount of data transferred (i.e., message size) by each remains constant, thus decreasing the computation-to-communication ratio. In contrast, a problem can be scaled up by increasing the problem size as processors are added. In this case, the amount of work done by each processor, as well as the communication time, can be made to remain constant, all independent of the number of processors added. In this way the computation-to-communication ratio can also be fixed with changing problem size.

Single-dimension decomposition experiments were done with decomposition in the x direction and in the z direction. Two-dimensional decomposition experiments were done with decomposition in the x and y directions. Subdomain sizes were restricted to the maximum that would fit in the memory of each processor, that is, 15,872 grid points for the machines used here. Thus, a typical subdomain contained $16 \times 31 \times 32$ points.

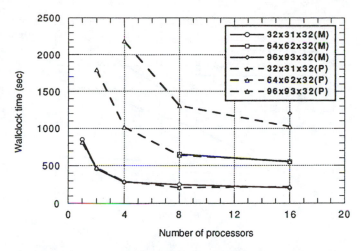

Figure 3.5   Measured (M) and predicted (P) wallclock time for fixed-size problem.

Subdomains larger than this caused time-consuming paging of data in and out of memory. However, the larger memory of the host machine allowed sequential jobs to run with grids as large as $32 \times 62 \times 32$ points.

Subdomain arrangements for two-dimensional decomposition were restricted to those producing whole grids with square dimensions. This restriction, although arbitrary, is reasonable since whole grids with rectangular dimensions are more efficiently decomposed with one-dimensional decompositions in the direction of the long axis. The two-dimensional experiments used either 4 or 16 processors, in each case with one machine serving as the host node.

The timestep, grid increment, and number of time steps were held constant for all decomposition experiments, regardless of the number of grid points used. Thus, as the number of points increased in a given direction, so did the physical extent of the grid in that direction. This was done to avoid computational stability problems associated with the Courant–Friedrichs–Levy (CFL) condition.

Fixed-size experiments   The fixed-size runs showed a speedup with increasing numbers of processors (subdomains). The results of the fixed-size experiments for one-dimensional decomposition in the x direction are shown in Figure 3.5 for three different grid sizes: $32 \times 31 \times 32$, $64 \times 62 \times 32$ and $96 \times 93 \times 32$. Shown are the measured timings obtained by running the code on the cluster, and predicted timings obtained from the analytic performance model. In all cases, the former were obtained by placing calls to the system clock around the calls to the communication routines at the application level. All predicted communication times were obtained from the performance model.

The predicted timings agree closely with the measured timings. The timings for the $32 \times 31 \times 32$ case show a result similar to that predicted by Amdahl's law in that the timing curve appears to approach an asymptote. Timings for the $64 \times 62 \times 32$ and $96 \times 93 \times 32$ grids suggest asymptotic behavior similar to that for the $32 \times 31 \times 32$ case (Figure 3.5). Again, predicted versus measured timings are in close agreement. The

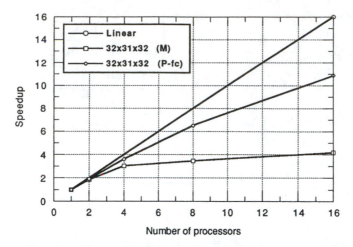

Figure 3.6   Measured (M) and predicted (P) speedup for fixed-size problem. The predicted speedup (P) is for communication 100 times faster than can be obtained with PVM or clustered RISC System 6000s connected via Ethernet.

experiments for the $64 \times 62 \times 32$ grid could not use fewer than 8 processors due to memory constraints. Similarly, experiments for the $96 \times 93 \times 32$ grid case could not be run with fewer than 16 processors.

The fixed-size speedup measured in these runs was 4.11 using 16 processors and $32 \times 31 \times 32$ total grid points (Figure 3.6), and 2.19 using 8 processors and $16 \times 31 \times 32$ total grid points. The fixed-size speedup of 4.11 was 25.7% of the linear speedup. Under ideal conditions with no limiting factors, the wallclock time would have been 52 s instead of the measured 204 s. Analysis of the 152 s loss shows that 125 s were due to interprocessor communication, 21 s to duplicate calculations, and 6 s to initialization. This sort of loss for fixed-size problems, where communication is responsible for the biggest loss and duplicate computations for the next biggest loss, is typical.

The effect of communication can be further illustrated by comparing calculation time with communication time as a function of the number of processors (Figure 3.7). Calculation times (solid curves) decrease with increasing numbers of processors since the number of points per subdomain also decreases. However, because of the dependence of the communication time on the number of processors, the communication time increases. As stated earlier, this is a characteristic of the joint communication network hardware/software systems, including protocols and operating system drivers. Faster network speeds (where network includes both software and hardware) would permit the use of more processors before the communication bottleneck becomes a serious impediment.

Wallclock times for the two-dimensional decomposition experiments are shorter than for comparable one-dimensional decomposition experiments with equal numbers of processors and grid points. For example, the wallclock time for the case of $32 \times 32 \times 31$ total grid points over 16 processors ($8 \times 8 \times 31$ subdomains) was 192 s. This is 6% faster

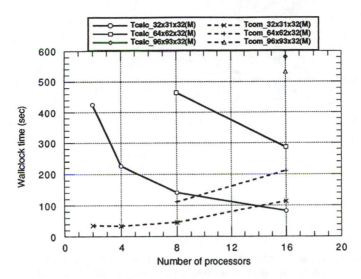

Figure 3.7 **Calculation versus communication time for three fixed-size problems.**

than the one-dimensional decomposition run. This speedup results from shorter messages that, in turn, result in less communication time and fewer duplicate computations.

Scaled-size experiments   The scaled-speedup experiments used one- and two-dimensional domain decompositions similar to those in the fixed-size experiments. The size of
the subdomain on each processor was fixed as more processors were added. Consider a
one-dimensional decomposition in the x direction for the case of an $8 \times 62 \times 32$ grid
point subdomain with up to 16 processors, giving a total grid size of $128 \times 62 \times 32$
points. The results for this case are shown in Figures 3.8 and 3.9. As seen in Figure 3.8,
the wallclock time increases as the number of processors increases. Theoretically, the time
to run the ARPS should not change with the number of processors, P, unless the serial
part of the code depends upon P. For this decomposition, the serial initialization portion
of the ARPS is a function of grid size and thus a function of P. Also, the communication
time is a function of P. Thus, these two factors contribute to an increase in wallclock
time as P increases. This is evident in both the measured and predicted timings. The
scaled-problem speedup of 8.2 for the case of $128 \times 62 \times 32$ total points on 16 processors is 51.2% of the possible linear speedup of 16. The 390 s difference between the ideal
wallclock time and the measured time is attributable primarily to communication costs.
Of the total wallclock time of 800 s, interprocessor communications take 319 s, duplicate calculations take 43 s, and initialization takes 28 s.

The scaled-size experiments using two-dimensional decomposition behaved similarly
to that of the one-dimensional decompositions. However, for similar sized grids, the
wallclock times for the two-dimensional decompositions were smaller. For example, a
$32 \times 31 \times 32$ grid decomposed in the x direction over 4 processors had a wallclock time
of 282 s versus 241 s for the two-dimensional decomposition of a $32 \times 32 \times 31$ grid
point run on 4 processors. This difference is primarily the result of shorter messages.

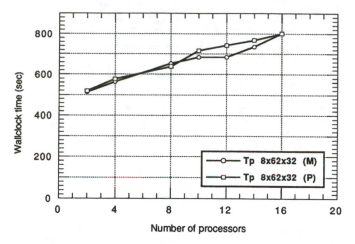

Figure 3.8 Measured (M) and predicted (P) wallclock time when using a communications network (hardware and software) 100 times faster can be obtained with PVM or clustered RISC System 6000s connected via Ethernet.

This leads to less communication time even though there are more messages in the latter. Also, as mentioned earlier, duplicate calculations are a factor in the decreased time. The length of the subdomain borders is also shorter, implying shorter messages and leading to fewer grid points where duplicate calculations are required.

Problems and alternatives Clearly the biggest obstacle to achieving significant speedups with the ARPS (and, most likely, with other models of a similar type) when run on a workstation cluster is communication associated with transferring data to adjacent processors. Next in importance is the effect of redundant calculations, followed by computations for generating the initial fields, and synchronization between processors due to load imbalances. These effects are tied to the serial portion of the program, and limit speedup in a fashion analogous to the serial portion of Amdahl's law. Remedies to these problems are discussed below.

Interprocessor communication time can be reduced by choosing appropriate decompositions and using faster networks. Some decomposition strategies have advantages over others when considering communication costs. As mentioned above, decomposing in two or more dimensions leads to less data transfer than in one dimension. A rule of thumb is to select subdomains that minimize the surface area while maximizing the volume, thereby increasing the computation-to-communications ratio. For highly non-isotropic computational domains, decomposing along the larger dimensions leads to greater efficiency.

Faster communication networks (including both hardware and software) are likely to produce the greatest speedup improvements on workstation clusters. Increasing the communication speed by a factor of 100 in the analytic performance model suggests an increase in speedup by a factor of two over the Ethernet results presented in Figures 3.6 and

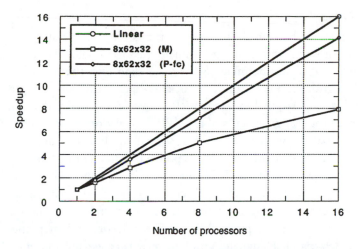

Figure 3.9   Measured (M) and predicted (P) speedup for scaled problem. The predicted
speedup is for a communications network (hardware and software) 100
times faster can be obtained with PVM or clustered RISC System 6000s
connected via Ethernet.

3.9. Software/hardware network systems with this speed will be available for clusters in
the near future, and considerable improvement in network speed is also anticipated on
MPPs, though at a significantly greater cost than for clusters of loosely coupled processors.

The issue of load balancing across processors did not arise in the parallel experiments
conducted here because all subdomains were of equal size and no data-dependent process
existed; thus, all processors, being of equal speed, performed equivalent amounts of
computation.

Future Work

Several issues remain to be addressed for the parallelization of the ARPS model. The
parallelized code needs to be run on a workstation cluster with faster communications
in order to verify the performance projected by the analytic model. The issue of load
balancing needs to be studied for those instances where data-dependent physical processes exist. Finally, the portability to MPPs of programs developed in a cluster environment must also be examined, and we plan to do so initially by running the PVM version
of ARPS on the Cray T3D.

3.7 Evaluation of the ARPS Using Fortran-P

Having established basic performance statistics for the ARPS using a small number of
loosely coupled processors, we move now to a tightly coupled network of higher-per-
formance processors and use a translation tool known as Fortran-P to convert ARPS
Fortran 77 into domain-decomposed CMF for the Connection Machine.

Basic Fortran-P Model

Fortran-P is a subset of Fortran 77 that allows the coding of self-similar applications programs, that is, those in which the algorithm applied to the global data domain is the same as that applied to each subdomain. Self-similarity implies the following properties: a logically regular grid, local communications, and equal work for each processor. Applications with this property, including the ARPS, have data domains that can be divided evenly among the processing elements of an MPP. This is done at compile time so that no run-time load balancing is required. Self-similar applications are well suited for MPPs, so very good performance should be possible. They contain multiple levels of parallelism that can be exploited both among and within nodes. Grid algorithms employing explicit, finite difference numerical schemes often fit the self-similar model.

Fortran-P was developed to exploit this self-similarity property and automatically generate an equivalent program for an MPP.[34] The current implementation generates CM Fortran,[35] a data-parallel language with Fortran 90 array extensions and data layout directives. A future implementation will also generate message-passing code. A 1024-node CM-200 and a 544-node CM-5 from Thinking Machines are available at the University of Minnesota, where most Fortran-P work occurs. Our earlier research was mainly targeted at the CM-200, but most of our attention has now been shifted to the CM-5, which was recently upgraded with vector units.

In the Fortran-P environment, codes are developed and maintained in (implicitly parallel) Fortran 77 and converted to MPP form only when the large memory and performance of the MPP is required. Application developers can continue to work in the familiar workstation or vector supercomputer environment, yet have full portability to MPPs through translation tools.

Fortran-P translation can be divided into two stages: parallelization and data layout, and performance-enhancing optimizations. We discuss each of these below.

Parallelization and data layout In this stage, the code is parallelized for MPP execution. Data layout directives are generated that partition the data domain equally among the processors (e.g., see Figure 3.3). Additional parallel dimensions are added to each array reference to distribute subdomains among the processors.

As mentioned before, our current target MPP language for Fortran-P translation is CMF, in which scalar objects reside on the front-end processor while array objects may reside on the front-end or be distributed across processing nodes. Compiler directives are provided to allow the user to specify whether a dimension of a distributed array is within a node (:SERIAL) or spread across the nodes (:NEWS). This meshes well with the Fortran-P model; the original dimensions remain :SERIAL and the added dimensions are labeled as :NEWS. Consequently, the serial dimensions address elements within the subdomain, ensuring that the subdomains are not split among processors. The remaining dimensions form a processor address and specify the particular subdomain.[34, 36]

When the data domain is partitioned, a picture frame of fake zones that consist of redundant data from neighboring nodes is added to each subdomain to help improve communication efficiency (see Figure 3.3). During execution, these fake zones must occasionally be updated to reflect modified data on neighboring nodes.

Statements to implement and update the boundary zones of interior subdomains are added during this phase in connection with the handling of boundary conditions. Very close attention must be paid to this portion of code since it involves interprocessor communication. The original boundary condition code is modified so that these conditions are only applied to the boundaries that are actually on the exterior of the whole problem domain.

Once these transformations are complete, the code can be compiled and executed on an MPP. However, additional transformations (described next) can improve performance considerably.

Performance-enhancing optimizations With immature compilers, restricted programming styles must often be used to achieve efficient execution, and this seems especially true on MPPs. In certain cases we have seen a 100-times difference in performance between two different but equivalent loop-coding styles. In developing the Fortran-P translator, many timing experiments were performed on different loops to arrive at source forms having the best performance. These forms have been incorporated into the CM Fortran code generated by the translator. More traditional compiler source transformations such as loop unrolling and forward substitution are also applied to improve performance. Forward substitution is applied to vectorizable loops; scalar temporaries are substituted directly into expressions, leaving only assignments into array references. This results in larger sequences of conformant array operations,[34, 36] giving performance improvements on the order of 10–30%.

Subgrid Virtual Processor Ratio Problem

One feature critical to the performance of CM Fortran codes is the virtual processor (VP) ratio,[35] which is the number of parallel nodes assumed in the program divided by the actual number of physical nodes made available at run time; in another words, the number of subdomains assigned to each processor node. Early versions of the CMF compiler parallelized within a CM-200 or CM-5 node across the multiple subgrids, but would not vectorize across the serial dimensions within individual subdomains. As a result, a high VP ratio was necessary for good performance. In the Fortran-P model, each subdomain has at least one fake zone on each boundary, and as the subgrid ratio increases via further divisions to the subdomain, the ratio of real zones to fake zones plummets. In such cases, considerable memory is wasted on the fake zones, and the real megaflop rate (i.e., neglecting the redundant boundary data) is high only for very large problems. Fortunately, Thinking Machines has responded to this problem and has removed this constraint in the latest release of CM Fortran.

ARPS Results

The computational kernel of the ARPS code fits the self-similar model well. To understand some of the potential problems associated with converting the full ARPS code, a nonlinear two-dimensional shallow water model, simpler in physical formulation but of equivalent computational structure to ARPS, was translated first. Nearly all of the shallow water application, with the exception of boundary conditions and fake zone

Problem Size	Subdomain Size	Processor Grid	Processors	VP	Memory (MB)
$32 \times 32 \times 32$	$8 \times 8 \times 8$	$4 \times 4 \times 4$	32	2	578
$40 \times 40 \times 40$	$5 \times 5 \times 5$	$8 \times 8 \times 8$	32	16	243
$80 \times 80 \times 80$	$5 \times 5 \times 5$	$16 \times 16 \times 16$	128	32	977

Table 3.1 Problem size, subdomain size, number of processors, memory use, and resulting VP ratios for three experiments.

handling, was translated automatically using Fortran-P. Additional procedures have since been added to deal with the other parts.

The converted two-dimensional shallow water code was run and the performance measured in a nondedicated mode on one quadrant of the University of Minnesota CM-200 (i.e., 256 FPUs, 1 gigabyte of memory) using release 1.2 of the CM Fortran slice-wise compiler. Given the compiler limitations, the performance was found to be linked directly to the subgrid ratio; the megaflop rating increased from 132 for a 1:1 subgrid ratio (256 subgrids of a size of 64×32) to 924 for a subgrid ratio of 8:1 (2048 subdomains of the same size). Apparently, large problems are required to obtain acceptable performance with the given compiler.

The three-dimensional ARPS code was then translated and executed on the CM-5. Again, with the earlier version of CM Fortran, high VP ratios had to be used for good performance. Since ARPS uses three boundary points (one on the left and two on the right) due to grid staggering, each subdomain also required 3 boundary points. Because of the ARPS memory requirements (approximately 60 full-domain-sized three-dimensional arrays), the subdomains needed to be small to avoid memory limitations on the CM-5. A reasonable size turned out to be 5^3 real points per subdomain, or 8^3 total points per subdomain. This means that only $5^3/8^3 = 24.4\%$ of the memory used was for real points, the remainder associated with the fake boundary zones.

This memory inefficiency, associated with large VP ratios, resulted in speeds only 25% of real time on 32 nodes of a 544-node CM-5 for a problem size of $40 \times 40 \times 40$ grid points. A 128-node run using $80 \times 80 \times 80$ points ran at about the same speed relative to real time.

Table 3.1 shows problem size, subdomain size, processor grid, memory used, and VP ratios for three experiments. The so-called rule of eight on the CM Fortran compiler is important here, namely, that non-multiple-of-eight array sizes are padded to a multiple of eight. This explains why the $32 \times 32 \times 32$ problem takes considerably more memory than the $40 \times 40 \times 40$ problem; with the three boundary zones used by ARPS, the subdomain arrays of the former are $11 \times 11 \times 11$ and were probably padded to $16 \times 16 \times 16$ for the latter.

Preliminary Results with CMF 2.1 Beta 1.0 and Beta Fortran-P Translator

As mentioned earlier, CM Fortran compiler versions prior to CMF 2.1 Beta 1.0 (which was unfortunately not available for our preliminary study) yielded poor memory efficiency and hence poor computational efficiency as well. The alpha version of the Fortran-P translator did not generate the appropriate loop form for the CM Fortran 2.1 Beta 1.0 compiler; this has been corrected in the beta Fortran-P translator.[34]

Early results with the CMF 2.1 Beta 1.0 compiler are very encouraging. In particular, high subgrid ratios become much less important and replication of subgrids on processors (which leads directly to memory inefficiency) was not critical to performance. We have also employed an early version of the beta Fortran-P translator to generate Fortran 90–styled loops (instead of the serial DO loop structure employed in the alpha version) and used the Cray FPP in-liner to reduce the significant subroutine overheads present in ARPS due to its operator-based style. These translation improvements led to significant performance increases; early results indicate that a $40 \times 40 \times 40$ grid size now runs at twice the speed of the weather on 32-nodes, a factor of 8 increase in speed over our earlier results.

Future Work with Fortran-P

With the release of ARPS 3.2 (and later versions) and the availability of CMF Version 2.1 Beta 1.0, which vectorizes across the serial dimensions, we are concentrating on developing a more modular, beta version of the Fortran-P translator that can be targeted for the Fortran 90 coding style that the CMF compiler prefers. Our experience with the ARPS pointed out many important properties of other self-similar finite difference codes, including the use of staggered grids. We intend to incorporate these and other new features in our translators, and retranslate the latest version of ARPS to study its performance.

3.8 Parallel Execution of ARPS on CM-5 Using CMAX Translator

We have used a second code translator, CMAX, to port the ARPS to the Connection Machine CM-5. In contrast to Fortran-P, which is designed around a subset of Fortran-77, CMAX is a commercial product that seeks to address a broader range of applications, including "dusty decks" written using much older versions of Fortran.

The CMAX Translator

The CM Automated X-lator[37] is a software tool that converts standard Fortran 77 code into CM Fortran (CMF), a modern Fortran which incorporates the array expression syntax of Fortran 90 (F90). It is based on Forge technology from Applied Parallel Research (APR).[38] Thinking Machines Corporation is now continuing its development. When applied to a program written in *scalable* Fortran 77 (see Chapter 8), the output of CMAX exhibits good performance on distributed-memory, massively parallel systems like the CM. Thus, CMAX provides a migration path for serial programs onto the CM.

CMAX can be used to assist in a one-time porting effort, at the conclusion of which the user discards the old Fortran 77 code and maintains the CMF output. Alternatively, users can continue to maintain their scalable software in Fortran 77 for maximum portability to multiple systems and can run CMAX as a preprocessor before regular compilation by the CMF compiler. Development of new code might also be done in Fortran 77 using CMAX either for portability or because developers familiar with Fortran 77 prefer to continue using it rather than CMF.

Porting ARPS to CMF

The translation of scalable Fortran 77 into CMF for execution on distributed memory CMs consists of two components. The first involves substituting array operations for statements that operate on array elements within Fortran 77 loops.[39] This issue has been addressed by a number of previous translators. Second, and of equal importance, is the translation of constructs arising from the Fortran 77 linear memory model into code that does not rely on storage or sequence association. Interprocedural analysis is performed by CMAX (the first translator having this capability) to detect and remedy this problem. A side benefit is the improvement of loop vectorization.

The ARPS code fits the scalable Fortran model (see Chapter 8 and also Wholey et al.[40]) quite well. The entire ARPS 3.1 application, consisting of over 65,000 lines of Fortran 77 including comments, was translated using CMAX, run on the CM-5, and verified against the original Fortran 77 code on a Cray Y-MP.

In the translation, a number of modifications were made to both the original code and the CMAX-generated output. In order for scientists to understand and appreciate the steps required, we present below a brief synopsis or diary of the principal modifications made during the initial porting phase. Readers unconcerned with these details may proceed directly to "ARPS Performance on the CM-5" in Section 3.8.

- ARPS was translated using CMAX version 0.8. Fifty-nine CMF$LAYOUT array data distribution directives were inserted to improve performance by shifting the time index such that it could be distributed across the processors. (Experience gained from working with the ARPS resulted in many improvements to CMAX. For example, the manually inserted directives described in this section can now be added automatically.)

- A bug in CMAX that prevented vectorization of certain reduction loops was found and corrected.

- Six CMAX$NODEPENDENCE directives were inserted to allow vectorization of six dependence-free loops that CMAX incorrectly diagnosed as having dependencies. CMAX 1.0 now vectorizes the loops without the directives.

At this point, the ARPS was executed on a problem of size $35 \times 35 \times 35$ points using a 32-processor CM-5, and achieved a speed of 9.9 s per iteration for a single timestep of 6 s. The data distribution was parallel along the three spatial dimensions, but not along the time dimension, as described above.

The serial time dimension of length 3 (for 3 time levels) was the rightmost dimension. Unfortunately, the current version of CM Fortran, CMF 2.1 Beta 1.0, is more efficient when nonparallel dimensions are gathered on the left. The makefile was modified to call a CMAX utility to automatically permute the array dimensions in ARPS, moving the time dimension to the leftmost position. This reduced the time per iteration to 4.9 s.

CMAX translated the differencing and averaging operators into expressions containing several EOSHIFTs (end off shift). The boundary was later set and its shifted value never used. Unfortunately, the latest version of CSHIFT (circular shift) in the CM Fortran run time library is more optimized than EOSHIFT. The Fortran 77 code was, therefore, modified to perform a circular shift. The execution time dropped to 4.0 s per iteration with this change.

As discussed earlier, many of the calculations in the ARPS are done by operators in separate subroutines containing loops over entire arrays. CMAX can vectorize these loops, which are then implemented by CMF. However, CMF is unable to fuse the loops *between* subroutines since it does not operate interprocedurally. This was overcome by implementing a simple tool that both searched for directives of the form "C$INLINE function from file" and executed the requested subroutine in-lining. Fifteen INLINE directives were added to the program based on the profiling results, and the program was recompiled. The in-lining improved execution speed by 12%.

The next problem highlighted by the profiling was the treatment of boundary conditions. A large amount of time was spent computing various equations along the domain boundaries. The boundary computations used several two-dimensional arrays that contain the time tendencies of prognostic variables. These time tendencies were applied to the two-dimensional faces of a three-dimensional array. In order to bring the two-dimensional data into the three-dimensional array, CM Fortran was forced to use expensive, general purpose communication. A decision was made to trade space for time: the Fortran 77 code was modified to store the time tendencies in the outer faces of a new three-dimensional array rather than in multiple two-dimensional arrays. This change wastes the interior of the new array, but by itself improves execution on the CM by about 15%. When combined with in-lining, the improvement is 26%.

The next change again involved boundary conditions. Six expensive calculations (x, y, and z momentum, pressure, and potential temperature) were identified along four two-dimensional faces and four one-dimensional columns of a three-dimensional array. Each associated subroutine contained eight loop nests, and six such subroutines were found. Space was again traded for time by using a three-dimensional bitmask array that indicated, for each element, the relative spatial location (e.g., interior, corner, or face). Eight loop nests were then fused and the eight single-line loop bodies converted to a single line in the fused loops; the line used the bitmask array. This effort also exposed multiply–adds to the CMF scheduler that had previously been obscured, improving execution time by an additional 12%.

The final change was to perform all computations in double precision rather than single precision. Double precision uses twice as much memory and thus halves the largest solvable problem (and the vector length) for a fixed-size memory; however, switching to double precision still improved performance by 15% because the CM-5 memory system is optimized for 64-bit operands.

ARPS Performance on the CM-5

With the aforementioned changes now in place, the translated ARPS was put through a set of timing tests on the CM-5. These experiments used the environment from a well-studied supercell storm to define the model base state, and a warm thermal perturbation near the ground to trigger the initial storm.

All times presented below are wallclock times on a dedicated machine for a complete execution of 600 timesteps of 6 s each, corresponding to 1 h of real weather, and include the input/output and initialization. Initialization took several minutes on the larger problems. The latest beta releases of all Thinking Machines software were used.

Due to our limited access to larger machines, we were unable to complete the desired matrix of run times. The 1024-processor machine at the Los Alamos National Laboratory (LANL) was the most difficult to schedule time on. Therefore, we ran one problem to completion on it, and made two other partial runs which were then extrapolated into full run timings (the initialization and the timestepping timing were properly handled in the extrapolation; therefore, the timings should be reasonably accurate). These two partial runs are italicized in Table 3.2.

The single-processor timing used the Sun f77 compiler and executed on a single processor of a CM-5, in single precision. All other timings used CMAX to translate Fortran 77 to CMF, followed by CMF compilation, and are double precision. The difference favors the single-processor run time, reducing speedups.

The speed relative to real time for simulating 1 h of weather on the CM-5 for different domain sizes is plotted against the number of processors in Figure 3.10. Another index of performance is the rate at which grid point values are updated, that is, the number of grid points updated per wallclock second. These rates are presented in Table 3.2. As shown in the table, the best rate for a single CM-5 processor run was 1264 and the best rate for a 512-processor CM-5 run was 402,267, the ratio of which gives a speedup of 318. For a 1024-processor CM-5 run, the best rate was 1,146,542, giving a speedup of 907.

Problem Size/NP	1	4	32	64	128	256	512	1024
$32 \times 32 \times 32$	1171	4697	20696	34312	—	—	—	—
$40 \times 40 \times 40$	1264	4868	27288	54957	112993	111393	112027	—
$80 \times 80 \times 80$	—	4472	34428	60693	—	—	286496	—
$40 \times 40 \times 40$	—	—	—	—	—	—	—	609047
$80 \times 80 \times 80$	—	—	—	—	—	—	402267	*991379*
$1024 \times 1024 \times 32$	—	—	—	—	—	—	—	*1146542*

Table 3.2 Simulated grid point updates per wallclock second as a function of problem size (number of grid points) and number of processors, NP (*top line in table*). Italicized numbers are estimates extrapolated from short runs; others are based on measured wallclock time for full runs.

Figure 3.10 clearly shows consistent speedups for problems of size $32 \times 32 \times 32$ up to 64 processors (this small problem was not run on larger machines); the moderately sized $64 \times 64 \times 32$ problem did not bottom out until more than 128 processors. For the workstation cluster experiments reported earlier, a $32 \times 31 \times 32$ problem bottomed out at 8 processors due to the associated slower communication network (hardware and software).

To demonstrate the value of MPP and the CMAX utility, Figure 3.11 shows, for four three-dimensional ARPS simulations differing only in their spatial resolution,[41] horizontal cross sections of rainwater content at an altitude of 4 km above the ground for a well-documented severe storm. In each case, the domain extends 64 km laterally and 16 km vertically. In the three panels labeled 2 km, 1 km, and 500 m—the numbers indicating the horizontal resolution—a vertical resolution of 500 m was used. In the lower right panel, a uniform grid spacing of 250 m was used in all three dimensions. Horizontal resolutions of 1 to 2 km, shown in the upper part of Figure 3.11, are typical for simulation studies of storm-scale phenomena.

It is clear from Figure 3.11 that as the grid is refined the model captures significantly more detail, including turbulent structures related to the entrainment of environmental air. Although the usefulness of small-scale features in storm prediction remains to be shown, they are absolutely essential for representing phenomena such as tornadoes. An early analysis of these experiments shows that the solutions were beginning to converge only at resolutions higher than 1 km, and only at the highest resolution did the peak updraft strength approach that predicted by inviscid linear theory.

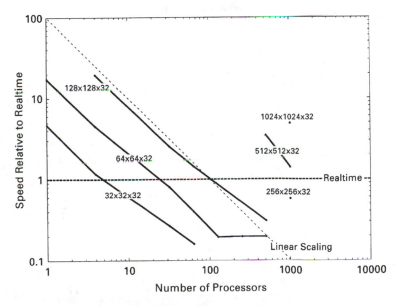

Figure 3.10   Speed relative to real time for simulating 1 h of weather on the CM-5 as a function of the number of processors ($\Delta x = 1$ km, $\Delta y = 1$ km, and $\Delta z = 0.5$ km). Each connected line represents a single problem size. Points below the horizontal dashed line represent runs that predict weather faster than real-time. The diagonal dashed line represents linear scaling.

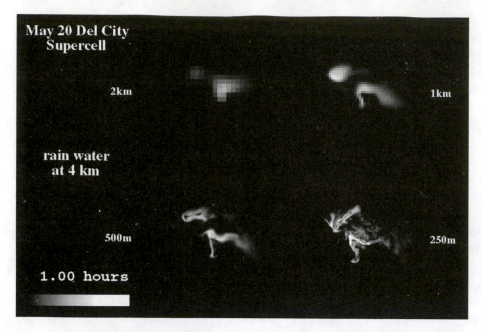

Figure 3.11 Horizontal cross sections of rainwater content at an altitude of 4 km above the ground for a well-documented severe storm simulated using four different spatial resolutions in the ARPS.[41] In each experiment, the domain extends 64 km laterally and 16 km vertically. In the three panels labeled 2 km, 1 km, and 500 m—the numbers indicating the horizontal resolution—a vertical resolution of 500 m was used. In the lower right panel, a uniform grid spacing of 250 m was used in all three dimensions.

By virtue of CMAX, the long-desired goal of simulating a severe storm in three-dimensional with uniformly high spatial resolution has been achieved, and efforts are now underway to explore the utility of the results, in particular to estimate minimum resolutions nominally for various types of events, and the impact of resolution on atmospheric predictability. Instead of using the power of CMAX and the CM-5 to attain extremely high spatial resolutions, one can use coarser resolutions but much larger domain sizes—an essential requirement for operational storm-scale NWP that has also now been achieved.

Summary and Outlook

We have reported here the porting of the entire ARPS 3.1 Fortran 77 application to CMF, and the timing results obtained on the CM-5. The execution of the ARPS on the CM-5 was possible because of new parallelizing compiler technology called CMAX. A speedup of 907 was achieved on a 1024-processor CM-5 for a $1024 \times 1024 \times 32$ problem, which represents the "ultimate" domain size necessary for storm-scale prediction. The speed of parallel execution opens up new possibilities for the operational testing and research capabilities of the ARPS, both with respect to the areal extent of the domain as well as the spatial resolution. The CMAX strategy will allow future versions of the ARPS to be ported to the CM with little additional investment of time. Other issues that may arise from the use of implicit algorithms and certain physics calculations will be the subject of future investigations.

3.9 Evaluation of the ARPS Using Fortran-D

The final port of the ARPS uses a message-passing approach, in which a programmer explicitly defines the decomposition of the model domain for the particular hardware system, and manages the communication of messages among processor nodes. We use Fortran 77 plus message passing as a standard of comparison for our data-parallel and Fortran 90D/High Performance Fortran now under development.

Introduction

To develop parallel applications, one must first understand the structure of the problem and then use software to map the problem onto an appropriate parallel system.[42] The Fortran-D approach used at the Northeast Parallel Architectures Center (NPAC) is based on the recognized need for close communication and synergism between domain scientists and their applications, and computer scientists/engineers and software development tools. We view the lack of appropriate software tools as the most important obstacle to developing parallel applications. To be useful for solving real-world problems, extensions and improvements to software must be guided by the evaluation of challenging application problems.[43] For this reason, we have incorporated the ARPS into the Fortran-D benchmark suite of industrial and scientific application codes. By developing a set of ARPS models for MIMD and SIMD architectures, and data-parallel and message-passing software, we will be able to identify strategies for the ARPS model development effort and define those extensions needed in Fortran-D to accommodate it. It is our belief that such strategies are also applicable to other disciplines and applications.

Description of Fortran-D

Fortran-D is a software development project sponsored by the National Science Foundation (NSF) and the Advanced Research Project Agency (ARPA), and being carried out jointly by the Center for Research on Parallel Computation (CRPC) at Rice University, and NPAC at Syracuse University. The goal is to produce a machine-independent parallel programming model and a language to implement it. Fortran-D is built upon Fortran 77 and Fortran 90, and contains extensions to help the programmer express parallelism in the application and then map the application to a specific machine architecture. For example, decomposition and alignment statements define the sizes, shapes, and mappings between arrays. Distribution statements specify the mapping of a problem to physical machine characteristics including topology, the communication network, the size of local memory, and the number of processors. The user is involved in this process by design since the user is the one who best understands the details of the application code; and Fortran-D attempts to take advantage of this information.[44] High Performance Fortran (HPF)[45] will become the industry standard data-parallel Fortran, and a subset of Fortran 90D will be built into HPF.

Computational Models

Data-parallel computing is particularly suited for the ARPS because this approach is well established, and because current versions of data-parallel Fortran and C can express applications having regular structure.[46] Additionally, programmer-written directives can be added to advise the compiler on data structure decomposition and minimization of data movement. Finally, data-parallel code tends to be easier to understand, write, and debug than applications that use a message-passing strategy.

Message passing works well for a large set of applications on MIMD machines, but is not completely portable. The programmer must provide explicitly the message-passing constructs and choose appropriate strategies for domain decomposition as well as overlapping of communication and computation. Message passing is indeed viable, but a more easily implemented approach is perhaps desirable. NPAC is developing a message-passing version of the ARPS to serve as a standard for comparison against other dialects of Fortran.

Using Fortran-D with the ARPS model provides portability and a link to future software development. Fortran 77 plus message passing provides portability to all MIMD machines, and Fortran 90D/HPF will provide portability to all SIMD and MIMD machines. A goal of our work with the ARPS is to examine the usefulness of Fortran-D extensions to programmers and advanced compilers, and at the same time to define the features of an evolving ARPS model which cannot be expressed using current software. The latter issue will become more important as subsequent versions of the code involving major changes to the physics and data assimilation/ingest algorithms become available.

Model Implementation: Fortran 77 Plus Message Passing on the CM-5

In the first of two principal experiments, we implemented a portion of the ARPS code in Fortran 77 plus message passing on the CM-5. We selected only those subroutines associated with the differencing and averaging operators, and used a host–node programming model, wherein a main program runs on the host processor and passes input to multiple independent nodes. Each node runs independent subroutine or node programs. Nodes do the bulk of the computation, pass data to other nodes, and pass output back to the host.

Because the ARPS is a grid-based model using second-order spatial differences, relevant parallel computing issues include domain partitioning, update ordering, interprocessor communication, and scalability. The uniform structure of the current version of ARPS is well understood and leads to a simple decomposition strategy (see Figure 3.3 and the related discussion). In this first experiment, we chose to distribute the model computational domain among physical processors so as to minimize the subdomain area/volume ratio. For example, using a $4 \times 4 \times 2$ processor grid on NPAC's 32-node

CM-5, the $32 \times 32 \times 32$ point ARPS domain mapped into subdomains of size $8 \times 8 \times 16$. We follow the methodology for storing redundant boundary data in the subdomains, as described in "Decomposition strategies" in the "Implementation" subsection of Section 3.6 (see Figure 3.3). For efficient communication, we pass messages that contain a plane of grid points rather than a single value.

All processors send and receive messages concurrently. For example, in a two-dimensional processor array, a given processor simultaneously receives an array of nodal values from the processor to the left while sending an array to the processor on the right. Separate communication functions are used for each type of message, including host-to-node and node-to-node, message direction (right, left, up, down, front, back), and message shape (two-, three-, and four-dimensional arrays).

Preliminary Results

Two related experiments were conducted based on an explicit message-passing approach to parallel programming. In the first, we implemented a set of the ARPS discrete numerical operators in Fortran 77 plus message passing on the CM-5. Following the model development approach of CAPS, we emphasized the use of fine-grained communication modules that are easy to understand and modify. In the second, larger experiment called mpARPS (message-passing ARPS), we implemented the full ARPS application, with the exception of initialization and input/output routines, in Fortran 77 plus message passing on the Intel Delta.

In the first experiment, communication time, as measured at the application level by system calls, accounted for a very small percentage (of order 1%) of the total computation time per timestep. However, because this simple test involved only the operators, communication-intensive aspects were neglected. Thus, in the second experiment with message passing applied to the full application, we examined one-, two-, and three-dimensional decompositions of size $1024 \times 1024 \times 32$ points in the x, y, and z directions, respectively, and found that, similar to the workstation cluster implementation using PVM, a one-dimensional decomposition represented the most effective communication strategy. Additionally, we were able to use a mapping function to process the boundary conditions, and overlap communication with computation though the use of asynchronous messages.

Based on a 512-node Intel Delta, our initial results show that the mpARPS can update 1.6 million grid points per second with a maximum possible size of 20 million points.[47] This represents a speedup of 553 relative to a single node on the Delta, and should be compared to 0.4 million points per second and a maximum problem size of 8 million points for a 512-node CM-5. Relative to a single-processor Cray Y-MP, the CMAX versions of the ARPS and the mpARPS achieve speedups of 2.7 and 11.5, respectively, for equivalent experiments.

Ongoing Research

Our immediate goal is to establish a set of ARPS codes in the following dialects of Fortran: Fortran 77, Fortran 77 plus message passing, and Fortran 90. We will then add

Fortran 90D compiler directives to produce a Fortran 90D/High Performance Fortran version. Additionally, we may investigate the possibility of producing a Fortran 90 plus message passing version to run on CM-5 vector nodes.

We further wish to represent the ARPS on both SIMD and MIMD machine architectures, and message-passing and data-parallel software architectures, so as to evaluate the performance characteristics of and level of work required to implement portable, parallel versions of such codes. Future improvements in model physics modules will require new parallel algorithms, and to tackle these and other issues, we plan to take advantage of the extensive work now being done by members of the parallel computing research community.

3.10 Summary and Future Research Directions

We have described the development and implementation of a new three-dimensional atmospheric model designed for the operational prediction of thunderstorms and related weather. This code, known as the Advanced Regional Prediction System (ARPS), is the first full-physics, general-purpose mesoscale atmospheric model developed specifically for broad classes of scalable-parallel architectures. Results from four complementary ports of the ARPS to parallel systems were described:

1 Explicit message passing using a portable communications library, Parallel Virtual Machine (PVM), on a networked cluster of IBM RISC (reduced instruction set computer) System 6000 workstations (Section 3.6)

2 A data-parallel approach in which serial Fortran 77 is translated into Connection Machine Fortran (CMF) on the CM-200 and CM-5 using the Fortran-P translator (Section 3.7)

3 A data-parallel approach in which serial Fortran 77 is translated into Connection Machine Fortran (CMF) on the CM-5 using the Thinking Machines CMAX translator (Section 3.8)

4 Explicit message passing applied to the original Fortran 77 ARPS on the CM-5 and Intel Delta, which is the first step toward a port using Fortran-D/High Performance Fortran (Section 3.9).

The principal impediment to performance on workstation clusters was interprocessor communication overhead, as verified by our analytic performance model, suggesting enhanced scalability for the ARPS with the use of faster communication (both hardware and software). Although workstation clusters appear to be extremely useful for the development of parallel codes, and for running moderate-sized problems as a low-cost alternative to supercomputers, one should be very cautious in extrapolating performance from clusters to machines having significantly faster networks.

The early success of parallel architectures will depend largely on the ability to port, and show significant speedups with, existing codes in a relatively straightforward manner. To facilitate this process, considerable effort is being expended in both the academic and commercial sectors to develop appropriate code translation tools. We applied two translation tools, Fortran-P and CMAX, to port the ARPS to the Connection Machine CM-200 and CM-5. Both tools convert Fortran 77 to Connection Machine Fortran (CMF), insert data layout directives, and implement various performance-enhancing options. Although the full ARPS code translated by both tools was unable to yield performance greater than approximately 10% of machine peak, the ease with which our Fortran 77 was translated to the CM was encouraging. It is important to note that, although overall code performance was marginal on the CM-5 (32 nodes of the CM-5 yielded a performance approximately equal to a single Cray Y-MP processor for the ARPS), our timings were performed without the benefit of hand tuning. Further, the large memory of the CM-5 allowed us to run much larger problems than was possible with many other machines, including our "ultimate" domain size of order $1024 \times 1024 \times 32$ grid points, for which we attained a speedup of 907 on a 1024-node machine. The nearly linear speedups achieved for large problem sizes on the CM-5 validated the scalable-coding strategies used by the ARPS, making our code a good role model for similar codes in science and engineering.

The fourth implementation of the ARPS on dedicated MPPs, the CM-5 and Intel Delta, relied on Fortran 77 plus message passing. This work was the first step toward a Fortran-D implementation which, when complete, will include versions of the ARPS on SIMD and MIMD hardware architectures, and data-parallel and explicit message-passing software architectures. Based on a 512-node Intel Delta, our initial results show that the message-passing version of ARPS (mpARPS) can update 1.6 million grid points per second with a maximum possible size of 20 million points.[47] This represents a speedup of 553 relative to a single node on the Delta, and should be compared to 0.4 million points per second and a maximum problem size of 8 million points for a 512-node CM-5. Relative to a single-processor Cray Y-MP, the CMAX versions of the ARPS and the mpARPS achieve speedups of 2.7 and 11.5, respectively, for equivalent experiments.

The operational numerical prediction of storm-scale weather will require a model system that can run 50 to 100 times faster than real time on domains of size $1000 \times 1000 \times 40$ grid points. Based on extrapolations of current model performance, a sustained teraflop of computing power, coupled with gigabit capacity networks, will be required to achieve this goal. We will continue to explore a variety of parallel-computing strategies with the ARPS during the next several years, with emphasis on using a broad spectrum of platforms ranging from relatively inexpensive workstations and clusters to the fastest massively parallel machines available. The results presented herein, though somewhat preliminary, have set the stage for further collaborations among our interdisciplinary team. Although we believe that message-passing paradigms represent the best approach for using distributed-memory processors in the near term, our code will remain flexible so as to accommodate new techniques and architectures as they become available.

Acknowledgments

Funding for this study was provided by the National Science Foundation through Grants ATM88-09862 and ATM91-20009 to the Center for Analysis and Prediction of

Storms at the University of Oklahoma, by the U.S. Department of Energy through Contract DE-FC05-85ER250000 to the Supercomputer Computations Research Institute at Florida State University, and by the U.S. Army Research Office under contract number DAAL03-89-C-0038 to the University of Minnesota Army High Performance Computing Research Center. The Northeast Parallel Architecture Center is supported by DARPA, NSF, NASA, the U.S. Army, and the state of New York. The CMAX work was supported by Thinking Machines Corporation. The authors wish to acknowledge discussions with and the assistance of Dennis Duke, Tom Green, Jeff Bauer, Gregory Riccardi, and Randy Langley of Florida State University; Neil Lincoln of SSESCO; Terence Parr and Henry Dietz of Purdue University; Olivier Meirhaeghe, Tom Varghese, and Paul Woodward of the University of Minnesota; and Nikos Chrisochoides, Geoffrey Fox, and Nancy McCracken of NPAC.

A special acknowledgment is in order for our colleagues who compose the ARPS Model Development team at the Center for Analysis and Prediction of Storms. They include, during the early versions of the code, Paula Reid, Joe Bradley, and Robert Lindsey, and more recently, Drs. Alan Shapiro and Vince Wong, Mr. and Mrs. Hao Jin, Keith Brewster, Dan Weber, Norman Lin, Xiaoguang Song, David Jahn, Steve Lazarus, Jason Levit, Adwait Sathye, Yuhe Liu, Yifeng Tang, Dr. Gene Bassett, Steve Weygandt, and Sue Weygandt.

Portions of this chapter were reprinted from *Parallel Supercomputing in Atmospheric Science*, Proceedings of the 5th ECMWF Workshop on the Use of Parallel Processors in Meteorology (G.-R. Hoffman and T. Kauranne, Eds.) World Scientific Publishing Co. Pte. Ltd., 1993, p. 99–129, and from Reference 31.

References

1 G. Sabot, S. Wholey, J. Berlin, and P. Oppenheimer. "Parallel Execution of a Fortran-77 Weather Prediction Model," *Proceedings*. Supercomputing '93, pp. 538–545.

2 J. G. Charney, R. Fjørtøft, and J. von Neumann. "Numerical Integration of the Barotropic Vorticity Equation," *Tellus*. **2**, 237–254, 1950.

3 L. F. Richardson. *Weather Prediction by Numerical Process*. Cambridge University Press, New York, 1992. Also available from Dover, New York, 1965.

4 F. G. Shuman. "History of Numerical Weather Prediction at the National Meteorological Center," *Wea. and Forecasting*. **4**, 286–296, 1989.

5 H. E. Brooks, C. A. Doswell III, and R. A. Maddox. "On the Use of Mesoscale and Cloud-Scale Models in Operational Forecasting," *Wea. and Forecasting*. **7**, 120–132, 1992.

6 K. Droegemeier and J. Levit. "The Sensitivity of Numerically Simulated Storm Evolution to Initial Conditions." 17th Conf. on Severe Local Storms, St. Louis, MO, Amer. Meteor. Soc., 1993, pp. 431-435.

7   K. Droegemeier. "Toward a Science of Storm-Scale Prediction." 16th Conf. on Severe Local Storms, Kananaskis Provincial Park, Alberta, Amer. Meteor. Soc., 1990, pp. 256–262.

8   D. K. Lilly. "Numerical Prediction of Thunderstorms—Has Its Time Come?" *Quart. J. Roy. Meteor. Soc.* **116**, 779–798, 1990.

9   M. Xue, K. Brewster, K. Droegemeier, V. Wong, Y. Liu, and M. Zou. "Application of the Advanced Regional Prediction System (ARPS) to Real-Time Operational Forecasting," *Proceedings.* 14th Conference on Weather and Forecasting, 1995.

10 P. R. Janish, K. K. Droegemeier, M. Xue, K. Brewster, and J. Levit. "Evaluation of the Advanced Regional Prediction System (ARPS) for Storm-Scale Modeling Applications in Operational Forecasting," *Proceedings.* 14th Conference on Weather and Forecasting, 1995.

11 O. Talagrand. "The Use of Adjoint Equations in Numerical Modeling of Atmospheric Circulation," *Automatic Differentiation of Algorithms: Theory, Implementation, and Application.* Proceedings of the First SIAM Workshop on Automatic Differentiation, Breckenridge, CO, January 6–8, 1991, pp. 169–180.

12 C. Bischof, A. Carle, G. Corliss, A. Griewank, and P. Hovland. "ADIFOR—Generating Derivative Codes from Fortran Programs," *Scientific Programming.* **1**, 11–29, 1992.

13 J. Smagorinsky. "General Circulation Experiments with the Primitive Equations," *Mon. Wea. Rev.* **91**, 99–164, 1963.

14 D. K. Lilly. "On the Numerical Simulation of Buoyant Convection," *Tellus.* **14**, 168–172, 1962.

15 M. Germano, U. Piomelli, P. Moin, and W. H. Cabot. "A Dynamic Subgrid-Scale Eddy Viscosity Model," *Phys. Fluids A.* **3**, 1760–1765, 1991.

16 V. Wong. "A Proposed Statistical-Dynamical Closure Method for the Linear or Nonlinear Subgrid-Scale Stresses," *Phys. Fluids A.* **4**, 1080–1082, 1992.

17 D. K. Lilly. "A Proposed Modification of the Germano Subgrid-Scale Closure Method," *Phys. Fluids A.* **4**, 633–635, 1992.

18 W. C. Skamarock and J. B. Klemp. "Adaptive Grid Refinement for Two-Dimensional and Three-Dimensional Nonhydrostatic Atmospheric Flow," *Mon. Wea. Rev.* **121**, 788–804, 1993.

19 M. Xue, K. K. Droegemeier, and P. R. Woodward. "Simulation of Tornado Vortices Within a Supercell Storm Using Adaptive Grid Refinement Technique." 17th Conf. on Severe Local Storms, St. Louis, MO, Amer. Meteor. Soc., 1993, pp. 362–365.

20 M. Xue, K. K. Droegemeier, V. Wong, A. Shapiro, and K. Brewster. *ARPS Version 4.0 User's Guide.* Center for Analysis and Prediction of Storms, University of Oklahoma, Norman, OK, 1995.

21 J. B. Klemp and R. B. Wilhelmson. "The Simulation of Three-Dimensional Convective Storm Dynamics," *J. Atmos. Sci.* **35**, 1070–1096, 1978.

22 W. C. Skamarock and J. B. Klemp. "The Stability of Time-Split Numerical Methods for the Hydrostatic and the Nonhydrostatic Elastic Equations," *Mon. Wea. Rev.* **120**, 2109–2127, 1992.

23 Y. Ogura and N. A. Phillips. "A Scale Analysis of Deep and Shallow Convection in the Atmosphere," *J. Atmos. Sci.* **19**, 173–179, 1962.

24 D. K. Lilly. "On the Computational Stability of Numerical Solutions of Time-Dependent Non-Linear Geophysical Fluid Dynamics Problems," *Mon. Wea. Rev.* **93**, 11–26, 1965.

25 F. B. Hildebrand. *Introduction to Numerical Analysis.* 2nd ed., Dover, New York, 1987.

26 A. Shapiro. "On the Use of an Exact Solution of the Navier-Stokes Equations in a Validation Test of a Three-Dimensional Nonhydrostatic Numerical Model." *Mon. Wea. Rev.* **121**, 2420–2425, 1992.

27 K. Droegemeier. "Cooperative Regional Assimilation and Forecast Test (CRAFT): Preliminary Field Evaluation '93." Center for Analysis and Prediction of Storms, University of Oklahoma, 1993.

28 D. W. Duke. "Cluster Computing Exploits Performance and Cost Advantages," *Computers in Physics.* **7**, 176–183, 1993.

29 V. S. Sunderam. "PVM: A Framework for Parallel Distributed Computing," *Con: Pract. and Exp.* **2**, 315–339, 1990.

30 T. Kauranne. "An Introduction to Parallel Processing in Meteorology." *The Dawn of Massively Parallel Processing in Meteorology.* (G.-R. Hoffman and D. K. Maretis, Eds.) Springer-Verlag, New York, 1990, pp. 3–20.

31 K. W. Johnson, J. Bauer, G. A. Riccardi, K. K. Droegemeier, and M. Xue. "Distributed Processing of a Regional Prediction Model." *Mon. Wea. Rev.* **122**, 2558–2572, 1994.

32 T. Kauranne. "Asymptotic Parallelism of Weather Models," *The Dawn of Massively Parallel Processing in Meteorology.* (G.-R. Hoffman and D. K. Maretis, Eds.) Springer-Verlag, New York, 1990, pp. 303–314.

33 G. C. Fox, M. A. Johnson, G. A. Lyzenga, S. W. Otto, J. K. Salmon, and D. W. Walker. *Solving Problems on Concurrent Processors. Volume I. General Techniques and Regular Problems.* Prentice Hall, Englewood Cliffs, NJ, 1988.

34 P. R. Woodward, M. O'Keefe, S. Anderson, T. Parr, D. Porter, and K. Edgar. "The Fortran-P Programming Paradigm." Army High Performance Computing Research Center, University of Minnesota, in preparation.

35 "CM Fortran Reference Manual," Version 1.0. Thinking Machines Corporation (TMC), Cambridge, MA, 1991.

36 M. O'Keefe, T. Parr, B. K. Edgar, S. Anderson, P. Woodward, and H. Dietz. "The Fortran-P Translator: Automatic Translation of Fortran-77 Programs for Massively Parallel Processors," Preprint No. 93-021, Army High Performance Computing Research Center, University of Minnesota, 1993.

37 G. Sabot and S. Wholey. "A Fortran Translator for the Connection Machine System," *Proceedings.* 7th International Conference on Supercomputing, 1993, pp. 147–156.

38 J. Levesque and R. Friedman. "The State of the Art in Automatic Parallelization," *Proceedings.* Supercomputing Europe, 1993.

39 J. R. Allen and K. Kennedy. "Automatic Translation of Fortran Programs to Vector Form," *ACM Transactions on Programming Languages and Systems.* **9**, 491–542, 1987.

40 S. Wholey, C. Lasser, and G. Bhanot. "Flo67: A Case Study in Scalable Programming," *Int. J. of Supercomputer Applications.* 6, 1992.

41 K. K. Droegemeier, G. Bassett, and M. Xue. "Very High-Resolution, Uniform-Grid Simulations of Deep Convection on a Massively Parallel Processor: Implications for Small-Scale Predictability." Preprint from 10th Conference on Numerical Weather Prediction, American Meteorollgical Society, Portland, 1994.

42 G. C. Fox. "Achievements and Prospects for Parallel Computing." Syracuse Center for Computational Science-29, Center for Research on Parallel Computation-TR90083, NPAC, Syracuse University, Syracuse, NY, 1990.

43 G. C. Fox. "The Architecture of Problems and Portable Parallel Software Systems." Syracuse Center for Computational Science-134, Center for Research on Parallel Computation-TR91172, NPAC, Syracuse University, Syracuse, NY, 1991.

44 G. C. Fox, S. Hiranadani, K. Kennedy, C. Koelbel, U. Kremer, C.-W. Tseng, and M.-Y. Wu. "Fortran D Language Specification." Syracuse Center for Computational Science-42c, Rice COMP TR90-141, NPAC, Syracuse University, Syracuse, NY, 1991.

45 High-Performance Fortran Language Specifications, Version 1.0. High-Performance Fortran Forum, Rice University, Houston, 1993.

46 G. C. Fox. "Hardware and Software Architectures for Irregular Problem Architectures." Center for Computational Science-111, Center for Research on Parallel Computation-TR91164, NPAC, Syracuse University, Syracuse, NY, 1990.

47 N.-T. Lin, K. Mills, Y.-C. Chen, K. Droegemeier, and M. Xue. "A Message-Passing Version of the Advanced Regional Prediction System (mpARPS)." Technical Report SCCS-529, Center for Computational Science, Syracuse University, Syracuse, NY, 1993.

4

Libraries for Linear Algebra

JACK DONGARRA and DAVID WALKER

Contents

Even more so than an application like ARPS, a library is designed for portability and reuse. Unlike a single application, a library is reused with many applications, which makes both efficiency and maintainability even more important than it is with an individual application. As is obvious from the success of EISPACK, LINPACK, LAPACK, and the BLAS, the techniques described in this chapter have resulted in efficient libraries that are used with virtually all high performance computers. The issues encountered in the design of these libraries, such as communication latency, pipelining, and load balancing, are general in nature and should be understood by anyone who must design highly efficient parallel algorithms.

4.1 Introduction

The increasing availability of advanced-architecture computers is having a very significant effect on all spheres of scientific computation, including algorithm research and software development in numerical linear algebra. Linear algebra—in particular, the solution of linear systems of equations—lies at the heart of most calculations in scientific computing. This chapter discusses some of the recent developments in linear algebra designed to exploit these advanced-architecture computers. Particular attention will be paid to dense factorization routines, such as the Cholesky and LU factorizations, and these will be used as examples to highlight the most important factors that must be considered in designing linear algebra software for advanced-architecture computers. We use these factorization routines for illustrative purposes not only because they are relatively simple, but also because of their importance in several scientific and engineering applications that make use of boundary element methods. These applications include electromagnetic scattering and computational fluid dynamics problems, which are discussed in Section 4.4 (see "Uses of LU Factorization in Science and Engineering").

Much of the work in developing linear algebra software for advanced-architecture computers is motivated by the need to solve large problems on the fastest computers available. In this chapter, we focus on four basic issues: (1) the motivation for the work; (2) the development of standards for use in linear algebra and the building blocks for a library; (3) aspects of algorithm design and parallel implementation; and (4) future directions for research.

For the past 15 years or so, there has been a great deal of activity in the area of algorithms and software for solving linear algebra problems. The linear algebra community has long recognized the need for help in developing algorithms into software libraries, and several years ago, as a community effort, put together a de facto standard for identifying basic operations required in linear algebra algorithms and software. The hope was that the routines making up this standard, known collectively as the Basic Linear Algebra Subprograms (BLAS), would be efficiently implemented on advanced-architecture computers by many manufacturers, making it possible to reap the portability benefits of their being efficiently implemented on a wide range of machines. This goal has been largely realized.

The key insight of our approach to designing linear algebra algorithms for advanced-architecture computers is that the frequency with which data are moved between different levels of the memory hierarchy must be minimized in order to attain high performance. Thus, our main algorithmic approach for exploiting both vectorization and parallelism in our implementations is the use of block-partitioned algorithms, particularly in conjunction with highly tuned kernels for performing matrix–vector and matrix–matrix operations (the Level 2 and 3 BLAS). In general, the use of block-partitioned algorithms requires data to be moved as blocks, rather than as vectors or scalars, so that although the total amount of data moved is unchanged, the latency (or startup cost) associated with the movement is greatly reduced because fewer messages are needed to move the data.

A second key idea is that the performance of an algorithm can be tuned by a user by varying the parameters that specify the data layout. On shared-memory machines this is controlled by the block size, while on distributed-memory machines it is controlled by the block size and the configuration of the logical process mesh, as described in more detail in Section 4.5.

In this section we give an overview of some of the major software projects aimed at solving dense linear algebra problems. Next, we describe the types of machines that benefit most from the use of block-partitioned algorithms, and discuss what is meant by high-quality, reusable software for advanced-architecture computers. Section 4.2 discusses the role of the BLAS in portability and performance on high performance computers. We discuss the design of these building blocks and their use in block-partitioned algorithms in Section 4.3. Section 4.4 focuses on the design of a block-partitioned algorithm for LU factorization, and Sections 4.5, 4.6, and 4.7 use this example to illustrate the most important factors in implementing dense linear algebra routines on MIMD, distributed-memory, concurrent computers. Section 4.5 deals with the issue of mapping the data onto the hierarchical memory of a concurrent computer. The layout of an application's data is crucial in determining the performance and scalability of the parallel code. In Sections 4.6 and 4.7, details of the parallel implementation and optimization issues are discussed. Section 4.8 presents some future directions for investigation.

Dense Linear Algebra Libraries

Over the past 25 years, the first author of this chapter has been directly involved in the development of several important packages of dense linear algebra software: EISPACK, LINPACK, LAPACK, and the BLAS. In addition, both authors are currently involved in the development of ScaLAPACK, a scalable version of LAPACK for distributed-memory concurrent computers. In this section, we give a brief review of these packages—their history, their advantages, and their limitations on high performance computers.

EISPACK EISPACK is a collection of Fortran subroutines that compute the eigenvalues and eigenvectors of nine classes of matrices: complex general, complex Hermitian, real general, real symmetric, real symmetric banded, real symmetric tridiagonal, special real tridiagonal, generalized real, and generalized real symmetric. In addition, two routines are included that use singular value decomposition to solve certain least-squares problems.

EISPACK is primarily based on a collection of Algol procedures developed in the 1960s and collected by J. H. Wilkinson and C. Reinsch in a volume entitled *Linear Algebra* in the *Handbook for Automatic Computation*[1] series. This volume was not designed to cover every possible method of solution; rather, algorithms were chosen on the basis of their generality, elegance, accuracy, speed, or economy of storage.

Since the release of EISPACK in 1972, over 10,000 copies of the collection have been distributed worldwide.

LINPACK   LINPACK is a collection of Fortran subroutines that analyze and solve linear equations and linear least-squares problems. The package solves linear systems whose matrices are general, banded, symmetric indefinite, symmetric positive definite, triangular, and tridiagonal square. In addition, the package computes the QR and singular value decompositions of rectangular matrices, and applies them to least-squares problems.

LINPACK is organized around four matrix factorizations: LU factorization, pivoted Cholesky factorization, QR factorization, and singular value decomposition. The term LU factorization is used here in a very general sense to mean the factorization of a square matrix into a lower triangular part and an upper triangular part, perhaps with pivoting. These factorizations will be treated at greater length later, when the actual LINPACK subroutines are discussed. But first a digression on organization and factors influencing LINPACK's efficiency is necessary.

LINPACK uses column-oriented algorithms to increase efficiency by preserving locality of reference. This means that if a program references an item in a particular block, the next reference is likely to be in the same block. By column orientation we mean that the LINPACK codes always reference arrays down columns, not across rows. This works because Fortran stores arrays in column major order. Thus, as one proceeds down a column of an array, the memory references proceed sequentially in memory. On the other hand, as one proceeds across a row, the memory references jump across memory, the length of the jump being proportional to the length of a column. The effects of column orientation are quite dramatic: on systems with virtual or cache memories, the LINPACK codes will significantly outperform codes that are not column oriented. We note, however, that textbook examples of matrix algorithms are seldom column oriented.

Another important factor influencing the efficiency of LINPACK is the use of the Level 1 BLAS; there are three effects.

First, the overhead entailed in calling the BLAS reduces the efficiency of the code. This reduction is negligible for large matrices, but it can be quite significant for small matrices. The matrix size at which it becomes unimportant varies from system to system; for square matrices it is typically between $n = 25$ and $n = 100$. If this seems like an unacceptably large overhead, remember that on many modern systems the solution of a system of order 25 or less is itself a negligible calculation. Nonetheless, it cannot be denied that a person whose programs depend critically on solving small matrix problems in inner loops will be better off with BLAS-less versions of the LINPACK codes. Fortunately, the BLAS can be removed from the smaller, more frequently used program in a short editing session.

Second, the BLAS improve the efficiency of programs when they are run on non-optimizing compilers. This is because doubly subscripted array references in the inner loop of the algorithm are replaced by singly subscripted array references in the appropriate BLAS. The effect can be seen for matrices of quite small order, and for large orders the savings are quite significant.

Finally, improved efficiency can be achieved by coding a set of BLAS[2] to take advantage of the special features of the computers on which LINPACK is being run. For most computers, this simply means producing machine language versions. However, the code can also take advantage of more exotic architectural features, such as vector operations.

Further details about the BLAS are presented in Section 4.2.

LAPACK LAPACK[3] provides routines for solving systems of simultaneous linear equations, least-squares solutions of linear systems of equations, eigenvalue problems, and singular value problems. The associated matrix factorizations (LU, Cholesky, QR, SVD, Schur, generalized Schur) are also provided, as are related computations such as reordering of the Schur factorizations and estimating condition numbers. Dense and banded matrices are handled, but not general sparse matrices. In all areas, similar functionality is provided for real and complex matrices, in both single and double precision.

The original goal of the LAPACK project was to make the widely used EISPACK and LINPACK libraries run efficiently on shared-memory vector and parallel processors. On these machines, LINPACK and EISPACK are inefficient because their memory access patterns disregard the multilayered memory hierarchies of the machines, thereby spending too much time moving data instead of doing useful floating-point operations. LAPACK addresses this problem by reorganizing the algorithms to use block matrix operations, such as matrix multiplication, in the innermost loops.[3, 4] These block operations can be optimized for each architecture to account for its memory hierarchy,[5] and so provide a transportable way to achieve high efficiency on diverse modern machines. Here we use the term "transportable" instead of "portable" because, for fastest possible performance, LAPACK requires that highly optimized block matrix operations be already implemented on each machine. In other words, the correctness of the code is portable, but high performance is not—if we limit ourselves to a single Fortran source code.

LAPACK can be regarded as a successor to LINPACK and EISPACK. It has virtually all the capabilities of these two packages and much more besides. LAPACK improves on LINPACK and EISPACK in four main respects: speed, accuracy, robustness, and functionality. While LINPACK and EISPACK are based on the vector operation kernels of the Level 1 BLAS, LAPACK was designed at the outset to exploit the Level 3 BLAS— a set of specifications for Fortran subprograms that do various types of matrix multiplication and the solution of triangular systems with multiple right-hand sides. Because of the coarse granularity of the Level 3 BLAS operations, their use tends to promote high efficiency on many high performance computers, particularly if specially coded implementations are provided by the manufacturer.

ScaLAPACK The ScaLAPACK software library, which was released in December of 1994, extends the LAPACK library to run scalably on MIMD, distributed-memory, concurrent computers.[6, 7] For such machines the memory hierarchy includes the off-processor memory of other processors, in addition to the hierarchy of registers, cache, and local memory on each processor. Like LAPACK, the ScaLAPACK routines are based on block-partitioned algorithms in order to minimize the frequency of data movement between different levels of the memory hierarchy. The fundamental building blocks of the ScaLAPACK library are distributed-memory versions of the Level 2 and Level 3 BLAS, and a set of Basic Linear Algebra Communication Subprograms[8, 9] (BLACS) for communication tasks that arise frequently in parallel linear algebra computations. In the ScaLAPACK routines, all interprocessor communication occurs within the distributed BLAS and the BLACS, so the source code of the top software layer of ScaLAPACK looks very similar to that of LAPACK.

We envisage a number of user interfaces to ScaLAPACK. Initially, the interface will be similar to that of LAPACK, with some additional arguments passed to each routine to specify the data layout. Once this is in place, we intend to modify the interface to make the arguments to each ScaLAPACK routine the same as in LAPACK. This will require information about the data distribution of each matrix and vector to be hidden from the user. This may be done by means of a ScaLAPACK initialization routine. This interface will be fully compatible with LAPACK. Provided "dummy" versions of the ScaLAPACK initialization routine and the BLACS are added to LAPACK, there will be no distinction between LAPACK and ScaLAPACK at the application level, though each will link to different versions of the BLAS and BLACS. Following on from this, we will experiment with object-based interfaces for LAPACK and ScaLAPACK, with the goal of developing interfaces compatible with Fortran 90[6] and C++.[10]

Target Architectures

The EISPACK and LINPACK software libraries were designed for supercomputers used in the 1970s and early 1980s, such as the CDC-7600, Cyber 205, and Cray-1. These machines featured multiple functional units pipelined for good performance.[11] The CDC-7600 was basically a high performance scalar computer, while the Cyber 205 and Cray-1 were early vector computers.

The development of LAPACK in the late 1980s was intended to make the EISPACK and LINPACK libraries run efficiently on shared-memory vector supercomputers. The ScaLAPACK software library will extend the use of LAPACK to distributed-memory concurrent supercomputers. The development of ScaLAPACK began in 1991, and software was released in December of 1994.

The underlying concept of both the LAPACK and ScaLAPACK libraries is the use of block-partitioned algorithms to minimize data movement between different levels in hierarchical memory. Thus, the ideas discussed in this chapter for developing a library for dense linear algebra computations are applicable to any computer with a hierarchical memory that (1) imposes a sufficiently large startup cost on the movement of data between different levels in the hierarchy, and for which (2) the cost of a context switch is too great to make fine grain size multithreading worthwhile. Our target machines are, therefore, medium and large grain size advanced-architecture computers. These include "traditional" shared-memory vector supercomputers, such as the Cray Y-MP and C90, and MIMD distributed-memory concurrent supercomputers, such as the Intel Paragon, Thinking Machines CM-5, and the more recently announced IBM SP1™ and Cray T3D™ concurrent systems. Since these machines have only very recently become available, most of the ongoing development of the ScaLAPACK library is being done on a 128-node Intel iPSC/860 hypercube and on the 520-node Intel Delta™ system.

The Intel Paragon supercomputer can have up to 2000 nodes, each consisting of an i860 processor and a communications processor. The nodes each have at least 16 MB of memory and are connected by a high-speed network with the topology of a two-dimensional mesh. The CM-5 from Thinking Machines Corporation[12] supports both SIMD and MIMD programming models, and may have up to 16,000 processors, though the largest CM-5 currently installed has 1024 processors. Each CM-5 node is a Sparc processor and up to four associated vector processors. Point-to-point communication between nodes is supported by a data network with the topology of a "fat tree."[13] Global communication operations, such as synchronization and reduction, are supported by a separate control network. The IBM SP1 system is based on the same RISC chip used in the IBM RS/6000™ workstations and uses a multistage switch to connect processors. The Cray T3D uses the Alpha™ chip from Digital Equipment Corporation, and connects the processors in a three-dimensional torus.

Future advances in compiler and hardware technologies in the mid to late 1990s are expected to make multithreading a viable approach for masking communication costs. Since the blocks in a block-partitioned algorithm can be regarded as separate threads, our approach will still be applicable on machines that exploit medium and coarse grain size multithreading.

High-Quality Reusable Mathematical Software

In developing a library of high-quality subroutines for dense linear algebra computations the design goals fall into three broad classes:

- performance

- ease of use

- range of use.

Performance Two important performance metrics are *concurrent efficiency* and *scalability*. We seek good performance characteristics in our algorithms by eliminating, as much as possible, overhead due to load imbalance, data movement, and algorithm restructuring. The way the data are distributed (or decomposed) over the memory hierarchy of a computer is of fundamental importance to these factors. Concurrent efficiency, ϵ, is defined as the concurrent speedup per processor,[14] where the concurrent speedup is the execution time, T_{seq}, for the best sequential algorithm running on one processor of the concurrent computer, divided by the execution time, T, of the parallel algorithm running on N_p processors. When direct methods are used, as in LU factorization, the concurrent efficiency depends on the problem size and the number of processors; so on a given parallel computer and for a fixed number of processors, the running time should not vary greatly for problems of the same size. Thus, we may write

$$\epsilon(N, N_p) = \frac{1}{N_p} \frac{T_{seq}(N)}{T(N, N_p)} \tag{4.1}$$

where N represents the problem size. In dense linear algebra computations, the execution time is usually dominated by the floating-point operation count, so the concurrent efficiency is related to the performance, G, measured in floating-point operations per second, by

$$G(N, N_p) = \frac{N_p}{t_{calc}} \epsilon(N, N_p) \tag{4.2}$$

where t_{calc} is the time for one floating-point operation. For iterative routines, such as eigensolvers, the number of iterations and hence the execution time depends not only on the problem size, but also on other characteristics of the input data, such as condition number. A parallel algorithm is said to be scalable[15] if the concurrent efficiency depends on the problem size and number of processors only through their ratio. This ratio is simply the problem size per processor, often referred to as the granularity. Thus for a scalable algorithm, the concurrent efficiency is constant as the number of processors increases while keeping the granularity fixed. Alternatively, Equation 4.2 shows that this is equivalent to saying that for a scalable algorithm the performance depends linearly on the number of processors for fixed granularity.

Ease of use Ease of use is concerned with factors such as portability and the user interface to the library. Portability, in its most inclusive sense, means that the code is written in a standard language such as Fortran, and that the source code can be compiled on an arbitrary machine to produce a program that will run correctly. We call this the "mail-order software" model of portability, since it reflects the model used by software servers such as *netlib*.[16] This notion of portability is quite demanding. It requires that all relevant properties of the computer's arithmetic and architecture be discovered at run time within the confines of a Fortran code. For example, if it is important to know the overflow threshold for scaling purposes, it must be determined at run time *without overflowing*, since overflow is generally fatal. Such demands have resulted in quite large and sophisticated programs[17, 18] which must be modified frequently to deal with new architectures and software releases. This mail-order notion of software portability also means that codes generally must be written for the worst possible machine expected to be used, thereby often degrading performance on all others. Ease of use is also enhanced if implementation details are largely hidden from the user, for example, through the use of an object-based interface to the library.[10]

Range of use Range of use may be gauged by how numerically stable the algorithms are over a range of input problems, and the range of data structures the library will support. For example, LINPACK and EISPACK deal with dense matrices stored in a rectangular array, packed matrices where only the upper or lower half of a symmetric matrix is stored, and banded matrices where only the nonzero bands are stored. In addition, some special formats such as Householder vectors are used internally to represent orthogonal matrices. There are also sparse matrices, which may be stored in many different ways; but in this paper we focus on dense and banded matrices, the mathematical types addressed by LINPACK, EISPACK, and LAPACK.

4.2 The BLAS as the Key to Portability

At least three factors affect the performance of portable Fortran code:

1 Vectorization: Designing vectorizable algorithms in linear algebra is usually straightforward. Indeed, for many computations there are several variants, all vectorizable, but with different characteristics in performance (see, for example, Dongarra[19]). Linear algebra algorithms can approach the peak performance of many machines, principally because peak performance depends on some form of chaining of vector addition and multiplication operations, and this is just what the algorithms require. However, when the algorithms are realized in straightforward Fortran 77 code, the performance may fall well short of the expected level, usually because vectorizing Fortran compilers fail to minimize the number of memory references—that is, the number of vector load and store operations.

2 Data movement: What often limits the actual performance of a vector, or scalar, floating-point unit is the rate of transfer of data between different levels of memory in the machine. Examples include the transfer of vector operands in and out of vector registers, the transfer of scalar operands in and out of a high-speed scalar processor, the movement of data between main memory and a high-speed cache or local memory, paging between actual memory and disk storage in a virtual memory system, and interprocessor communication on a distributed-memory concurrent computer.

3 Parallelism: The nested loop structure of most linear algebra algorithms offers considerable scope for loop-based parallelism. This is the principal type of parallelism that LAPACK and ScaLAPACK presently aim to exploit. On shared-memory concurrent computers, this type of parallelism can sometimes be generated automatically by a compiler, but often requires the insertion of compiler directives. On distributed-memory concurrent computers, data must be moved between processors. This is usually done by explicit calls to message-passing routines, although parallel language extensions such as Coherent Parallel C[20] and Split-C[21] do the message passing implicitly.

The question arises, "How can we achieve sufficient control over these three factors to obtain the levels of performance that machines can offer?" The answer is through use of the BLAS.

There are now three levels of BLAS:

- Level 1 BLAS[22]:   for vector operations, such as $y \leftarrow \alpha x + y$
- Level 2 BLAS[23]:   for matrix–vector operations, such as $y \leftarrow \alpha A x + \beta y$
- Level 3 BLAS[2]:   for matrix–matrix operations, such as $C \leftarrow \alpha A B + \beta C$.

Here, A, B, and C are matrices, x and y are vectors, and α and β are scalars.

The Level 1 BLAS are used in LAPACK, but for convenience rather than for performance: they perform an insignificant fraction of the computation, and they cannot achieve high efficiency on most modern supercomputers.

The Level 2 BLAS can achieve near-peak performance on many vector processors, such as a single processor of a Cray X-MP or Y-MP, or Convex C-2 machine. However, on other vector processors such as a Cray-2 or an IBM 3090 VF, the performance of the Level 2 BLAS is limited by the rate of data movement between different levels of memory.

The Level 3 BLAS overcome this limitation. This third level of BLAS performs $O(n^3)$ floating-point operations on $O(n^2)$ data, whereas the Level 2 BLAS perform only $O(n^2)$ operations on $O(n^2)$ data. The Level 3 BLAS also allow us to exploit parallelism in a way that is transparent to the software that calls them. While the Level 2 BLAS offer some scope for exploiting parallelism, greater scope is provided by the Level 3 BLAS, as Table 4.1 illustrates.

4.3 Block Algorithms and Their Derivation

It is a comparatively straightforward task to recode many of the algorithms in LINPACK and EISPACK so that they call Level 2 BLAS. Indeed, in the simplest cases the same floating-point operations are done, possibly even in the same order: it is just a matter of

	Speed (megaflops)			
BLAS Operation	1 Processor	2 Processors	4 Processors	8 Processors
Level 2: $y \leftarrow \alpha A x + \beta y$	311	611	1197	2285
Level 3: $C \leftarrow \alpha A B + \beta C$	312	623	1247	2425
Level 2: $x \leftarrow U x$	293	544	898	1613
Level 3: $B \leftarrow U B$	310	620	1240	2425
Level 2: $x \leftarrow U^{-1} x$	272	374	479	584
Level 3: $B \leftarrow U^{-1} B$	309	618	1235	2398

Table 4.1   Speed (in megaflops) of Level 2 and Level 3 BLAS operations on a Cray Y-MP. All matrices are of order 500; *U* is upper triangular.

reorganizing the software. To illustrate this point, we consider the Cholesky factorization algorithm used in the LINPACK routine SPOFA, which factorizes a symmetric positive definite matrix as $A = U^T U$. We consider Cholesky factorization because the algorithm is simple, and no pivoting is required. In Section 4.4 we shall consider the slightly more complicated example of LU factorization.

Suppose that after $j-1$ steps the block A_{00} in the upper lefthand corner of A has been factored as $A_{00} = U_{00}^T U_{00}$. The next row and column of the factorization can then be computed by writing $A = U^T U$ as

$$\begin{pmatrix} A_{00} & b_j & A_{02} \\ \cdot & a_{jj} & c_j^T \\ \cdot & \cdot & A_{22} \end{pmatrix} = \begin{pmatrix} U_{00}^T & 0 & 0 \\ v_j^T & u_{jj} & 0 \\ U_{02}^T & w_j & U_{22}^T \end{pmatrix} \begin{pmatrix} U_{00} & v_j & U_{02} \\ 0 & u_{jj} & w_j^T \\ 0 & 0 & U_{22} \end{pmatrix}$$

where b_j, c_j, v_j, and w_j are column vectors of length $j-1$, and a_{jj} and u_{jj} are scalars. Equating coefficients of the jth column, we obtain

$$b_j = U_{00}^T v_j$$

$$a_{jj} = v_j^T v_j + u_{jj}^2$$

Since U_{00} has already been computed, we can compute v_j and u_{jj} from the equations

$$U_{00}^T v_j = b_j$$

$$u_{jj}^2 = a_{jj} - v_j^T v_j$$

The body of the code of the LINPACK routine SPOFA that implements the above method is shown in Figure 4.1. The same computation recoded in "LAPACK-style" to

```
do j = 0, n - 1
info = j + 1
   s = 0.0e0
   jm1 = j
   if (jm1 .ge.  1) then
      do k = 0, jm1 - 1
         t = a(k,j) - sdot(k,a(0,k),1,a(0,j),1)
         t = t/a(k,k)
         a(k,j) = t
         s = s + t*t
      end do
   end if
   s = a(j,j) - s
   if (s .le.  0.0e0) go to 40
   a(j,j) = sqrt(s)
end do
```

Figure 4.1   **The body of the LINPACK routine SPOFA for Cholesky factorization.**

```
do j = 0, n - 1
   call strsv( 'upper', 'transpose', 'non-unit', j, a, lda, a(0,j), 1 )
   s = a(j,j) - sdot( j, a(0,j), 1, a(0,j), 1 )
   if ( s .le.  zero ) go to 20
   a(j,j) = sqrt( s )
end do
```

Figure 4.2   The body of the "LAPACK-style" routine SPOFA for Cholesky factorization.

use the Level 2 BLAS routine STRSV (which solves a triangular system of equations) is shown in Figure 4.2. The call to STRSV has replaced the loop over K which made several calls to the Level 1 BLAS routine SDOT. (For reasons given below, this is not the actual code used in LAPACK—hence the term LAPACK-style.)

This change by itself is sufficient to result in large gains in performance on a number of machines—for example, from 72 to 251 megaflops for a matrix of order 500 on one processor of a Cray Y-MP. Since this is 81% of the peak speed of matrix–matrix multiplication on this processor; we cannot hope to do very much better by using Level 3 BLAS.

We can, however, restructure the algorithm at a deeper level to exploit the faster speed of the Level 3 BLAS. This restructuring involves recasting the algorithm as a *block algorithm*—that is, an algorithm that operates on *blocks* or submatrices of the original matrix.

Deriving a Block Algorithm

To derive a block form of Cholesky factorization, we partition the matrices as shown in Figure 4.3, in which the diagonal blocks of A and U are square, but of differing sizes. We assume that the first block has already been factored as $A_{00} = U_{00}^T U_{00}$, and that we now want to determine the second block column of U consisting of the blocks U_{01} and U_{11}. Equating submatrices in the second block of columns, we obtain

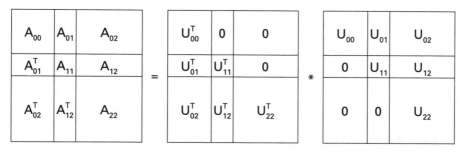

Figure 4.3   Partitioning of A, U^T, and U into blocks. It is assumed that the first block has already been factored as $A_{00} = U_{00}^T U_{00}$, and we next want to determine the block column consisting of U_{01} and U_{11}. Note that the diagonal blocks of A and U are square matrices.

```
do j = 0, n - 1, nb
  jb = min( nb, n-j )
  call strsm( 'left', 'upper', 'transpose', 'non-unit', j, jb, one,
              a, lda, a(0,j), lda )
  call ssyrk( 'upper', 'transpose', jb, j, -one, a(0,j), lda, one,
              a(j,j), lda )
  call spotf2( 'upper', jb, a(j,j), lda, info )
  if( info .ne.  0 ) go to 20
end do
```

Figure 4.4   The body of the "LAPACK-style" routine SPOFA for block Cholesky factorization. In this code fragment, nb denotes the width of the blocks.

$$A_{01} = U_{00}^T U_{01}$$
$$A_{11} = U_{01}^T U_{01} + U_{11}^T U_{11}$$

Since U_{00} has already been computed, we can compute U_{01} as the solution to the equation

$$U_{00}^T U_{01} = A_{01}$$

by a call to the Level 3 BLAS routine STRSM; and then we can compute U_{11} from

$$U_{11}^T U_{11} = A_{11} - U_{01}^T U_{01}$$

This involves first updating the symmetric submatrix A_{11} by a call to the Level 3 BLAS routine SSYRK, and then computing its Cholesky factorization. Since Fortran does not allow recursion, a separate routine must be called (using Level 2 BLAS rather than Level 3), named SPOTF2 in Figure 4.4. In this way, successive blocks of columns of U are computed. The LAPACK-style code for the block algorithm is shown in Figure 4.4. This code runs at 49 megaflops on an IBM 3090, more than double the speed of the LINPACK code. On a Cray Y-MP, the use of Level 3 BLAS squeezes a little more performance out of one processor, but makes a large improvement when using all eight processors.

But that is not the end of the story, and the code given above is not the code actually used in the LAPACK routine SPOTRF. We mentioned earlier that for many linear algebra computations there are several algorithmic variants, often referred to as *i, j,* and *k* variants, according to a convention introduced in Dongarra[19] and used in Golub and Van Loan.[24] The same is true of the corresponding block algorithms.

It turns out that the *j* variant chosen for LINPACK, and used in the above examples, is not the fastest on many machines, because it performs most of the work in solving triangular systems of equations, which can be significantly slower than matrix–matrix multiplication. The variant actually used in LAPACK is the *i* variant, which relies on matrix–matrix multiplication for most of the work.

Table 4.2 summarizes the results.

4.3 BLOCK ALGORITHMS AND THEIR DERIVATION   **105**

	Speed (megaflops)		
	IBM 3090 VF, 1 Processor	CRAY Y-MP, 1 Processor	CRAY Y-MP, 8 Processors
j variant: LINPACK	23	72	72
j variant: using Level 2 BLAS	24	251	378
j variant: using Level 3 BLAS	49	287	1225
i variant: using Level 3 BLAS	50	290	1414

Table 4.2   Speed (megaflops) of Cholesky factorization $A = U^T U$ for $n = 500$.

Examples of Block Algorithms in LAPACK

Having discussed in detail the derivation of one particular block algorithm, we now describe examples of the performance achieved with two well-known block algorithms: LU and Cholesky factorizations. Neither extra floating-point operations nor extra working storage are required for these simple block algorithms. (See Gallivan et al.[25] and Dongarra et al.[26] for surveys of algorithms for dense linear algebra on high performance computers.)

Table 4.3 illustrates the speed of the LAPACK routine for LU factorization of a real matrix, SGETRF in single precision on Cray machines, and DGETRF in double precision on all other machines. Thus, 64-bit floating-point arithmetic is used on all machines tested. A block size of 1 means that the unblocked algorithm is used, since it is faster than—or at least as fast as—a block algorithm.

Machine	No. of Proc.	Block Size	Speed (megaflops) at Values of n				
			100	200	300	400	500
IBM RISC/6000-530	1	32	19	25	29	31	33
Alliant FX/8	8	16	9	26	32	46	57
IBM 3090J VF	1	64	23	41	52	58	63
Convex C-240	4	64	31	60	82	100	112
Cray Y-MP	1	1	132	219	254	272	283
Cray-2	1	64	110	211	292	318	358
Siemens/Fujitsu VP 400-EX	1	64	46	132	222	309	397
NEC SX2	1	1	118	274	412	504	577
Cray Y-MP	8	64	195	556	920	1188	1408

Table 4.3   Speed (megaflops) of SGETRF/DGETRF for square matrices of order n.

Machine	No. of Proc.	Block Size	Speed (megaflops) at Values of n				
			100	200	300	400	500
IBM RISC/6000-530	1	32	21	29	34	36	38
Alliant FX/8	8	16	10	27	40	49	52
IBM 3090J VF	1	48	26	43	56	62	67
Convex C-240	4	64	32	63	82	96	103
Cray Y-MP	1	1	126	219	257	275	285
Cray-2	1	64	109	213	294	318	362
Siemens/Fujitsu VP 400-EX	1	1	53	145	237	312	369
NEC SX2	1	1	155	387	589	719	819
Cray Y-MP	8	32	146	479	845	1164	1393

Table 4.4 Speed (megaflops) of `SPOTRF`/`DPOTRF` for matrices of order n. Here UPLO = "U"; so the factorization is of the form $A = U^T U$.

LAPACK is designed to give high efficiency on vector processors, high performance "superscalar" workstations, and shared-memory multiprocessors. LAPACK in its present form is less likely to give good performance on other types of parallel architectures (for example, massively parallel SIMD machines, or MIMD distributed memory machines), but the ScaLAPACK project, described in Section 4.1 (see "ScaLAPACK"), is intended to adapt LAPACK to these new architectures. LAPACK can also be used satisfactorily on all types of scalar machines (PCs, workstations, mainframes).

Table 4.4 gives similar results for Cholesky factorization, extending the results given in Table 4.2.

LAPACK, like LINPACK, provides LU and Cholesky factorizations of band matrices. The LINPACK algorithms can easily be restructured to use Level 2 BLAS, though restructuring has little effect on performance for matrices of very narrow bandwidth. It is also possible to use Level 3 BLAS, at the price of doing some extra work with zero elements outside the band.[27] This process becomes worthwhile for large matrices and semibandwidths greater than 100 or so.

4.4 LU Factorization

In this section, we discuss the uses of dense LU factorization in several fields, and develop a block-partitioned version of the k, or right-looking, variant of the LU factorization algorithm. In subsequent sections, the parallelization of this algorithm is described in detail in order to highlight the issues and considerations that must be taken into account in developing an efficient, scalable, and transportable dense linear algebra library for MIMD, distributed-memory, concurrent computers.

Uses of LU Factorization in Science and Engineering

A major source of large dense linear systems is problems involving the solution of boundary integral equations. These are integral equations defined on the boundary of a region of interest. All examples of practical interest compute some intermediate quantity on a two-dimensional boundary and then use this information to compute the final desired quantity in three-dimensional space. The price one pays for replacing three dimensions with two is that what started as a sparse problem in $O(n^3)$ variables is replaced by a dense problem in $O(n^2)$.

Dense systems of linear equations are found in numerous applications, such as

- airplane wing design
- radar cross-section studies
- supercomputer benchmarking
- flow around ships and other offshore constructions
- diffusion of solid bodies in a liquid
- noise reduction
- diffusion of light through small particles.

The electromagnetics community is a major user of dense linear systems solvers. Of particular interest to this community is the solution of the so-called radar cross-section problem. In this problem, a signal of fixed frequency bounces off an object; the goal is to determine the intensity of the reflected signal in all possible directions. The underlying differential equation may vary, depending on the specific problem. In the design of stealth aircraft, the principal equation is the Helmholtz equation. To solve this equation, researchers use the *method of moments*.[28, 29] In the case of fluid flow, the problem often involves solving the Laplace or Poisson equation. Here, the boundary integral solution is known as the *panel method*,[30, 31] so named from the quadrilaterals that discretize and approximate a structure such as an airplane. Generally, these methods are called *boundary element methods*.

Use of these methods produces a dense linear system of size $O(N)$ by $O(N)$, where N is the number of boundary points (or panels) being used. It is not unusual to see size $3N$ by $3N$, because of three physical quantities of interest at every boundary element.

A typical approach to solving such systems is to use LU factorization. Each entry of the matrix is computed as an interaction of two boundary elements. Often, many integrals must be computed. In many instances, the time required to compute the matrix is considerably larger than the time for solution.

Only the builders of stealth technology who are interested in radar cross sections are considering using direct Gaussian elimination methods for solving dense linear systems. These systems are always symmetric and complex, but not Hermitian.

For further information on various methods for solving large dense linear algebra problems that arise in computational fluid dynamics, see the report by Alan Edelman.[32]

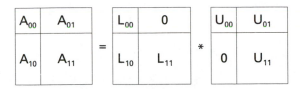

Figure 4.5   **Block LU factorization of the partitioned matrix A. A_{00} is $r \times r$, A_{01} is $r \times (N - r)$, A_{10} is $(M - r) \times r$, and A_{11} is $(M - r) \times (N - r)$. L_{00} and L_{11} are lower triangular matrices with 1's on the main diagonal, and U_{00} and U_{11} are upper triangular matrices.**

Derivation of a Block Algorithm for LU Factorization

Suppose the $M \times N$ matrix A is partitioned as shown in Figure 4.5, and we seek a factorization $A = LU$, where the partitioning of L and U is also shown in Figure 4.5. Then we may write

$$L_{00} U_{00} = A_{00} \tag{4.3}$$

$$L_{10} U_{00} = A_{10} \tag{4.4}$$

$$L_{00} U_{01} = A_{01} \tag{4.5}$$

$$L_{10} U_{01} + L_{11} U_{11} = A_{11} \tag{4.6}$$

where A_{00} is $r \times r$, A_{01} is $r \times (N - r)$, A_{10} is $(M - r) \times r$, and A_{11} is $(M - r) \times (N - r)$. L_{00} and L_{11} are lower triangular matrices with 1's on the main diagonal, and U_{00} and U_{11} are upper triangular matrices.

Equations 4.3 and 4.4 taken together perform an LU factorization on the first $M \times r$ panel of A (i.e., A_{00} and A_{10}). Once this is completed, the matrices L_{00}, L_{10}, and U_{00} are known, and the lower triangular system in Equation 4.5 can be solved to give U_{01}. Finally, we rearrange Equation 4.6 as

$$A'_{11} = A_{11} - L_{10} U_{01} = L_{11} U_{11} \tag{4.7}$$

From this equation we see that the problem of finding L_{11} and U_{11} reduces to finding the LU factorization of the $(M - r) \times (N - r)$ matrix A'_{11}. This can be done by applying the steps outlined above to A'_{11} instead of to A. Repeating these steps K times, where

$$K = \min \left(\lceil M/r \rceil, \lceil N/r \rceil \right) \tag{4.8}$$

we obtain the LU factorization of the original $M \times N$ matrix A. For an in-place algorithm, A is overwritten by L and U—the 1's on the diagonal of L do not need to be stored explicitly. Similarly, when A is updated by Equation 4.7 this may also be done in place.

After k of these K steps, the first kr columns of L and the first kr rows of U have been evaluated, and matrix A has been updated to the form shown in Figure 4.6, in which panel B is $(M - kr) \times r$ and C is $r \times (N - (k - 1)r)$. Step $k + 1$ then proceeds as follows:

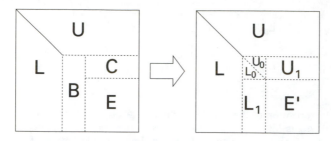

Figure 4.6 Stage *k* + 1 of the block LU factorization algorithm showing how the panels *B* and *C*, and the trailing submatrix *E* are updated. The trapezoidal submatrices *L* and *U* have already been factored in previous steps. *L* has *kr* columns, and *U* has *kr* rows. In the step shown, another *r* columns of *L* and *r* rows of *U* are evaluated.

1 Factor *B* to form the next panel of *L*, performing partial pivoting over rows if necessary (see Figure 4.14). This evaluates the matrices L_0, L_1, and U_0 in Figure 4.6.

2 Solve the triangular system $L_0 U_1 = C$ to get the next row of blocks of *U*.

3 Do a rank-*r* update on the trailing submatrix *E*, replacing it with $E' = E - L_1 U_1$.

The LAPACK implementation of this form of LU factorization uses the Level 3 BLAS routines xTRSM and xGEMM to perform the triangular solve and rank-*r* update. We can regard the algorithm as acting on matrices that have been partitioned into blocks of *r* × *r* elements, as shown in Figure 4.7.

4.5 Data Distribution

The fundamental data object in the LU factorization algorithm presented in Section 4.4 (see "Derivation of a Block Algorithm for LU Factorization") is a block-partitioned matrix. In this section, we describe the block cyclic method for distributing such a matrix over a two-dimensional mesh of processes, or template. In general, each process has an

$A_{0,0}$	$A_{0,1}$	$A_{0,2}$	$A_{0,3}$	$A_{0,4}$	$A_{0,5}$
$A_{1,0}$	$A_{1,1}$	$A_{1,2}$	$A_{1,3}$	$A_{1,4}$	$A_{1,5}$
$A_{2,0}$	$A_{2,1}$	$A_{2,2}$	$A_{2,3}$	$A_{2,4}$	$A_{2,5}$
$A_{3,0}$	$A_{3,1}$	$A_{3,2}$	$A_{3,3}$	$A_{3,4}$	$A_{3,5}$
$A_{4,0}$	$A_{4,1}$	$A_{4,2}$	$A_{4,3}$	$A_{4,4}$	$A_{4,5}$
$A_{5,0}$	$A_{5,1}$	$A_{5,2}$	$A_{5,3}$	$A_{5,4}$	$A_{5,5}$

Figure 4.7 Block-partitioned matrix *A*. Each block $A_{i,j}$ consists of *r* × *r* matrix elements.

m	0	1	2	3	4	5	6	7	8	9
p	0	0	0	0	1	1	1	1	2	2
i	0	1	2	3	0	1	2	3	0	1

(a) Block

m	0	1	2	3	4	5	6	7	8	9
p	0	1	2	0	1	2	0	1	2	0
i	0	0	0	1	1	1	2	2	2	3

(b) Cyclic

Figure 4.8 Examples of block and cyclic decompositions of $M = 10$ data objects over $P = 3$ processes.

independent thread of control, and with each process is associated some local memory directly accessible only by that process. The assignment of these processes to physical processors is a machine-dependent optimization issue, and will be considered later in Section 4.7.

An important property of the class of data distribution we shall use is that independent decompositions are applied over rows and columns. We shall, therefore, begin by considering the distribution of a vector of M data objects over P processes. This can be described by a mapping of the global index, m, of a data object to an index pair (p, i), where p specifies the process to which the data object is assigned and i specifies the location in the local memory of p at which it is stored. We shall assume $0 \le m < M$ and $0 \le p < P$.

Two common decompositions are the *block* and the *cyclic* decompositions.[14, 33] The block decomposition, which is often used when the computational load is distributed homogeneously over a regular data structure such as a cartesian grid, assigns contiguous entries in the global vector to the processes in blocks.

$$m \longrightarrow (\lfloor m/L \rfloor, m \bmod L) \tag{4.9}$$

where $L = \lceil M/P \rceil$. The cyclic decomposition (also known as the wrapped or scattered decomposition) is commonly used to improve load balance when the computational load is distributed inhomogeneously over a regular data structure. The cyclic decomposition assigns consecutive entries in the global vector to successive different processes:

$$m \longrightarrow (m \bmod P, \lfloor m/P \rfloor) \tag{4.10}$$

Examples of the block and cyclic decompositions are shown in Figure 4.8.

The block cyclic decomposition is a generalization of the block and cyclic decompositions in which blocks of consecutive data objects are distributed cyclically over the processes. In the block cyclic decomposition the mapping of the global index, m, can be expressed as $m \longrightarrow (p, b, i)$, where p is the process number, b is the block number in process p, and i is the index within block b to which m is mapped. Thus, if the number of data objects in a block is r, the block cyclic decomposition may be written

$$m \longrightarrow \left(\left\lfloor \frac{m \bmod T}{r} \right\rfloor, \left\lfloor \frac{m}{T} \right\rfloor, m \bmod r \right) \tag{4.11}$$

where $T = rP$. It should be noted that this reverts to the cyclic decomposition when $r = 1$, with local index $i = 0$ for all blocks. A block decomposition is recovered when

$r = L$, in which case there is a single block in each process with block number $b = 0$. The inverse mapping of the triplet (p, b, i) to a global index is given by

$$(p, b, i) \longrightarrow Br + i = pr + bT + i \tag{4.12}$$

where $B = p + bP$ is the global block number. The block cyclic decomposition is one of the data distributions supported by High Performance Fortran (HPF),[34] and has been previously used in one form or another by several researchers (see References 35–43 for examples of its use). The block cyclic decomposition is illustrated in Figure 4.9.

The form of the block cyclic decomposition given by Equation 4.11 ensures that the block with global index 0 is placed in process 0, the next block is placed in process 1, and so on. However, it is sometimes necessary to offset the processes relative to the global block index so that, in general, the first block is placed in process p_0, the next in process $p_0 + 1$, and so on. We, therefore, generalize the block cyclic decomposition by replacing m on the right-hand side of Equation 4.11 by $m' = m + rp_0$ to give

$$m \longrightarrow \left(\left\lfloor \frac{m' \bmod T}{r} \right\rfloor, \left\lfloor \frac{m'}{T} \right\rfloor, m' \bmod r \right)$$

$$= \left(\left(\left\lfloor \frac{m \bmod T}{r} \right\rfloor + p_0 \right) \bmod P, \left\lfloor \frac{m + rp_0}{T} \right\rfloor, m \bmod r \right) \tag{4.13}$$

Equation 4.12 may also be generalized to

$$(p, b, i) \longrightarrow Br + i = (p - p_0)r + bT + i \tag{4.14}$$

where the global block number is given by $B = (p - p_0) + bP$. It should be noted that in processes with $p < p_0$, block 0 is not within the range of the block cyclic mapping, and it is therefore an error to reference it in any way.

In decomposing an $M \times N$ matrix we apply independent block cyclic decompositions in the row and column directions. Thus, suppose the matrix rows are distributed

m	0	1	2	3	4	5	6	7	8	9	10	11	12	13	14	15	16	17	18	19	20	21	22
p	0	0	1	1	2	2	0	0	1	1	2	2	0	0	1	1	2	2	0	0	1	1	2
b	0	0	0	0	0	0	1	1	1	1	1	1	2	2	2	2	2	2	3	3	3	3	3
i	0	1	0	1	0	1	0	1	0	1	0	1	0	1	0	1	0	1	0	1	0	1	0

(a)　$m \rightarrow (p, b, i)$

p	0	0	0	0	0	0	0	0	1	1	1	1	1	1	1	1	2	2	2	2	2	2	2
b	0	0	1	1	2	2	3	3	0	0	1	1	2	2	3	3	0	0	1	1	2	2	3
i	0	1	0	1	0	1	0	1	0	1	0	1	0	1	0	1	0	1	0	1	0	1	0
m	0	1	6	7	12	13	18	19	2	3	8	9	14	15	20	21	4	5	10	11	16	17	22

(b)　$(p, b, i) \rightarrow m$

Figure 4.9　An example of the block cyclic decomposition of $M = 23$ data objects over $P = 3$ processes for a block size of $r = 2$. (a) shows the mapping from global index m to the triplet (p, b, i), and (b) shows the inverse mapping.

with block size r and offset p_0 over P processes by the block cyclic mapping $\mu_{r,p_0,P}$, and the matrix columns are distributed with block size s and offset q_0 over Q processes by the block cyclic mapping $\nu_{s,q_0,Q}$. Then the matrix element indexed globally by (m, n) is mapped as follows:

$$m \xrightarrow{\mu} (p, b, i)$$

$$n \xrightarrow{\nu} (q, d, j) \tag{4.15}$$

The decomposition of the matrix can be regarded as the tensor product of the row and column decompositions, and we can write

$$(m, n) \rightarrow ((p, q), (b, d), (i, j)) \tag{4.16}$$

The block cyclic matrix decomposition given by Equations 4.15 and 4.16 distributes blocks of size $r \times s$ to a mesh of $P \times Q$ processes. We shall refer to this mesh as the *process template*, and refer to processes by their position in the template. Equation 4.16 says that global index (m, n) is mapped to process (p, q), where it is stored in the block at location (b, d) in a two-dimensional array of blocks. Within this block it is stored at location (i, j). The decomposition is completely specified by the parameters r, s, p_0, q_0, P, and Q. In Figure 4.10 an example is given of the block cyclic decomposition of a 36×80 matrix for block size 3×5, a process template 3×4, and a template offset $(p_0, q_0) = (0,0)$. Figure 4.11 shows the same example but for a template offset of $(1,2)$.

The block cyclic decomposition can reproduce most of the data distributions commonly used in linear algebra computations on parallel computers. For example, if $Q = 1$ and $r = \lceil M/P \rceil$ the block row decomposition is obtained. Similarly, $P = 1$ and $s = \lceil N/Q \rceil$ gives a block column decomposition. These decompositions, together with row and column cyclic decompositions, are shown in Figure 4.12. Other commonly used block cyclic matrix decompositions are shown in Figure 4.13.

4.6 Parallel Implementation

In this section we describe the parallel implementation of LU factorization, with partial pivoting over rows, for a block-partitioned matrix. The matrix, A, to be factored is assumed to have a block cyclic decomposition, and at the end of the computation is overwritten by the lower and upper triangular factors, L and U. This implicitly determines the decomposition of L and U. Quite a high-level description is given here since the details of the parallel implementation involve optimization issues that will be addressed in Section 4.7.

The sequential LU factorization algorithm described in Section 4.4 (see "Derivation of a Block Algorithm for LU Factorization") uses square blocks. Although in the parallel algorithm we could choose to decompose the matrix using nonsquare blocks, this would result in a more complicated code and additional sources of concurrent overhead. For LU factorization we therefore restrict the decomposition to use only square blocks, so that the blocks used to decompose the matrix are the same as those used to partition the

p,q	0	1	2	3	4	5	6	7 D	8	9	10	11	12	13	14	15
0	0,0	0,1	0,2	0,3	0,0	0,1	0,2	0,3	0,0	0,1	0,2	0,3	0,0	0,1	0,2	0,3
1	1,0	1,1	1,2	1,3	1,0	1,1	1,2	1,3	1,0	1,1	1,2	1,3	1,0	1,1	1,2	1,3
2	2,0	2,1	2,2	2,3	2,0	2,1	2,2	2,3	2,0	2,1	2,2	2,3	2,0	2,1	2,2	2,3
3	0,0	0,1	0,2	0,3	0,0	0,1	0,2	0,3	0,0	0,1	0,2	0,3	0,0	0,1	0,2	0,3
4	1,0	1,1	1,2	1,3	1,0	1,1	1,2	1,3	1,0	1,1	1,2	1,3	1,0	1,1	1,2	1,3
B 5	2,0	2,1	2,2	2,3	2,0	2,1	2,2	2,3	2,0	2,1	2,2	2,3	2,0	2,1	2,2	2,3
6	0,0	0,1	0,2	0,3	0,0	0,1	0,2	0,3	0,0	0,1	0,2	0,3	0,0	0,1	0,2	0,3
7	1,0	1,1	1,2	1,3	1,0	1,1	1,2	1,3	1,0	1,1	1,2	1,3	1,0	1,1	1,2	1,3
8	2,0	2,1	2,2	2,3	2,0	2,1	2,2	2,3	2,0	2,1	2,2	2,3	2,0	2,1	2,2	2,3
9	0,0	0,1	0,2	0,3	0,0	0,1	0,2	0,3	0,0	0,1	0,2	0,3	0,0	0,1	0,2	0,3
10	1,0	1,1	1,2	1,3	1,0	1,1	1,2	1,3	1,0	1,1	1,2	1,3	1,0	1,1	1,2	1,3
11	2,0	2,1	2,2	2,3	2,0	2,1	2,2	2,3	2,0	2,1	2,2	2,3	2,0	2,1	2,2	2,3

(a) Assignment of global block indices (B,D) to processes (p,q)

B,D	0				1 q				2				3			
0	0,0	0,4	0,8	0,12	0,1	0,5	0,9	0,13	0,2	0,6	0,10	0,14	0,3	0,7	0,11	0,15
	3,0	3,4	3,8	3,12	3,1	3,5	3,9	3,13	3,2	3,6	3,10	3,14	3,3	3,7	3,11	3,15
	6,0	6,4	6,8	6,12	6,1	6,5	6,9	6,13	6,2	6,6	6,10	6,14	6,3	6,7	6,11	6,15
	9,0	9,4	9,8	9,12	9,1	9,5	9,9	9,13	9,2	9,6	9,10	9,14	9,3	9,7	9,11	9,15
	1,0	1,4	1,8	1,12	1,1	1,5	1,9	1,13	1,2	1,6	1,10	1,14	1,3	1,7	1,11	1,15
p 4	4,0	4,4	4,8	4,12	4,1	4,5	4,9	4,13	4,2	4,6	4,10	4,14	4,3	4,7	4,11	4,15
	7,0	7,4	7,8	7,12	7,1	7,5	7,9	7,13	7,2	7,6	7,10	7,14	7,3	7,7	7,11	7,15
	10,0	10,4	10,8	10,12	10,1	10,5	10,9	10,13	10,2	10,6	10,10	10,14	10,3	10,7	10,11	10,15
	2,0	2,4	2,8	2,12	2,1	2,5	2,9	2,13	2,2	2,6	2,10	2,14	2,3	2,7	2,11	2,15
8	5,0	5,4	5,8	5,12	5,1	5,5	5,9	5,13	5,2	5,6	5,10	5,14	5,3	5,7	5,11	5,15
	8,0	8,4	8,8	8,12	8,1	8,5	8,9	8,13	8,2	8,6	8,10	8,14	8,3	8,7	8,11	8,15
	11,0	11,4	11,8	11,12	11,1	11,5	11,9	11,13	11,2	11,6	11,10	11,14	11,3	11,7	11,11	11,15

(b) Global blocks (B,D) in each process (p,q)

Figure 4.10   Block cyclic decomposition of a 36 × 80 matrix with a block size of 3 × 5 onto a 3 × 4 process template. Each small rectangle represents one matrix block—individual matrix elements are not shown. In (a), shading is used to emphasize the process template that is periodically stamped over the matrix, and each block is labeled with the process to which it is assigned. In (b), each shaded region shows the blocks in one process, and is labeled with the corresponding global block indices. In both figures, the black rectangles indicate the blocks assigned to process (0,0).

computation. If the block size is $r \times r$, then an $M \times N$ matrix consists of $M_b \times N_b$ blocks, where $M_b = \lceil M/r \rceil$ and $N_b = \lceil N/r \rceil$.

As discussed in Section 4.4 (see "Derivation of a Block Algorithm for LU Factorization"), LU factorization proceeds in a series of sequential steps indexed by $k = 0$, $\min(M_b, N_b) - 1$, in each of which the following three tasks are performed:

p,q	0	1	2	3	4	5	6	7	8	9	10	11	12	13	14	15
0	1,2	1,3	1,0	1,1	1,2	1,3	1,0	1,1	1,2	1,3	1,0	1,1	1,2	1,3	1,0	1,1
1	2,2	2,3	2,0	2,1	2,2	2,3	2,0	2,1	2,2	2,3	2,0	2,1	2,2	2,3	2,0	2,1
2	0,2	0,3	0,0	0,1	0,2	0,3	0,0	0,1	0,2	0,3	0,0	0,1	0,2	0,3	0,0	0,1
3	1,2	1,3	1,0	1,1	1,2	1,3	1,0	1,1	1,2	1,3	1,0	1,1	1,2	1,3	1,0	1,1
4	2,2	2,3	2,0	2,1	2,2	2,3	2,0	2,1	2,2	2,3	2,0	2,1	2,2	2,3	2,0	2,1
5	0,2	0,3	0,0	0,1	0,2	0,3	0,0	0,1	0,2	0,3	0,0	0,1	0,2	0,3	0,0	0,1
6	1,2	1,3	1,0	1,1	1,2	1,3	1,0	1,1	1,2	1,3	1,0	1,1	1,2	1,3	1,0	1,1
7	2,2	2,3	2,0	2,1	2,2	2,3	2,0	2,1	2,2	2,3	2,0	2,1	2,2	2,3	2,0	2,1
8	0,2	0,3	0,0	0,1	0,2	0,3	0,0	0,1	0,2	0,3	0,0	0,1	0,2	0,3	0,0	0,1
9	1,2	1,3	1,0	1,1	1,2	1,3	1,0	1,1	1,2	1,3	1,0	1,1	1,2	1,3	1,0	1,1
10	2,2	2,3	2,0	2,1	2,2	2,3	2,0	2,1	2,2	2,3	2,0	2,1	2,2	2,3	2,0	2,1
11	0,2	0,3	0,0	0,1	0,2	0,3	0,0	0,1	0,2	0,3	0,0	0,1	0,2	0,3	0,0	0,1

(B label at left, between rows 5 and 6)

(a) Assignment of global block indices (B,D) to processes (p,q)

B,D		0					1			q	2				3			
	—	—	—	—	—	—	—	—	—	—	—	—	—	—	—	—	—	—
0	—	2,2	2,6	2,10	2,14	—	2,3	2,7	2,11	2,15	2,0	2,4	2,8	2,12	—	2,1	2,5	2,9	2,13	—
	—	5,2	5,6	5,10	5,14	—	5,3	5,7	5,11	5,15	5,0	5,4	5,8	5,12	—	5,1	5,5	5,9	5,13	—
	—	8,2	8,6	8,10	8,14	—	8,3	8,7	8,11	8,15	8,0	8,4	8,8	8,12	—	8,1	8,5	8,9	8,13	—
	—	11,2	11,6	11,10	11,14	—	11,3	11,7	11,11	11,15	11,0	11,4	11,8	11,12	—	11,1	11,5	11,9	11,13	—
p 1	—	0,2	0,6	0,10	0,14	—	0,3	0,7	0,11	0,15	0,0	0,4	0,8	0,12	—	0,1	0,5	0,9	0,13	—
	—	3,2	3,6	3,10	3,14	—	3,3	3,7	3,11	3,15	3,0	3,4	3,8	3,12	—	3,1	3,5	3,9	3,13	—
	—	6,2	6,6	6,10	6,14	—	6,3	6,7	6,11	6,15	6,0	6,4	6,8	6,12	—	6,1	6,5	6,9	6,13	—
	—	9,2	9,6	9,10	9,14	—	9,3	9,7	9,11	9,15	9,0	9,4	9,8	9,12	—	9,1	9,5	9,9	9,13	—
	—	—	—	—	—	—	—	—	—	—	—	—	—	—	—	—	—	—
	—	1,2	1,6	1,10	1,14	—	1,3	1,7	1,11	1,15	1,0	1,4	1,8	1,12	—	1,1	1,5	1,9	1,13	—
	—	4,2	4,6	4,10	4,14	—	4,3	4,7	4,11	4,15	4,0	4,4	4,8	4,12	—	4,1	4,5	4,9	4,13	—
2	—	7,2	7,6	7,10	7,14	—	7,3	7,7	7,11	7,15	7,0	7,4	7,8	7,12	—	7,1	7,5	7,9	7,13	—
	—	10,2	10,6	10,10	10,14	—	10,3	10,7	10,11	10,15	10,0	10,4	10,8	10,12	—	10,1	10,5	10,9	10,13	—
	—	—	—	—	—	—	—	—	—	—	—	—	—	—	—	—	—	—

(b) Global blocks (B,D) in each process (p,q)

Figure 4.11 The same matrix decomposition as in Figure 4.10, but for a template offset of (p_0, q_0) = (1,2). Dashed entries in (b) indicate that the block does not contain any data. In both figures, the black rectangles indicate the blocks assigned to process (0,0).

1 Factor the kth column of blocks, performing pivoting if necessary. This evaluates the matrices L_0, L_1, and U_0 in Figure 4.6.

2 Evaluate the kth block row of U by solving the lower triangular system $L_0 U_1 = C$.

3 Do a rank-r update on the trailing submatrix E, replacing it with $E' = E - L_1 U_1$.

We now consider the parallel implementation of each of these tasks. The computation in the factorization step involves a single column of blocks, and these lie in a single

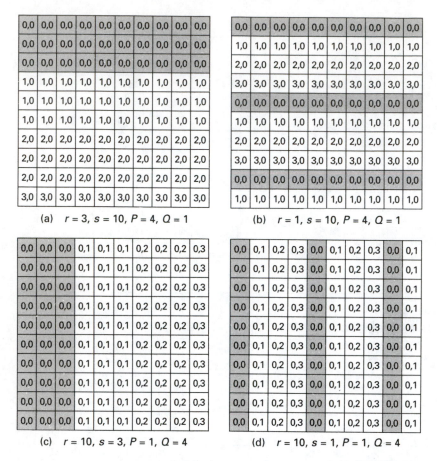

(a) $r = 3$, $s = 10$, $P = 4$, $Q = 1$

(b) $r = 1$, $s = 10$, $P = 4$, $Q = 1$

(c) $r = 10$, $s = 3$, $P = 1$, $Q = 4$

(d) $r = 10$, $s = 1$, $P = 1$, $Q = 4$

Figure 4.12   **Four different ways of decomposing a 10 × 10 matrix. Each cell represents a matrix element and is labeled by the position (p, q) in the template of the process to which it is assigned. To emphasize the pattern of decomposition, the matrix entries assigned to the process in the first row and column of the template are shown shaded, and each separate shaded region represents a matrix block. Parts (a) and (b) show block and cyclic row-oriented decompositions, respectively, for 4 nodes. In parts (c) and (d) the corresponding column-oriented decompositions are shown. Below each figure we give the values of r, s, P, and Q corresponding to the decomposition. In all cases $p_0 = q_0 = 0$.**

column of the process template. In the kth factorization step, each of the r columns in block column k is processed in turn. Consider the ith column in block column k. The pivot is selected by finding the element with largest absolute value in this column between row $kr + i$ and the last row, inclusive. The elements involved in the pivot search at this stage are shown shaded in Figure 4.14. Having selected the pivot, the value of the pivot and its row are broadcast to all other processors. Next, pivoting is performed by exchanging the entire row $kr + i$ with the row containing the pivot. We exchange entire rows, rather than just the part to the right of the columns already factored, in order to simplify the application of the pivots to the right-hand side in any subsequent solve

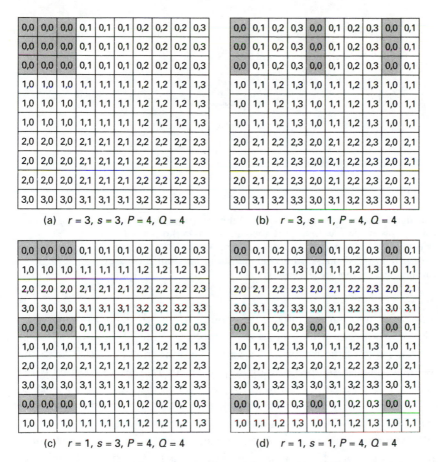

Figure 4.13 Four different ways of decomposing a 10 × 10 matrix over 16 processes arranged as a 4 × 4 template. Below each part are the values of r, s, P, and Q corresponding to the decomposition. In all cases $p_0 = q_0 = 0$.

phase. Finally, each value in the column below the pivot is divided by the pivot. If a cyclic column decomposition is used, like that shown in Figure 4.12d, only one processor is involved in the factorization of the block column, and no communication is necessary between the processes. However, in general P processes are involved, and communication is necessary in selecting the pivot and exchanging the pivot rows.

The solution of the lower triangular system $L_0 U_1 = C$ to evaluate the kth block row of U involves a single row of blocks, and these lie in a single row of the process template. If a cyclic row decomposition is used, like that shown in Figure 4.12b, only one processor is involved in the triangular solve and no communication is necessary between the processes. However, in general Q processes are involved and communication is necessary to broadcast the lower triangular matrix, L_0, to all processes in the row. Once this has been done, each process in the row independently performs a lower triangular solve for the blocks of C that it holds.

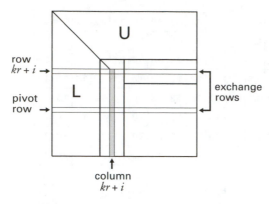

Figure 4.14 This figure shows pivoting for step *i* of the *k*th stage of LU factorization. The element with largest absolute value in the shaded part of column *kr* + *i* is found, and the row containing it is exchanged with row *kr* + *i*. If the rows exchanged lie in different processes, communication may be necessary.

The communication necessary to update the trailing submatrix at step k takes place in two steps. First, each process holding part of L_1 broadcasts these blocks to the other processes in the same row of the template. This may be done in conjunction with the broadcast of L_0 mentioned in the preceding paragraph so that all of the factored panel is broadcast together. Next, each process holding part of U_1 broadcasts these blocks to the other processes in the same column of the template. Each process can then complete the update of the blocks that it holds with no further communication.

A pseudocode outline of the parallel LU factorization algorithm is given in Figure 4.15. There are two points worth noting in Figure 4.15. First, the triangular solve and update phases operate on matrix blocks and may, therefore, be done with parallel versions of the Level 3 BLAS (specifically, xTRSM and xGEMM, respectively). The factorization of the column of blocks, however, involves a loop over matrix columns. Hence, it is not a block-oriented computation and cannot be performed using the Level 3 BLAS. The second point is that most of the parallelism in the code comes from updating the trailing submatrix, since this is the only phase in which all the processes are busy.

Figure 4.15 also shows quite clearly where communication is required: in finding the pivot, exchanging pivot rows, and performing various types of broadcast. The exact way in which these communications are done and interleaved with computation generally has an important effect on performance (this is discussed in more detail in Section 4.7).

Figure 4.15 refers to broadcasting data to all processes in the same row or column of the template. This is a common operation in parallel linear algebra algorithms, so the idea is described here in greater detail. Consider, for example, the task of broadcasting the lower triangular block, L_0, to all processes in the same row of the template, as required before solving $L_0 U_1 = C$. If L_0 is in process (p, q), then it will be broadcast to all processes in row p of the process template. As a second example, consider the broadcast of L_1 to all processes in the same template row, as required before updating the

```
pcol= $q_0$
prow= $p_0$
do k= 0, min($M_b$, $N_b$) − 1

        do i= 0, r − 1
            if ($q$ =pcol) find pivot value and location
            broadcast pivot value and location to all processes
            exchange pivot rows
            if ($q$ =pcol) divide column r below diagonal by pivot
        end do

        if ($p$ =prow) then
            broadcast $L_0$ to all processes in same template row
            solve $L_0 U_1 = C$
        end if

        broadcast $L_1$ to all processes in same template row
        broadcast $U_1$ to all processes in same template column
        update $E \leftarrow E - L_1 U_1$

    pcol= (pcol + 1)mod $Q$
    prow= (prow + 1)mod $P$
end do
```

Figure 4.15   **Pseudocode for the basic parallel block-partitioned LU factorization algorithm. This code is executed by each process. The first box inside the k loop factors the kth column of blocks. The second box solves a lower triangular system to evaluate the kth row of blocks of U, and the third box updates the trailing submatrix. The template offset is given by (p_0, q_0), and (p, q) is the position of a process in the template.**

trailing submatrix. This type of "rowcast" is shown schematically in Figure 4.16a. If L_1 is in column q of the template, then each process (p, q) broadcasts its blocks of L_1 to the other processes in row p of the template. Loosely speaking, we can say that L_0 and L_1 are broadcast along the rows of the template. This type of data movement is the same as that performed by the Fortran 90 routine SPREAD.[44] The broadcast of U_1 to all processes in the same template column is very similar. This type of communication is sometimes referred to as a "colcast," and is shown in Figure 4.16b.

4.7 Optimization, Tuning, and Tradeoffs

In this section, we examine techniques for optimizing the basic LU factorization code presented in Section 4.4 (see "Derivation of a Block Algorithm for LU Factorization").

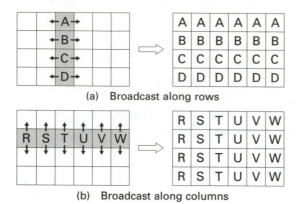

(a) Broadcast along rows

(b) Broadcast along columns

Figure 4.16   Schematic representation of broadcast along rows and columns of a 4 × 6 process template. In (*a*), each shaded process broadcasts to the processes in the same row of the process template. In (*b*), each shaded process broadcasts to the processes in the same column of the process template.

Among the issues to be considered are the assignment of processes to physical processors, the arrangement of the data in the local memory of each process, the tradeoff between load imbalance and communication latency, the potential for overlapping communication and calculation, and the type of algorithm used to broadcast data. Many of these issues are interdependent, and in addition the portability and ease of code maintenance and use must be considered. For further details of the optimization of parallel LU factorization algorithms for specific concurrent machines, together with timing results, the reader is referred to the work of Chu and George,[45] Geist and Heath,[46] Geist and Romine,[47] Van de Velde,[33] Brent,[48] Hendrickson and Womble,[49] Lichtenstein and Johnsson,[50] and Dongarra and co-workers.[6, 51]

Mapping Logical Memory to Physical Memory

In Section 4.5, a logical (or virtual) matrix decomposition was described in which the global index (m, n) is mapped to a position (p, q) in a logical process template, a position (b, d) in a logical array of blocks local to the process, and a position (i, j) in a logical array of matrix elements local to the block. Thus, the block cyclic decomposition is hierarchical, and attempts to represent the hierarchical memory of advanced-architecture computers. Although the parallel LU factorization algorithm can be specified solely in terms of this logical hierarchical memory, its performance depends on how the logical memory is mapped to physical memory.

Assignment of processes to processors   Consider first the assignment of processes, (p, q), to physical processors. In general, more than one process may be assigned to a processor, so the problem may be overdecomposed. To avoid load imbalance, the same number of processes should be assigned to each processor as nearly as possible. If this condition is satisfied, the assignment of processes to processors can still affect performance by influencing the communication overhead. On recent distributed-memory

LIBRARIES FOR LINEAR ALGEBRA   Chapter 4

machines, such as the Intel Delta and CM-5, the time to send a single message between two processors is largely independent of their physical location,[52-54] and hence the assignment of processes to processors does not have much direct effect on performance. However, when a collective communication task, such as a broadcast, is being done, contention for physical resources can degrade performance. Thus, the way in which processes are assigned to processors can affect performance if some assignments result in differing amounts of contention. Logarithmic contention-free broadcast algorithms have been developed for processors connected as a two-dimensional mesh[55, 56]; so on such machines, process (p,q) is usually mapped to the processor at position (p,q) in the mesh of processors. Such an assignment also ensures that the multiple one-dimensional broadcasts of L_1 and U_1 along the rows and columns of the template, respectively, do not give rise to contention.

Layout of local process memory   The layout of matrix blocks in the local memory of a process and the arrangement of matrix elements within each block can also affect performance. Here, tradeoffs among several factors need to be taken into account. When communicating matrix blocks, for example in the broadcasts of L_1 and U_1, we would like the data in each block to be contiguous in physical memory so there is no need to pack them into a communication buffer before sending them. On the other hand, when updating the trailing submatrix E, each process multiplies a column of blocks by a row of blocks to do a rank-r update on the part of E that it contains. If this were done as a series of separate block–block matrix multiplications, as shown in Figure 4.17a, the performance would be poor except for sufficiently large block sizes, r, since the vector and/or pipeline units on most processors would not be fully utilized, as may be seen in Figure 4.18 for the i860 processor. Instead, we arrange the loops of the computation as shown in Figure 4.17b. Now, if the data are laid out in physical memory first by running over the i index and then over the d index the inner two loops can be merged, so that the length of the inner loop is now rd_{max}. This generally results in much better vector/pipeline performance. The b and j loops in Figure 4.17b can also be merged, giving the algorithm shown in Figure 4.17c. This is just the outer product form of the multiplication of an $rd_{max} \times r$ by an $r \times rb_{max}$ matrix; it would usually be done by a call to the Level 3 BLAS routine xGEMM of which an assembly-coded sequential version is available on most machines. Note that in Figure 4.17c the order of the inner two loops is appropriate for a Fortran implementation. For the C language this order should be reversed, and the data should be stored in each process by rows instead of by columns.

We have found in our work on the Intel iPSC/860 hypercube and the Delta system that it is better to optimize for the sequential matrix multiplication with an (i,d,j,b) ordering of memory in each process rather than adopting an (i,j,d,b) ordering to avoid buffer copies when communicating blocks. However, there is another reason for doing this. On most distributed-memory computers the message startup cost is sufficiently large that it is preferable wherever possible to send data as one large message rather than as several smaller messages. Thus, when communicating L_1 and U_1, the blocks to be broadcast would be amalgamated into a single message, which requires a buffer copy. The emerging Message Passing Interface (MPI) standard[57] provides support for noncontiguous

```
do b = 0, b_max − 1
  do d = 0, d_max − 1
    do i = 0, r − 1
      do j = 0, r − 1
        do k = 0, r − 1
          E(b,d;i,j) = E(b,d;i,j) − L_1(b,d;i,k) U_1(b,d;k,j)
end all do loops
```

(a)   Block–block multiplication

```
do k = 0, r − 1
  do b = 0, b_max − 1
    do j = 0, r − 1
      do d = 0, d_max − 1
        do i = 0, r − 1
          E(b,d;i,j) = E(b,d;i,j) − L_1(b,d;i,k) U_1(b,d;k,j)
end all do loops
```

(b)   Intermediate form of algorithm

```
do k = 0, r − 1
  do x = 0, rb_max − 1
    do y = 0, rd_max − 1
      E(x,y) = E(x,y) − L_1(x,k) U_1(k,y)
end all do loops
```

(c)   Outer product form of algorithm

Figure 4.17 **Pseudocode for different versions of the rank-r update, $E \leftarrow E − L_1 U_1$, for one process. The number of row and column blocks per process is given by b_{max} and d_{max}, respectively; r is the block size. Blocks are indexed by (b,d), and elements within a block by (i,j). In version (a) the $r \times r$ blocks are multiplied one at a time, giving an inner loop of length r. (b) shows the loops rearranged before merging the i and d loops, and the j and b loops. This leads to the outer product form of the algorithm shown in (c), in which the inner loop is now of length rd_{max}.**

messages, so in the future the need to avoid buffer copies will not be of such concern to the application developer.

Tradeoffs Between Load Balance and Communication Latency

We have discussed the mapping of the logical hierarchical memory to physical memory. In addition, we have pointed out the importance of maintaining long inner loops to get good sequential performance for each process, and the desirability of sending a few large messages rather than many smaller ones. We next consider load balance issues. Assuming that equal numbers of processes have been assigned to each processor, load imbalance

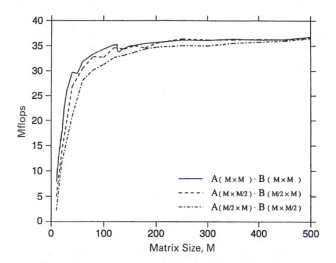

Figure 4.18 Performance of the assembly-coded Level 3 BLAS matrix multiplication routine DGEMM on one i860 processor of the Intel Delta system. Results for square and rectangular matrices are shown. Note that the peak performance of about 35 megaflops is attained only for matrices whose smallest dimension exceeds 100. Thus, performance is improved if a few large matrices are multiplied by each process, rather than many small ones.

arises in two phases of the parallel LU factorization algorithm: in factoring each column block, which involves only P processes, and in solving the lower triangular system to evaluate each row block of U, which involves only Q processes. If the time for data movement is negligible, the aspect ratio of the template that minimizes load imbalance in step k of the algorithm is

$$
\frac{P}{Q} = \frac{\text{Sequential time to factor column block}}{\text{Sequential time for triangular solve}}
$$

$$
= \frac{M_b - k - 1/3 + O(1/r^2)}{N_b - k - 1 + O(1/r^2)} \tag{4.17}
$$

where $M_b \times N_b$ is the matrix size in blocks, and r the block size. Thus, the optimal aspect ratio of the template should be the same as the aspect ratio of the matrix, that is, M_b/N_b in blocks, or M/N in elements. If the effect of communication time is included then we must take into account the relative times taken to locate and broadcast the pivot information, and the time to broadcast the lower triangular matrix, L_0, along a row of the template. For both tasks the communication time increases with the number of processes involved, and since the communication time associated with the pivoting is greater than that associated with the triangular solve, we would expect the optimum aspect ratio of the template to be less than M/N. In fact, for our runs on the Intel Delta system we found an aspect ratio, P/Q, of between $1/4$ and $1/8$ to be optimal for most

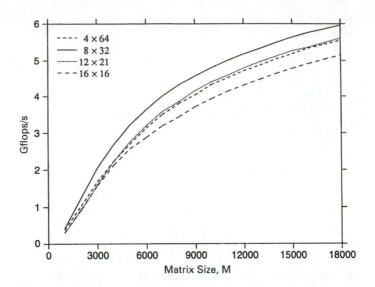

Figure 4.19 Performance of LU factorization on the Intel Delta as a function of square matrix size for different processor templates containing approximately 256 processors. The best performance is for an aspect ratio of 1/4, though the dependence on aspect ratio is rather weak.

problems with square matrices, and that performance depends rather weakly on the aspect ratio, particularly for large grain sizes. Some typical results are shown in Figure 4.19 for 256 processors, in which there is a variation of less than 20% in performance as P/Q varies between $1/16$ and 1 for the largest problem.

The block size, r, also affects load balance. Here the tradeoff is between the load imbalance that arises as rows and columns of the matrix are eliminated as the algorithm progresses, and communication startup costs. The block cyclic decomposition seeks to maintain good load balance by cyclically assigning blocks to processes, and the load balance is best if the blocks are small. On the other hand, cumulative communication startup costs are less if the block size is large since, in this case, fewer messages must be sent (although the total volume of data sent is independent of the block size). Thus, there is a block size that optimally balances the load imbalance and communication startup costs.

Optimality and Pipelining Tradeoffs

The communication algorithms used also influence performance. In the LU factorization algorithm, all the communication can be done by moving data along rows and/or columns of the process template. This type of communication can be done by passing from one process to the next along the row or column. We shall call this a "ring" algorithm, although the ring may, or may not, be closed. An alternative is to use a spanning tree algorithm, of which there are several varieties. The complexity of the ring algorithm is linear in the number of processes involved, whereas that of spanning tree algorithms is logarithmic (for example, see Reference 55). Thus, considered in isolation,

```
if (q =pcol) then
   do i= 0, r − 1
      find pivot value and location
      exchange pivot rows lying within panel
      divide column r below diagonal by pivot
   end do
end if
broadcast pivot information for r pivots along template rows
exchange pivot rows lying outside the panel for each of r pivots
```

Figure 4.20   **Pseudocode fragment for partial pivoting over rows. This may be regarded as replacing the first box inside the k loop in Figure 4.15. In the above code, pivot information is first disseminated within the template column doing the panel factorization. The pivoting of the parts of the rows lying outside the panel is deferred until the panel factorization has been completed.**

the spanning tree algorithms are preferable to a ring algorithm. However, in a spanning tree algorithm a process may take part in several of the logarithmic steps, and in some implementations these algorithms act as a barrier. In a ring algorithm each process needs to communicate only once and can then continue to compute, in effect overlapping the communication with computation. An algorithm that interleaves communication and calculation in this way is often referred to as a pipelined algorithm. In a pipelined LU factorization algorithm with no pivoting, communication and calculation would flow in waves across the matrix. Pivoting tends to inhibit this advantage of pipelining.

In the pseudocode in Figure 4.15 we do not specify how the pivot information should be broadcast. In an optimized implementation we need to finish with the pivot and triangular solve phases as soon as possible in order to begin the update phase, which is richest in parallelism. Thus, it is not a good idea to broadcast the pivot information from a single source process using a spanning tree algorithm, since this may occupy some of the processes involved in the panel factorization for too long. It is important to get the pivot information to the other processes in this template column as soon as possible, so the pivot information is first sent to these processes which subsequently broadcast it along the template rows to the other processes not involved in the panel factorization. In addition, the exchange of the parts of the pivot rows lying within the panel is done separately from that of the parts outside the pivot panel. Another factor to consider here is when the pivot information should be broadcast along the template columns. In Figure 4.15 the information is broadcast and rows are exchanged immediately after the pivot is found. An alternative is to store up the sequence of r pivots for a panel and broadcast them along the template rows when panel factorization is complete. This defers the exchange of pivot rows for the parts outside the panel until the panel factorization has been done, as shown in the pseudocode fragment in Figure 4.20. An advantage of this second approach is that only one message is used to send the pivot information for the panel along the template rows, instead of r messages.

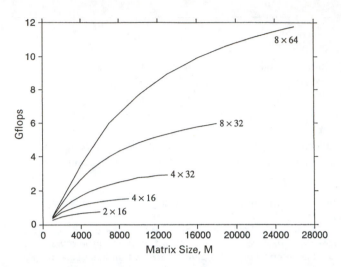

Figure 4.21 **Performance of LU factorization on the Intel Delta as a function of square matrix size for different numbers of processors. For each curve, results are shown for the process template configuration that gave the best performance for that number of processors.**

In our implementation of LU factorization on the Intel Delta system, we used a spanning tree algorithm to locate the pivot and to broadcast it within the column of the process template performing the panel factorization. This ensures that pivoting, which involves only P processes, is completed as quickly as possible. A ring broadcast is used to pipeline the pivot information and the factored panel along the template rows. Finally, after the triangular solve phase has completed, a spanning tree broadcast is used to send the newly formed block row of U along the template columns. Results for square matrices from runs on the Intel Delta system are shown in Figure 4.21. For each curve the results for the best process template configuration are shown. Recalling that for a scalable algorithm the performance should depend linearly on the number of processors for fixed granularity (see Equation 4.2), it is apparent that scalability may be assessed by the extent to which isogranularity curves differ from linearity. An isogranularity curve is a plot of performance against number of processors for a fixed granularity. The results in Figure 4.21 can be used to generate the isogranularity curves in Figure 4.22, which show that on the Delta system the LU factorization routine starts to lose scalability when the granularity falls below about 0.2×10^6. This corresponds to a matrix size of about $M = 10,000$ on 512 processors, or about 13% of the memory available to applications on the Delta, indicating that LU factorization scales well on the Intel Delta system.

4.8 Conclusions and Future Research Directions

Portability of programs has always been an important consideration. Portability was easy to achieve when there was a single architectural paradigm (the serial von Neumann

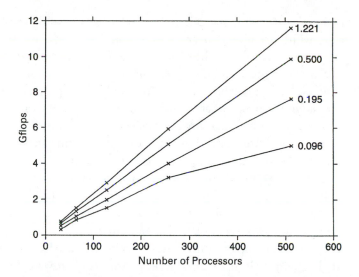

Figure 4.22   Isogranularity curves in the (N_p, G) plane for the LU factorization of square matrices on the Intel Delta system. The curves are labeled by the granularity in units of 10^6 matrix elements per processor. The linearity of the plots for granularities exceeding about 0.2×10^6 indicates that the LU factorization algorithm scales well on the Delta.

machine) and a single programming language for scientific programming (Fortran) embodying that common model of computation. Architectural and linguistic diversity have made portability much more difficult, but no less important, to attain. Users simply do not wish to invest significant amounts of time to create large-scale application codes for each new machine. Our answer is to develop portable software libraries that hide machine-specific details.

Portability, Scalability, and Standards

In order to be truly portable, parallel software libraries must be *standardized*. In a parallel computing environment in which the higher-level routines and/or abstractions are built upon lower-level computation and message-passing routines, the benefits of standardization are particularly apparent. Furthermore, the definition of computational and message-passing standards provides vendors with a clearly defined base set of routines that they can implement efficiently.

From the user's point of view, portability means that as new machines are developed they are simply added to the network, supplying cycles where they are most appropriate.

From the mathematical software developer's point of view, portability may require significant effort. Economy in development and maintenance of mathematical software demands that such development effort be leveraged over as many different computer systems as possible. Given the great diversity of parallel architectures, this type of portability is attainable to only a limited degree, but machine dependences can at least be isolated.

LAPACK is an example of a mathematical software package whose highest-level components are portable, while machine dependences are hidden in lower-level modules. Such a hierarchical approach is probably the closest one can come to software portability across diverse parallel architectures. And the BLAS that are used so heavily in LAPACK provide a portable, efficient, and flexible standard for applications programmers.

Like portability, *scalability* demands that a program be reasonably effective over a wide range of number of processors. The scalability of parallel algorithms, and software libraries based on them, over a wide range of architectural designs and numbers of processors will likely require that the fundamental granularity of computation be adjustable to suit the particular circumstances in which the software may happen to execute. Our approach to this problem is block algorithms with adjustable block size. In many cases, however, polyalgorithms[†] may be required to deal with the full range of architectures and processor multiplicity likely to be available in the future.

Scalable parallel architectures of the future are likely to be based on a distributed-memory architectural paradigm. In the longer term, progress in hardware development, operating systems, languages, compilers, and communications may make it possible for users to view such distributed architectures (without significant loss of efficiency) as having a shared memory with a global address space. For the near term, however, the distributed nature of the underlying hardware will continue to be visible at the programming level; therefore, efficient procedures for explicit communication will continue to be necessary. Given this fact, standards for basic message passing (send/receive), as well as higher-level communication constructs (global summation, broadcast, etc.), become essential to the development of scalable libraries that have any degree of portability. In addition to standardizing general communication primitives, it may also be advantageous to establish standards for problem-specific constructs in commonly occurring areas such as linear algebra.

The BLACS[8, 9] is a package that provides the same ease of use and portability for MIMD message-passing linear algebra communication that the BLAS[2, 22, 23] provide for linear algebra computation. Therefore, we recommend that future software for dense linear algebra on MIMD platforms consist of calls to the BLAS for computation and calls to the BLACS for communication. Since both packages will have been optimized for a particular platform, good performance should be achieved with relatively little effort. Also, since both packages will be available on a wide variety of machines, code modifications required to change platforms should be minimal.

Alternative Approaches

Traditionally, large, general-purpose mathematical software libraries have required users to write their own programs that call library routines to solve specific subproblems that arise during a computation. Adapted to a shared-memory parallel environment, this

---

[†] In a polyalgorithm, the actual algorithm used depends on the computing environment and the input data. The optimal algorithm in a particular instance is automatically selected at run time.

conventional interface still offers some potential for hiding underlying complexity. For example, the LAPACK project incorporates parallelism in the Level 3 BLAS, where it is not directly visible to the user.

But when going from shared-memory systems to the more readily scalable distributed-memory systems, the complexity of the distributed data structures required is more difficult to hide from the user. Not only must the problem decomposition and data layout be specified, but different phases of the user's problem may require transformations between different distributed data structures.

These deficiencies in the conventional user interface have prompted extensive discussion of alternative approaches for scalable parallel software libraries of the future. Possibilities include:

1 Traditional function library (i.e., minimum possible change to the status quo in going from serial to parallel environment). This will allow one to protect the programming investment that has been made.

2 Reactive servers on the network. A user would be able to send a computational problem to a server that was specialized in dealing with the problem. This fits well with the concepts of a networked, heterogeneous computing environment with various specialized hardware resources (or even the heterogeneous partitioning of a single homogeneous parallel machine).

3 General interactive environments like Matlab or Mathematica, perhaps with "expert" drivers (i.e., knowledge-based systems). With the growing popularity of the many integrated packages based on this idea, this approach would provide an interactive graphical interface for specifying and solving scientific problems. Both the algorithms and data structures are hidden from the user, because the package itself is responsible for storing and retrieving the problem data in an efficient, distributed manner. In a heterogeneous networked environment, such interfaces could provide seamless access to computational engines that would be invoked selectively for different parts of the user's computation according to which machine is most appropriate for a particular subproblem.

4 Domain-specific problem solving environments, such as those for structural analysis. Environments like Matlab and Mathematica have proven to be especially attractive for rapid prototyping of new algorithms and systems that may subsequently be implemented in a more customized manner for higher performance.

5 Reusable templates (i.e., users adapt "source code" to their particular applications). A template is a description of a general algorithm rather than the executable object code or the source code more commonly found in a conventional software library. Nevertheless, although templates are general descriptions of key data structures, they offer whatever degree of customization the user may desire.

Novel user interfaces that hide the complexity of scalable parallelism will require new concepts and mechanisms for representing scientific computational problems and for specifying how those problems relate to each other. Very high level languages and systems, perhaps graphically based, not only would facilitate the use of mathematical software from the user's point of view, but also would help to automate the determination of effective partitioning, mapping, granularity, data structures, etc. However, new concepts in problem specification and representation may also require new mathematical research on the analytic, algebraic, and topological properties of problems (e.g., existence and uniqueness).

We have already begun work on developing such templates for sparse matrix computations. Future work will focus on extending the use of templates to dense matrix computations.

We hope the insight we gained from our work will influence future developers of hardware, compilers, and systems software so that they provide tools to facilitate development of high quality portable numerical software.

The EISPACK, LINPACK, and LAPACK linear algebra libraries are in the public domain, and are available from *netlib*. For example, for more information on how to obtain LAPACK, send the following one-line email message to netlib@ornl.gov:

```
send index from lapack
```

Information for EISPACK, LINPACK, and ScaLAPACK can be similarly obtained.

Acknowledgments

This research was performed in part using the Intel Touchstone Delta System operated by the California Institute of Technology on behalf of the Concurrent Supercomputing Consortium. Access to this facility was provided through the Center for Research on Parallel Computing.

References

1 J. Wilkinson and C. Reinsch. *Handbook for Automatic Computation: Volume II—Linear Algebra.* Springer-Verlag, New York, 1971.

2 J. J. Dongarra, J. Du Croz, S. Hammarling, and I. Duff. "A Set of Level 3 Basic Linear Algebra Subprograms." *TOMS.* **16** (1), 1–17, 1990.

3 J. Demmel. "LAPACK: A Portable Linear Algebra Library for Supercomputers." In *Proceedings.* 1989 IEEE Control Systems Society Workshop on Computer-Aided Control System Design, Dec. 1989.

4 E. Anderson and J. Dongarra. "Evaluating Block Algorithm Variants in LAPACK." LAPACK Working Note 19, Computer Science Department, University of Tennessee, Knoxville, TN, 1990.

5 E. Anderson and J. Dongarra. "Results from the Initial Release of LAPACK." LAPACK Working Note 16, Computer Science Department, University of Tennessee, Knoxville, TN, 1989.

6 J. Choi, J. J. Dongarra, R. Pozo, and D. W. Walker. "ScaLAPACK: A Scalable Linear Algebra Library for Distributed Memory Concurrent Computers." In *Proceedings.* Fourth Symposium on the Frontiers of Massively Parallel Computation, IEEE Computer Society Press, 1992, pp. 120–127.

7 J. Choi, J. J. Dongarra, and D. W. Walker. "The Design of Scalable Software Libraries for Distributed Memory Concurrent Computers." In *Environments and Tools for Parallel Scientific Computing.* (J. J. Dongarra and B. Tourancheau, Eds.) Elsevier, New York, 1993.

8 J. J. Dongarra. "LAPACK Working Note 34: Workshop on the BLACS." Technical Report CS-91-134, Computer Science Department, University of Tennessee, Knoxville, TN, 1991.

9 J. J. Dongarra and R. A. van de Geijn. "Two-Dimensional Basic Linear Algebra Communication Subprograms." LAPACK Working Note 37, Computer Science Department, University of Tennessee, Knoxville, TN, 1991.

10 J. J. Dongarra, R. Pozo, and D. W. Walker. "An Object Oriented Design for High Performance Linear Algebra on Distributed Memory Architectures." In *Proceedings.* Object Oriented Numerics Conference, 1993.

11 R. W. Hockney and C. R. Jesshope. *Parallel Computers.* Adam Hilger Ltd., Bristol, UK, 1981.

12 CM-5 Technical Summary. Thinking Machines Corporation, Cambridge, MA, 1991.

13 C. Leiserson. "Fat Trees: Universal Networks for Hardware-Efficient Supercomputing." In *IEEE Transactions on Computers.* **C-34** (10), 892–901, 1985.

14 G. C. Fox, M. A. Johnson, G. A. Lyzenga, S. W. Otto, J. K. Salmon, and D. W. Walker. *Solving Problems on Concurrent Processors.* Vol. 1, Prentice Hall, Englewood Cliffs, NJ, 1988.

15 A. Gupta and V. Kumar. "On the Scalability of FFT on Parallel Computers." In *Proceedings.* Frontiers 90 Conference on Massively Parallel Computation, IEEE Computer Society Press, 1990. Also available as technical report TR 90-20 from the Computer Science Department, University of Minnesota, Minneapolis, MN.

16 J. J. Dongarra and E. Grosse. "Distribution of Mathematical Software via Electronic Mail." *Communications of the ACM.* **30** (5), 403–407, 1987.

17 J. Du Croz and M. Pont. "The Development of a Floating-Point Validation Package." In *Proceedings.* 8th Symposium on Computer Arithmetic, Como, Italy, 19–21 May 1987 (M. J. Irwin and R. Stefanelli, Eds.) IEEE Computer Society Press, 1987.

18 W. Kahan. "Paranoia." Available from netlib. See Reference 16.

19 J. J. Dongarra. "Increasing the Performance of Mathematical Software Through High-Level Modularity." In *Proceedings*. Sixth International Symp. Comp. Methods in Eng. & Applied Sciences, Versailles, France, North-Holland Press, 1984, pp. 239–248.

20 E. W. Felten and S. W. Otto. "Coherent Parallel C." In *Proceedings*. Third Conference on Hypercube Concurrent Computers and Applications. (G. C. Fox, Ed.) ACM Press, 1988.

21 D. E. Culler, A. Dusseau, S. C. Goldstein, A. Krishnamurthy, S. Lumetta, T. von Eicken, and K. Yelick. "Introduction to Split-C: Version 0.9." Computer Science Division—EECS, University of California, Berkeley, CA, Feb., 1993.

22 C. Lawson, R. Hanson, D. Kincaid, and F. Krogh. "Basic Linear Algebra Subprograms for Fortran Usage." *ACM Trans. Math. Softw.* **5**, 308–323, 1979.

23 J. J. Dongarra, J. Du Croz, S. Hammarling, and R. Hanson. "An Extended Set of Fortran Basic Linear Algebra Subroutines." *ACM Transactions on Mathematical Software.* **14** (1), 1–17, 1988.

24 G. H. Golub and C. F. Van Loan. *Matrix Computations.* 2nd ed. Johns Hopkins Press, Baltimore, 1989.

25 K. Gallivan, R. Plemmons, and A. Sameh. "Parallel Algorithms for Dense Linear Algebra Computations." *SIAM Review.* **32** (1), 54–135, 1990.

26 J. J. Dongarra, I. S. Duff, D. C. Sorensen, and H. A. Van der Vorst. *Solving Linear Systems on Vector and Shared Memory Computers.* SIAM Publications, Philadelphia, 1991.

27 J. J. Dongarra, P. Mayes, and G. Radicati di Brozolo. "The IBM RISC System/6000 and Linear Algebra Operations." *Supercomputer.* **44** (VIII-4), 15–30, 1991.

28 R. Harrington. "Origin and Development of the Method of Moments for Field Computation." *IEEE Antennas and Propagation Magazine.* June 1990.

29 J. J. H. Wang. *Generalized Moment Methods in Electromagnetics.* Wiley, New York, 1991.

30 J. L. Hess. "Panel Methods in Computational Fluid Dynamics." *Annual Reviews of Fluid Mechanics.* **22**, 255–274, 1990.

31 J. L. Hess and M. O. Smith. "Calculation of Potential Flows About Arbitrary Bodies." In *Progress in Aeronautical Sciences.* Vol. 8. (D. Küchemann, Ed.) Pergamon, New York, 1967.

32 A. Edelman. "Large Dense Numerical Linear Algebra in 1993: The Parallel Computing Influence." *International Journal Supercomputer Applications.* **3** (2), 113–128, 1993.

33 E. F. Van de Velde. "Data Redistribution and Concurrency." *Parallel Computing.* **16**, Dec. 1990.

34 High Performance Fortran Language Specification, Version 1.0. High Performance Fortran Forum, Jan. 1993.

35 E. Anderson, A. Benzoni, J. J. Dongarra, S. Moulton, S. Ostrouchov, B. Tourancheau, and R. van de Geijn. "LAPACK for Distributed Memory Architectures: Progress Report." In *Parallel Processing for Scientific Computing*, 5th SIAM Conference, SIAM, 1991.

36 C. C. Ashcraft. "The Distributed Solution of Linear Systems Using the Torus Wrap Data Mapping." Engineering Computing and Analysis Technical Report ECA-TR-147, Boeing Computer Services, Seattle, 1990.

37 C. C. Ashcraft. "A Taxonamy of Distributed Dense LU Factorization Methods." Engineering Computing and Analysis Technical Report ECA-TR-161, Boeing Computer Services, Seattle, 1991.

38 R. P. Brent. "The LINPACK Benchmark on the AP 1000: Preliminary Report." *Proceedings.* 2nd CAP Workshop, Nov. 1991.

39 J. J. Dongarra and S. Ostrouchov. "LAPACK Block Factorization Algorithms on the Intel iPSC/860." Technical Report CS-90-115. Computer Science Department, University of Tennessee, Knoxville, TN, 1990.

40 J. J. Dongarra and R. A. van de Geijn. "Reduction to Condensed Form for the Eigenvalue Problem on Distributed Memory Architectures." *Parallel Computing.* **18**, 973–982, 1992.

41 Y. Saad and M. H. Schultz. "Parallel Direct Methods for Solving Banded Linear Systems." YALEU/DCS/RR-387, Department of Computer Science, Yale University, New Haven, CT, 1985.

42 A. Skjellum and A. Leung. "LU Factorization of Sparse, Unsymmetric, Jacobian Matrices on Multicomputers." In *Proceedings.* 5th Distributed Memory Concurrent Computing Conference, (D. W. Walker and Q. F. Stout, Eds.) IEEE, 1990, pp. 328–337.

43 R. A. van de Geijn. "Massively Parallel LINPACK Benchmark on the Intel Touchstone Delta and iPSC/860 Systems." Computer Science Report TR-91-28, University of Texas, 1991.

44 W. S. Brainerd, C. H. Goldbergs, and J. C. Adams. *Programmers Guide to Fortran 90.* McGraw-Hill, New York, 1990.

45 E. Chu and A. George. "Gaussian Elimination with Partial Pivoting and Load Balancing on a Multiprocessor." *PC.* 5, 65–74, 1987.

46 A. Geist and M. Heath. "Matrix Factorization on a Hypercube Multiprocessor." In *Hypercube Multiprocessors, 1986.* (M. Heath, Ed.) SIAM, Philadelphia, 1986, pp. 161–180.

47 A. Geist and C. Romine. "LU Factorization Algorithms on Distributed-Memory Multiprocessor Architectures." *SISSC.* **9** (4), 639–649, 1988.

48 R. P. Brent. "The LINPACK Benchmark for the Fujitsu AP 1000." In *Proceedings*. 4th Symposium on the Frontiers of Massively Parallel Computation, IEEE Computer Society Press, 1992, pp. 128–135.

49 B. Hendrickson and D. Womble. "The Torus-Wrap Mapping for Dense Matrix Computations on Massively Parallel Computers." Technical Report SAND92-0792, Sandia National Laboratories, Albuquerque, April 1992.

50 W. Lichtenstein and S. L. Johnsson. "Block-Cyclic Dense Linear Algebra." Technical Report TR-04-92, Center for Research in Computing Technology, Harvard University, Cambridge, MA, Jan. 1992.

51 J. J. Dongarra, R. van de Geijn, and D. W. Walker. "A Look at Scalable Dense Linear Algebra Libraries." In *Proceedings*. Scalable High-Performance Computing Conference, IEEE, 1992, pp. 372–379.

52 T. H. Dunigan. "Communication Performance of the Intel Touchstone Delta Mesh." Technical Report TM-11983, Oak Ridge National Laboratory, Jan. 1992.

53 M. Lin, D. Du, A. E. Klietz and S. Saroff. "Performance Evaluation of the CM-5 Interconnection Network." Department of Computer Science, University of Minnesota, 1992.

54 R. Ponnusamy, A. Choudhary, and G. Fox. "Communication Overhead on CM-5: An Experimental Performance Evaluation." In *Proceedings*. 4th Symposium on the Frontiers of Massively Parallel Computation, IEEE Computer Society Press, 1992, pp. 108–115.

55 M. Barnett, D. G. Payne, and R. van de Geijn. "Broadcasting on Meshes with Worm-Hole Routing." Department of Computer Science, University of Texas, Austin, TX, April 1993. Submitted to *Supercomputing '93*.

56 S. R. Seidel. "Broadcasting on Linear Arrays and Meshes." Technical Report TM-12356, Oak Ridge National Laboratory, Oak Ridge, TN, April, 1993.

57 J. J. Dongarra, R. Hempel, A. J. G. Hey, and D. W. Walker. "A Proposal for a User-Level Message Passing Interface in a Distributed Memory Environment." Technical Report TM-12231, Oak Ridge National Laboratory, Oak Ridge, TN, Feb. 1993.

5

Dynamic Tree Searching

STEVE W. OTTO and EDWARD W. FELTEN

Contents

The previous chapters centered around grids; this chapter looks at algorithms used to write a parallel program to play chess. New basic issues encountered in this chapter include generating and searching a game tree efficiently, dynamic load balancing, scheduling, and emulation of shared memory on distributed-memory hardware.

5.1 Introduction

In this chapter, we discuss a parallel algorithm and program for playing chess on a 512-processor, distributed-memory parallel machine. We chose to study the problem of chess playing because it presented several interesting challenges that stretched the limits of our understanding of how to design, write, tune, and support parallel programs. Among the challenging (and often maddening) features of the problem are

- *Demanding performance requirements:* Chess is played against intelligent opponents, who have an uncanny knack of finding and exploiting the weaknesses in their opponent. In addition, the game is played with a time limit, so the performance of the parallel program is of utmost importance.

- *A large, highly asynchronous set of cooperating processes:* The program consists of over 500 processes, each synchronizing and communicating with several others. The relationships between these processes change dynamically in real time as the program's search proceeds. The activities of the processes must be coordinated so they work effectively together, without imposing unnecessary synchronization.

- *Extreme dynamic load imbalance:* The time required to perform the subtasks assigned to worker processes differs by several orders of magnitude, from tens of microseconds up to several minutes. This load imbalance is unpredictable, so the organization of processes must change rapidly to bring workers to bear on the available work.

- *Speculative parallelism:* The traditional algorithm is inherently sequential. *All* of the parallelism in the program is speculative—calculations are started before it is known whether the sequential algorithm would have performed them, in the hope that they will be useful. In order to minimize wasted work, we must be very careful exactly which opportunities for speculative parallelism are exploited and which are ignored.

- *A large, frequently accessed shared data structure:* Most of the available memory is used by a single, large data structure that is shared among all the processes. Accesses to this structure are frequent, and they exhibit neither spatial nor temporal locality. Yet this structure must be implemented efficiently on a distributed-memory machine.

Since we were interested only indirectly in issues specific to the game of chess, we spent most of our time attacking the problems of harnessing parallelism. On the other hand, a certain amount of attention to the program's output was required to make the program "real." As we will see below, several techniques for exploiting parallelism rely on properties of realistic, competitive programs; we would not have discovered these techniques if we had used only a toy program.

We will begin our discussion by reviewing the basic mechanisms by which sequential computers play chess; this will provide the necessary background for the discussion of parallel algorithms. We will then describe some of the problems we faced in designing and implementing our parallel program, and our solutions. Finally, we will discuss the performance of our program, and reflect on what we learned.

5.2 How Computers Play Chess

Competitive chess programs function by searching a tree of possible moves and countermoves from the current position.[1] A program starts with the current board position and generates all legal moves from that position, all legal responses to these moves, and so on until some fixed depth is reached. Each level of the tree is traditionally referred to as a "ply"; for example, a five-ply search examines the top five levels of the tree. (By contrast, when a chess player talks about thinking five moves ahead, he conventionally means five moves by each side, or ten ply.)

At each leaf node, the program applies an evaluation function that assigns a numerical score to that board position. These scores are then propagated towards the root of the tree by a process called minimaxing. Minimax is the algorithm that reflects the assumption that at all times each side will choose the line of play with the most favorable score. Figure 5.1 illustrates the concept. If positive scores favor white, then white picks the move of maximum score and black picks the move of minimum score.

The evaluation function is usually taken to be a combination of simple material balance, and several terms that represent positional or strategic factors. Material balance simply counts the total value of the pieces each side has on the board. The positional terms are relatively small but important, since material balance rarely changes during the course of most games. One of the classic research issues in computer chess has been the tradeoff between simple, material-dominated evaluation functions that run quickly and allow deep trees to be developed versus complex evaluation functions that measure more but are slow and thus restrict the search to shallow trees. The evidence from head-to-head competition has favored the simple, brute-force, deep-tree approach.

The dominant feature of tree searching as described so far is that the size of the tree grows exponentially with depth. The branching factor of the tree is given by the number of legal moves arising from a typical position. In the middle game of chess, this is about 35. A computational complexity growing as 35^n would limit even very fast computers to ply 5 or 6 searches and rather unimpressive play.

Fortunately, there is something better than full-width tree searching. Alpha-beta search is an algorithm that is guaranteed to give the same answer as full-width minimax search without looking at all nodes of the tree.[2] Intuitively, alpha-beta search works by ignoring subtrees that provably cannot be reached by best play on the part of both sides. This reduces the branching factor from 35 to an effective branching factor of about 6,

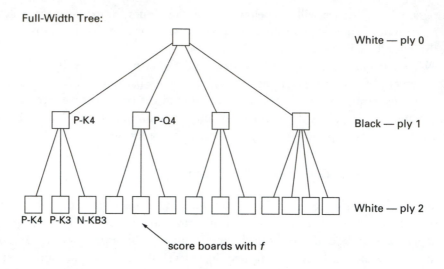

Full-Width Tree:

White — ply 0

P-K4   P-Q4   Black — ply 1

P-K4 P-K3 N-KB3   White — ply 2

score boards with *f*

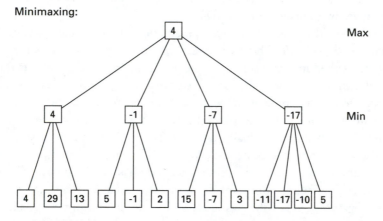

Minimaxing:

Max

Min

Figure 5.1   **Game playing by tree searching. The top half of the figure illustrates the general idea: develop a full-width tree to some depth, then score the leaves with the evaluation function, *f*. The bottom half shows minimaxing, which is based on the reasonable supposition that white (black) always chooses the line of play that maximizes (minimizes) the score.**

making deep trees and hence strong play possible. This is evidenced by the fact that many computer chess players are chess masters, and the very best, such as Deep Thought, play at grandmaster level.[3]

The idea behind alpha-beta pruning is shown in Figure 5.2 for a ply 2 tree. Assume that the child nodes are searched in the order of left to right in the figure. Alpha-beta is a depth-first searching technique, and it searches the leftmost subtree first. Suppose that minimizing yields a score of +4 for the first child of the root. Now move to the next subtree to the right. The first two children report scores of +5 and −1. The pruning

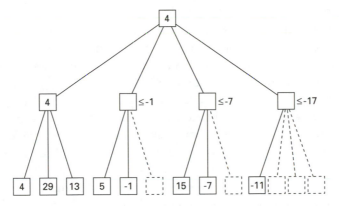

Figure 5.2 **Alpha-beta pruning for a ply 2 tree. The tree is generated in depth-first, left-to-right order. The first branch minimaxes to +4. In the second branch, as soon as the score –1 is computed, we immediately have a bound on the level above (≤ –1) which is below the score of the +4 subtree. We mark the level 1 node "≤ –1." A cutoff occurs, in that no more descendants of the ≤ –1 node need to be searched.**

happens after the score of −1 is returned. Since we are taking the minimum of the scores +5, −1, … we immediately have a bound on the scores of this subtree—we know the score will be no larger than −1. Since we are taking the maximum at the next level up (the root of the tree) and we already have a line of play better than −1 (namely, the +4 subtree), we need not explore this second subtree any further. Pruning occurs, as denoted by the dashed branch of the second subtree; pruning is safe because the scores of the pruned subtrees cannot possibly affect the score of the root, and hence cannot possibly affect the choice of which move to make in the root position. The process continues for the third branch. Again, as soon as the score can be bounded as less than the alpha cutoff of +4 (the bound is −7 in this case) the sub-branch prunes.

The amount of work saved in this small tree was insignificant, but alpha-beta pruning becomes very important for large trees. Remember, the real branching factor of the tree is about 35 rather than the 3 or 4 we have drawn. One consequence of this pruning is that sibling subtrees can have vastly different sizes.

Actually, what we have discussed so far is not full alpha-beta pruning, but merely "alpha-beta pruning without deep cutoffs." The algorithm described has only one bound, while the alpha-beta algorithm carries along two bounds, called alpha and beta. The additional pruning due to the second bound (the "deep cutoffs") shows up only in trees of depth 4 or greater. A discussion of full alpha-beta pruning can be found in Knuth and Moore.[4]

The effectiveness of pruning depends crucially on move ordering. If the best line of play is searched first, then other branches will prune rapidly; otherwise, the effectiveness of pruning is vastly reduced. As we will discuss, the method of iterative deepening and the transposition table data structure combine to give good move ordering for a modern alpha-beta searcher. Actual runs on real chess positions give branching factor reductions quite close to the theoretical best for perfect move ordering.

Competitive Programs

The description we've given so far covers only the basics of a computer chess program. To be *really* competitive, there are other important methods that lead to near-perfect move ordering in the alpha-beta tree, which is essential for the program's effectiveness. We next describe these important refinements.

Quiescence searching The evaluation function we have described so far is completely static—it takes a chess board as input, computes material balance and positional terms, and reports back a score. It really only makes sense to apply a static evaluation function to a position that is quiescent, or tactically quiet. That is, if our queen is about to be captured at a leaf node, it is wrong for the evaluator not to take this into account. As a result, most chess programs extend the tree search beyond nominal leaf nodes until a quiescent position is reached. Only at this point is the static evaluator actually applied.

We can think of the quiescence search as a dynamic evaluation function, which takes into account tactical possibilities. At each leaf node, the side to move has the choice of accepting the current static evaluation or trying to improve its position by tactics, which includes pawn promotions, most capture moves, some checks, and some pawn promotion threats. At each newly generated position the dynamic evaluator is applied again. At the nominal leaf nodes, therefore, a narrow (small branching factor) tactical search is done, with the static evaluator applied at all terminal points of this search (which end up being the true leaves). One consequence of quiescence search is an exaggeration of the load imbalance between subtrees.

Iterative deepening Tournament chess is played under a strict time control, and a program must make decisions about how much time to use for each move. Most chess programs do not set out to search to a fixed depth, but use a technique called iterative deepening. This means a program does a depth 1 search, then a depth 2 search, then a depth 3 search, and so on until the allotted time has run out. When the time is up, the program returns its current best guess at the move to make.

Iterative deepening has the additional advantage that it facilitates move ordering. The program knows which move was best in each position at the previous level of iterative deepening, and it searches this move first at the new level. This leads to very accurate move ordering. Since each iteration of iterative deepening takes about five times longer than the previous one, the extra cost of iterative deepening is small and is more than repaid by the gain due to more accurate move ordering.

The transposition table During the tree search, the same board position may occur several times. There are two reasons for this. The first is true transposition, or the fact that the same board position can be reached by different sequences of moves. The second reason is iterative deepening—the same position will be reached in the depth 2 search, the depth 3 search, etc. The transposition table is a way of storing information about positions that have already been searched; if the same position is reached again, the search can be sped up or eliminated entirely by using this information.

The transposition table plays a central role in a good chess program. It is essentially a cache for information about recent subtree searches. Each board position is mapped by a pseudorandom hash function[5] to a 128-bit signature that is assumed to be unique (the odds that two boards searched in the same game have the same signature are infinitesimal—much less than the odds of other catastrophic events like a conspiracy of three-bit errors in ECC-protected memory, or an earthquake). The cache is typically direct mapped, with low-order bits of the signature used to select a slot in the transposition table.

Each slot in the transposition table contains

- two status bits: "valid" and "stale"

- the signature of the position occupying the slot

- known upper and lower bounds on the score of the position

- the depth of search to which these bounds are valid

- a hint about what the best move is in the position.

The searcher uses the transposition table in the following way. Instead of just blindly generating all legal moves at a position and then going down these lines of play, the transposition table is first queried about the position. Occasionally, the transposition table provides bounds on the score tight enough to cause an immediate alpha-beta cutoff. More often, the transposition table merely has a suggested move to try, and this move is searched first. The 128-bit signature and the valid bit are used to ensure that the entry has information about the same position that the program is currently considering (more than one chess board can map to the same location in the table).

Whenever the program completes the search of a subtree of substantial size (i.e., one of depth greater than some minimum), the knowledge gained is written into the transposition table. If there is already a valid entry in that slot of the table we have a collision, and the program must decide which of the two entries to keep and which to discard. This is done by examining the depth of search and stale bits of each entry to estimate which entry is more valuable. If exactly one of the entries is stale, it is discarded; otherwise, the search of lower depth is discarded.

The stale bit allows us to keep information from one search to the next. When time runs out and a search is considered finished, the table is not simply cleared. Instead, the stale bit is set in all entries. If during the next search a valid read is done on a stale entry, the stale bit is cleared, the idea being that this position again seems to be useful. Since the replacement policy always discards stale entries first, the table does not become clogged with old, useless information.

Thinking on the opponent's time When it is the opponent's turn to move, the program does not wait idly but tries to do something useful. It uses information from the transposition table to guess which move the opponent will make, and then searches as if the opponent had already made the guessed move. If the guess turns out to be correct, the program will have gotten a headstart on its search for a response. The program guesses the opponent's move correctly about 40% of the time if the opponent is a computer and about 30% of the time if the opponent is a person.

The opening The opening is played by making use of an "opening book" of known positions. We used a database of about 18,000 positions, chosen by humans with the aid of books on chess theory. Since the database is referenced only a few times at the beginning of the game it is simply stored on disk.

5.3 The Parallel Program

Our goal was to write a massively parallel chess-tree searcher. The potentially large source of parallelism is the game tree. We decided to develop an algorithm to search multiple branches of the tree in parallel. Assuming that bottlenecks and overheads and the apparent sequentiality of alpha-beta search could be overcome, such a program could achieve large speedups when evaluating large game trees.

The target machine architectures are massively parallel distributed-memory MIMD machines. Each processor runs a program that acts as an asynchronous search server. Upon commands from a remote processor, which are expressed as asynchronous messages, the server performs alpha-beta searches of chess subtrees. The processors are organized in a master–slave hierarchy that is several levels deep.

Our parallel algorithm relies heavily on asynchronous techniques to achieve load balance. This shows up clearly in our use of self-scheduling by slave processors in obtaining work from master processors. Due to the large variation in search times for different subtrees, asynchronous self-scheduling is essential for acceptable load balance. Another source of asynchrony is the propagation of alpha-beta bounds. As tighter bounds are discovered, these bounds are propagated to sibling processors, leading to earlier alpha-beta cutoffs.

Because of the fundamental asynchrony of our program and the need for global load balancing, a mapping to SIMD architectures seems problematic.

Another essential feature of the target architecture and its system software is the availability of an active-message capability.[6, 7] We have found that the existence of a large shared transposition table mapped across all processors of the parallel machine is central to efficient game tree search. Random access to this global data structure (both remote reads and remote writes) is implemented as described in Section 5.5.

We developed our program on an nCUBE I multiprocessor, consisting of 512 processors connected by a network of hypercube topology. We modified the message-passing system of the machine, Vertex, to provide an interrupt-message capability.[6]

5.4 Parallel Control, Parallel Data Structures

This section explains how the basic data structures are mapped across the parallel machine. In contrast to most data-parallel scientific algorithms, our parallel control flow is also quite complex. At a high level, the program could be thought of as data parallel— each processor simply does alpha-beta searches on subtrees that are handed to it. On the other hand, the work is not statically scheduled to the processors, nor is the decision whether to "stay sequential" or to fan out into a parallel search at any subtree made in a simple or predictable way.

Self-Scheduled Master–Slave Hierarchy

We have been careful to keep the control of the program decentralized so as to avoid sequential bottlenecks. The parallelism comes from searching different parts of the chess tree at the same time. Processors are also organized into a tree, with each node of the tree representing a processor and each edge representing a master–slave relationship. At the top level there is a single master processor managing the root of the game tree search. This top-level master has several slaves to which it allocates work. These slaves, in turn, are actually the masters of entire teams of processors. The program is written to support an arbitrarily deep hierarchy of processors. When a "master" processor at one level hands off work to a processor at a level one step below, the master thinks of the slave as just a single processor and only sends a single message to the slave processor. If the slave is a true slave, that is, a leaf of the processor tree, it simply does the search requested and reports the result back to its master. If the "slave" is actually the master of a team of processors, it uses its own slaves to search the assigned subtree.

Processors travel down the chess tree by calling the function make(move) on the current board. To go back up the tree, the same move must be unmade by calling the function unmake(move) on the current board. Chess boards are not saved as the processors go up and down the tree, but are instead reconstructed by these relatively cheap operations. If a master processor wants to take all of its slaves down a single branch of the chess tree, it simply sends messages to the slaves that causes each of them to make the same move. In this way, the processors all go down a branch of the game tree but do not start parallel searches. If the master wants to invoke a parallel search, different moves are sent to each slave, and then a "search" message is sent to each.

The information that represents the chess tree is spread across all the processors. In master processors, lists are kept that describe, for each slave, what move that slave has made from the master's position in the chess tree and what alpha-beta search is running in the slave. The branches near the root of the chess tree are stored in these lists, across all the master processors. Once we get to the leaves of the processor hierarchy, we revert to a conventional chess program. This alpha-beta search is written recursively; this means that the analogous lists of legal moves at internal nodes of the game tree and partial search results are actually stored in the call stacks of the slave processors.

So far we have described the mechanics of how we represent the game tree in a distributed way and how we track where each processor is on this game tree. The parallelism occurs as masters start up independent subtree searches in their slaves. The basic parallel operation consists of one master coming to a node in the chess tree and assigning subtrees to its slaves in a self-scheduled way. Figure 5.3 shows a timeline of how this might happen with three slaves. Rather than deciding beforehand that each slave will do an equal number of searches, the master keeps a queue of remaining work. As the slaves return with answers, they request another item of work from the queue. Self-scheduling by the slaves helps to load-balance the computation, as can be seen in the figure. The method is effective as long as the dynamic range of the work times is not large in comparison to the number of searches that need to be performed. For

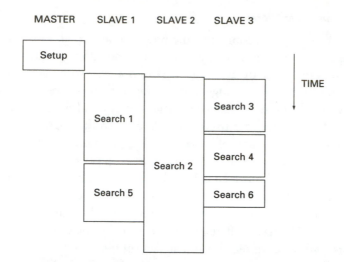

Figure 5.3   Slaves searching subtrees in a self-scheduled manner. Suppose one of the searches, in this case, search 2, takes a long time. The advantage of the self-scheduling is that while this search is proceeding in slave 2 the other slaves will have done all the remaining work. This technique works as long as the dynamic range of the computation times is not large when compared to the number of tasks.

example, if search 2 in Figure 5.3 were ten times as long as shown, the load balancing effect breaks down.

Figure 5.4 shows the "big picture"—what it looks like when many processors search the game tree. Since the branching factor is 35 and we want the load-balancing effect of self-scheduling, the "teams" of processors can't be very large. In our work a team size of eight seemed to be a good choice. To bring large numbers of processors into play, therefore, we must use a hierarchy of processors and do parallel searches at many levels of the chess tree simultaneously. This means that what appears to be a single self-scheduling slave at one level of the processor hierarchy may actually be an entire team of processors. Self-scheduling balances the load within a team, but load balancing on a larger scale, between teams, also occurs. It happens because of the self-scheduling one level higher up in the processor hierarchy.

5.5 Global Transposition Table

The transposition table is used to eliminate redundant searches and improve move ordering. It plays a central role in the search, and this implies that the table must be shared between all processors. Local transposition tables would not be adequate. A shared table is expensive on a distributed-memory machine, but in this case it is worthwhile.

Each processor contributes an equal amount of memory to the shared transposition table. Recall that each position is hashed to a 128-bit signature before accessing the transposition table. The low-order bits of this signature are used to choose a processor ID and

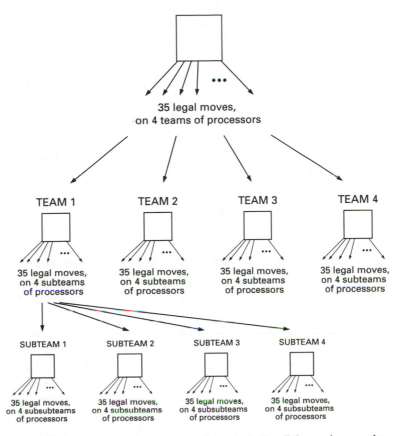

Figure 5.4 **A rough picture of the recursive parallel search. Parallel searches are begun, in a recursive fashion, down the chess tree to allow large numbers of processors to come into play. The topmost master has four slaves, which are each in turn a team of four processors, and so on.**

a local slot number on that processor; together, these determine where information about the position is stored. Remote memory is accessed by sending a message to the processor in which the desired memory resides. To insure prompt service to remote memory requests, these messages must be processed immediately upon arrival. nCUBE's native Vertex operating system does not support this feature, so we modified Vertex[8] to allow interrupt-time servicing of some messages without disturbing the running program.

When a processor wants to read a remote slot in the transposition table it sends a message containing the slot number and signature of the position to the appropriate processor. When this message arrives, the receiving processor is interrupted; it runs the read handler which sends the contents of the desired slot back to the requesting processor and updates the entry's *stale* flag if necessary. The processor that made the request waits until the answer comes back before proceeding.

Remote writing is a bit more complicated due to the possibility of collisions. As mentioned, collisions are resolved by a priority scheme; the decision of whether to overwrite the previous entry must be made by the processor that actually owns the relevant memory, because only it knows the previous contents of the slot. Remote writing is accomplished by sending a message containing the new transposition table entry to the appropriate processor. This message causes an interrupt, and the write handler examines the new data and the old contents of that transposition table slot and decides which one to keep.

Since transposition table data are shared among processors, any access to the table must be an atomic operation. This means we must guarantee that two accesses to the same slot cannot happen simultaneously. Our modified Vertex allows these critical sections to be protected while an access is in progress.

5.6 Using Speculative Parallelism

Alpha-beta pruning seems to imply a serialization of the parallel search. The result of searching one subtree determines the alpha-beta bounds for searches of subsequent subtrees and hence determines whether or not those subtrees will have to be searched at all. Thus, if one adheres strictly to the standard algorithm, there may be little opportunity for parallelism.

In order to achieve parallel speedup in alpha-beta search, we must make use of *speculative parallelism*. That is, we must search some subtrees before it is absolutely known whether those searches will be necessary. If a speculative search turns out to be necessary, we will have achieved useful parallelism; on the other hand, if it turns out to be unnecessary, the time and resources spent on the search will have been wasted. The performance of a parallel chess program is measured not in the number of positions per second searched but in the number of *useful* positions per second—the number of positions a sequential program would have searched to get the same result.

Fortunately, there are many more opportunities for speculative parallelism than there are processors to exploit them. This allows us to choose carefully when to apply parallelism and when to remain sequential. By making these choices wisely, we can use speculative parallelism only in places where the chances of a useful payoff are high and thus achieve a high rate of useful parallelism.

The algorithm for determining when to use speculative parallelism is one of the main innovations in our work. In order to understand this algorithm, we must first digress for a brief discussion of the properties of perfectly ordered alpha-beta trees. Since real searches exhibit almost perfect move ordering, this will provide valuable hints for designing a parallel search algorithm.

Properties of Perfectly Ordered Trees

Perfectly ordered alpha-beta trees are trees in which the best move in each position is always searched first. Knuth and Moore[4] have provided the most complete analysis of the behavior of alpha-beta search on perfectly ordered trees. We present here the results of Knuth and Moore, although we will use the more descriptive terminology suggested by Marsland.[9]

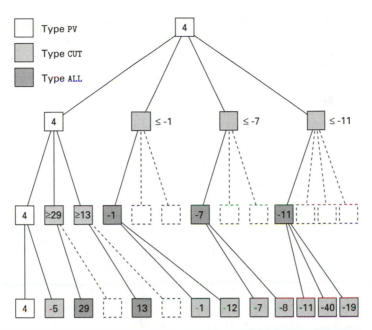

Figure 5.5 Pruning of a perfectly ordered tree. The example tree has been extended another ply, and also the move ordering has been rearranged so that the best move is always searched first. By classifying the nodes into types as described in the text, the following pattern emerges: all children of type PV and ALL nodes are searched, while only the first child of a type CUT node is searched.

Figure 5.5 shows a perfectly ordered alpha-beta tree. The tree's nodes can be divided into three classes, called PV, CUT, and ALL. Nodes of type PV are on the expected line of play; the first child of a PV node has type PV and all other children have type CUT. Nodes of type CUT represent positions where the first subtree searched will cause an alpha-beta cutoff; the child of a CUT node has type ALL. Nodes of type ALL represent positions at which all moves must be tried; the children of an ALL node have type CUT.

The implications of this for a parallel search are important. To efficiently search a perfectly ordered tree in parallel, we perform the following algorithm:

1 At PV nodes, the first child must be searched sequentially (in order to initialize the alpha-beta bounds), then the rest can be searched in parallel.

2 At CUT nodes there is no parallelism since only one child will be searched (time spent searching other children will be wasted).

3 ALL nodes, on the other hand, are fully parallel and all the children can be searched independently and simultaneously.

This algorithm is optimal for perfectly ordered trees.

The oscillating pattern between the node types is the principal reason for distinguishing them. The intuition behind the pattern is that only the first child of a CUT node is searched since this is a refutation move by our opponent to our move. We need not know about the details of the refutation (the exact score), just that there is one. The roles of CUT and ALL are reversed for branches off the principal variation (children of PV nodes), because the first move has in effect been forced.

Extending to Real Programs

A real program does not achieve perfect move ordering, so the clean distinction between node types breaks down in practice. However, real programs can achieve good move ordering in most cases, so the perfect-ordering case provides some useful insight.

In our parallel algorithm, information in the transposition table is used to guess the node type. Since the information in the table was mostly deposited by the previous iteration of iterative deepening, we are essentially guessing that each position will have the same node type that it had in the shallower search. Our algorithm works as follows:

1 If the previous search yielded both upper and lower bounds on the position's score, we guess the position has type PV. The suggested best move from the transposition table is searched sequentially, then the rest of the moves are searched in parallel.

2 If the previous search yielded only an upper bound on the position's score, we guess the position has type ALL, and search all subtrees in parallel.

3 If the previous search yielded only a lower bound, we guess the position has type CUT. The suggested move is searched first, sequentially. If this move unexpectedly fails to produce an alpha-beta cutoff, all other possibilities are searched in parallel.

4 If the position is not found in the transposition table, it is treated as type PV—the first move is searched sequentially, then all others in parallel.

Our algorithm reduces to the optimal algorithm in the case of perfect move ordering. In the realistic case, with good but not perfect move ordering, the algorithm makes good choices of when to apply speculative parallelism.

Previous computer chess researchers have emphasized the importance of the transposition table for providing good move ordering.[10] We have found it to have the additional importance of helping to schedule the parallel alpha-beta search.

Coordination of Processors

As indicated above, our program organizes processors in a multilevel hierarchy. A hierarchy with a branching factor between about 6 and 15 seems to work well in the middle game; in the end game a deeper, narrower hierarchy should be used. Control is decentralized; each processor only knows the identities of its parent and its slaves. A control program running on the front end takes care of time allocation and communication with the user so that the parallel machine serves only as a "search engine."

When a processor's slaves are searching it does not join them but stays where it is, monitoring their progress and passing them relevant information as it becomes available. For instance, if one slave finishes its search and returns a value to the master, this may narrow the alpha-beta bounds of the master and consequently also narrow the bounds of the slaves. The master notifies the slaves whenever new information narrows their alpha-beta bounds. The master also tells the slaves to abort their searches if an alpha-beta cutoff occurs. Aborts and updates of alpha-beta bounds are sent as interrupt messages to ensure rapid propagation down through the hierarchy.

5.7 Architectural Limitations

Due to the overhead of accessing the remote transposition table, we limited such accesses to only those game tree nodes a few ply up from the bottom of the tree. With this restriction, the program (on an nCUBE I) spent only a few percent of its time servicing the transposition table. The price paid was inaccurate move ordering near the leaves of the game tree. Better active-message performance or, perhaps, use of true hardware shared-memory would allow us to push the use of the transposition table to the bottom of the chess tree. This is probably the single most important limitation of this algorithm on distributed-memory MIMD architectures.

A secondary effect is the overhead associated with communications between master and slave processors. This affects the performance at the few-percent level but is less important than the potential payoff of improved load balancing (to be discussed in the next section) and better transposition table access.

In the design of our program, little attention was paid to the fact that the processor interconnect topology was that of a hypercube. We treated the machine as a flat topology, with each processor capable of sending messages to any other processor. The only place we took the physical topology into consideration was in the initial mapping of processor teams to physical processors. We did this in such a way that processors on the same team would be near one another in the hypercube. More modern architectures have hardware support for message forwarding, and this results in a true flattening of the topology since message times become nearly equal.[11]

5.8 Load Balancing, Tuning, Performance

As explained above, slaves get work from their masters in a self-scheduled way in order to achieve a simple type of load balancing. This turns out not to be enough, however. By the nature of alpha-beta search, the time to search two different subtrees of the same depth can vary quite dramatically—a factor of 100 variation in search times is common. Self-scheduling is nearly helpless in such a situation. In these cases a single slave would have to grind out the long search, while the other slaves (and conceivably, the rest of the machine) would merely sit idle. Another problem, near the bottom of the chess tree, is the extremely rapid time scales involved. Not only do the search times vary by a large factor, but this all happens at millisecond time scales. Any load-balancing procedure will, therefore, need to be quite fast and simple.

Our program was designed to handle such "chess hot spots" more intelligently. The master processors—besides waiting for search answers, updating alpha-beta bounds, and so forth—monitor what is going on with the slaves in terms of load balance. In particular, if some number of slaves are idle and if there has been a search proceeding for some minimum amount of time, the master halts the search in the slave containing the apparent hot spot, re-organizes all of its idle slaves into a single large team, and restarts the search in this new team. This process is entirely local to this master and its slaves and can happen recursively, at all levels of the processor tree.

This "shoot-down, restart" procedure is governed by two factors: the minimum number of slaves that must be idle and the minimum time for which they must be idle before declaring a search a hot spot. These factors are introduced as variables to prevent the halting, the processor rearrangement, and the associated overhead in cases that are not serious hot spots. The variables are tuned for maximum performance.

The payoff of dynamic load balancing has been quite large. Once we got the balancing code written, debugged, and tuned, the program was approximately three times faster than before load balancing. Through observing the speedup (discussed below) and by looking directly at the execution of the program across the nCUBE (using the parallel graphics display, also discussed below), we were convinced that the program is well load balanced, and we are optimistic about the prospects for scaling to larger speedups on larger machines.

Speedup Measurements

Speedup is defined as the ratio of sequential running time to parallel running time. We measure the speedup of our program by timing it directly with different numbers of processors on a standard suite of test searches. These searches are done from the Bratko–Kopec positions,[12] a well-known set of positions for testing chess programs. For each position we chose a depth of search which caused each search to take about the same amount of time, to mimic tournament conditions. Our benchmark consists of doing two successive searches from each position and adding up the total search time for all 24 searches. By varying the depth of search we can control the average search time of each benchmark.

The speedups measured are shown in Figure 5.6. Each curve corresponds to a different average search time. We find that speedup is a strong function of the depth of the search. This result is a reflection of the fact that deeper search trees have more potential parallelism and hence more speedup. Our main result is that at tournament speed (the uppermost curve of the figure) our program achieves a speedup of 101 out of a possible 256, and 170 out of a possible 512. These figures are not as high as for many numerical parallel programs, but are impressive for game tree search. As we've said before, the alpha-beta algorithm greatly constrains parallelism, and our parallel search algorithm is careful to stay sequential or go parallel at the correct places in the search tree. Even so, the parallel algorithm searches more tree nodes than a sequential alpha-beta algorithm. Therefore, our search speeds would sound better if we quoted them in terms of chess positions searched per second, but this wouldn't be fair. The sources of inefficiency of the parallel search algorithm are the larger number of nodes searched, the lack of transposition table access to the bottom of the tree, load imbalance, and communication overheads.

The "double hump" shape of the curves is also interesting. The dip at 16 processors is where the master in a one-level hierarchy has too many slaves, but a two-level hierarchy would be too narrow. This occurs again at 256 processors. Here, the processor hierarchy

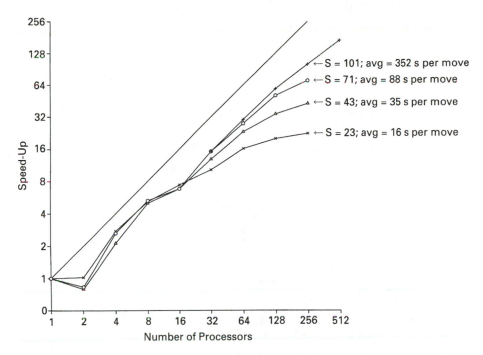

Figure 5.6 The speedup of the parallel chess program as a function of machine size and search depth. The results are averaged over a representative test set of 24 chess positions. The speedup increases dramatically with search depth, corresponding to the fact that there is more parallelism available in larger searches. The uppermost curve corresponds to tournament play—the program runs more than 100 times faster on 256 nodes as on a single nCUBE node when playing in tournament conditions, and the speedup is 170 for 512 processors.

needs to be three-level some of the time. Though the active load-balancing procedure does change the processor hierarchy this is only temporary, and the hierarchy is often reset to its starting state. Perhaps the speedup results indicate that a more flexible processor allocation scheme could do somewhat better.

Overall, the speedup results support our original hypothesis that large numbers of processors can be useful in a parallel alpha-beta search. Here, a "large" number of processors means many more processors than the branching factor of the game tree (the typical number of legal moves). A single-level hierarchy of processors, that is, a simple master–slave parallel program, cannot give scalable speedup for game tree search. By going to a multilevel, master–slave hierarchy of processors, we have evidence that scalable speedup for large search trees is achievable.

Real-Time Graphical Monitor

One tool we found extremely valuable in program development and tuning was a real-time performance monitor with color-graphics display. The nCUBE installation has a high-resolution color-graphics monitor driven by many parallel connections into the

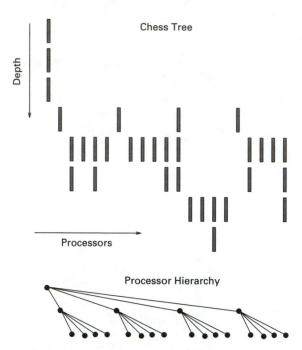

Figure 5.7 Schematic diagram of the real-time graphical monitor. The top half of the picture shows where the processors are (currently) on the chess tree. Depth into the tree grows downward and processor labels grow to the right. Each time a processor descends to another level on the game tree, it draws a rectangle to denote the fact. The bottom part of the picture shows the current processor hierarchy. This moves as active load balancing occurs.

hypercube. This gives sufficient bandwidth to support a status display from the hypercube processors in real time.[†]

A diagram of the monitor graphics is shown in Figure 5.7. The display shows where in the chess tree each processor is, and it draws the processor hierarchy as it changes. By watching the graphics screen we can see a load imbalance develop and observe dynamic load balancing as it tries to cope with the imbalance. Though intrusive (the search is slowed down by a factor of three), the performance monitor gave us the first evidence that dynamic load balancing was necessary, and it was invaluable in debugging and tuning the load balancing code.

5.9 Outlook

We developed the chess program over a period of two years on the 512-processor nCUBE I machine of the Caltech Concurrent Computation Program. The program, named Waycool, was entered in several of the ACM Computer Chess Championships.

[†] The performance monitoring software was written by Rod Morison.[13]

Though both our speedup results and our absolute speed were good (we searched at a speed of 10,000–20,000 chess boards per second at the tournaments), we were not able to match the standard of play of the powerful chess engines such as Deep Thought and Hitech,[3, 10] programs on a Cray (Cray Blitz),[14] or even the very carefully crafted programs such as Mephisto™ (a commercial chess program). We accepted this as the natural consequence of our decision to focus on issues of parallelism rather than the chess-specific parts of the problem.

For the future, we think our results will help in the construction of better parallel search programs. We hope to port the skeleton of our parallel alpha-beta search to current message-passing systems so that it can form the basis for future efforts.

Acknowledgments

We thank Geoffrey Fox and the Caltech Concurrent Computation Project for supporting us in this work. Eric Umland actually began the chess effort in 1985 but, tragically, died before it came to fruition. We also thank Rod Morison, Ken Barish, and Rob Fätland for helping with various phases of this project.

References

1 P. W. Frey. "An Introduction to Computer Chess," *Chess Skill in Man and Machine.* (P. W. Frey, Ed.) Springer-Verlag, New York, 1983.

2 A. Newell, J. Shaw, and H. Simon. "Chess Playing Programs and the Problem of Complexity," *IBM Journal of Research and Development.* **2**, 320–335, 1958.

3 F. Hsu, T. Anantharaman, M. Campbell, and A. Nowatzyk. "A Grandmaster Chess Machine," *Scientific American.* 44, Oct. 1990.

4 D. E. Knuth and R. W. Moore. "An Analysis of Alpha-Beta Pruning," *Artificial Intelligence.* **6**, 293–326, 1975.

5 A. L. Zobrist. A Hashing Method with Applications for Game Playing." Tech. Report No. 88, Computer Sciences Department, University of Wisconsin, Madison, WI, 1970.

6 S. Otto and E. Felten. "Chess on a Hypercube," *Proceedings.* 3rd Conf. on Hypercube Concurrent Computers and Applications. ACM Press, New York, 1988.

7 T. von Eicken, D. Culler, S. Goldstein, and K. Schauser. "Active Messages: A Mechanism for Integrated Communication and Computation," *Proceedings.* 19th Annual International Symposium on Computer Architecture, ACM Press, New York, 1992, pp. 256–266.

8 E. W. Felten. "Generalized Signals: An Interrupt-Based Communication System for Hypercubes," *Proceedings.* 3rd Conf. on Hypercube Concurrent Computers and Applications, ACM Press, New York, 1988, pp. 563–565.

9 T. A. Marsland and F. Popowich. "Parallel Game-Tree Search." Tech. Report No. TR-85-1, Department of Computing Science, University of Alberta, Edmonton, 1984.

10 C. Ebeling. *All the Right Moves: A VLSI Architecture for Chess.* MIT Press, Cambridge, MA, 1985.

11 W. Dally. "A VLSI Architecture for Concurrent Data Structures." PhD dissertation, Tech. Report No. 5209:TR:86, Department of Computer Science, California Institute of Technology, Pasadena, CA, 1986.

12 I. Bratko and D. Kopec. "A Test for Comparison of Human and Computer Performance in Chess," in *Advances in Computer Chess III.* (M. Clarke, Ed.) Pergamon, Oxford, U.K., 1982, pp. 31–55.

13 R. Morison. "Interactive Performance Display and Debugging Using the NCUBE Real-Time Graphics System," *Proceedings.* 3rd Conf. on Hypercube Concurrent Computers and Applications, ACM Press, New York, 1988, pp. 760–763.

14 "Cray Blitz," in *Computer Chess II.* (D. E. Welsh and B. Baczynskyj, Eds.) W. E. Brown, Dubuque, IA, 1985.

6

Connected Components Algorithms

JOHN GREINER and GUY E. BLELLOCH

Contents

In this chapter the authors discuss graphs and how they can be mapped onto parallel computers. Graphs are an exceedingly general data structure, with applications ranging from linear algebra and chess through economics and physics. This generality can lead to difficulties during implementation. In Chapter 5, trees, which are simply graphs, are discussed only in the context of a single application on a single target machine. Instead, this chapter describes how a single abstract graph algorithm—connected components—was implemented in its full generality on a variety of target machines.

6.1 Introduction

Many computational problems that arise in scientific and engineering applications can be naturally formulated in terms of *graphs*. Graphs are collections of *vertices* and *edges*, in which edges connect pairs of vertices. By abstracting a problem in terms of a graph it is often possible to use known algorithms or existing libraries, or gain insight from related graph problems.

One such example is in the solution of partial differential equations (PDEs) using finite element meshes, especially when the meshes are unstructured. Such PDEs can often be reduced to the solution of a sparse linear system. By viewing the sparse matrix as a graph, researchers have been able to make use of important results on finding graph separators with small cuts (a *graph separator* splits a graph into two almost equal parts, and the *cut size* is the number of edges that go between the parts). These separators in turn are used to pick a good elimination order in the direct solution of the linear systems. Such elimination orders can greatly reduce the fill-in (the number of nonzero terms that appear in the matrix during intermediate steps).

Another example is for the Swendsen–Wang algorithm, which is used to simulate the Ising model of theoretical physics.[1] In this method a system is modeled as a regular two- or three-dimensional lattice (mesh) in which each site can have a positive or negative spin. The algorithm works by recognizing *clusters* of sites and flipping the spin of each cluster as a whole. The clusters are determined by *bonds* between sites which are assigned as follows:

- If the spins of neighboring sites are in the same direction, then a bond is made between the sites with a probability that depends on the temperature.

- If spins are in opposite directions, no bond is made.

Once the bonds have been assigned, all sites attached by a bond are considered to be in the same cluster. Since it is possible to have long strings of bonds (typically true at lower temperatures), clusters can be large. The recognition of clusters is by far the most time-consuming step of the Swendsen–Wang algorithm. By viewing the lattice as a graph with the sites as vertices and bonds as edges, the problem of cluster formation is simply the problem of finding the *connected components* of a graph (one of the simplest graph problems).

Other examples of the use of graphs and graph algorithms are circuit simulation and layout, and the determination of the characteristics of various networks including the national power grid and communication networks.

In this chapter, we study the implementation of graph algorithms on parallel machines. In particular, we look at the connected components problem as a practical example, and compare several different algorithms for the problem in terms of efficiency and generality on the Connection Machines CM-2™ and the Cray Y-MP™. Many of the techniques used in these algorithms are useful for other graph algorithms. Such techniques include shortcutting (also called pointer-doubling), randomization (used to break symmetries), and hooking. A language called NESL is used to describe the algorithms. NESL allows a concise description and is very close to a high-level pseudocode. The overhead for learning the language is little more than that needed to understand the algorithms. The conversion of the code to High Performance Fortran (or a similar language) is relatively straightforward but somewhat messy because of the dynamic and irregular nature of the data structures.

Connected Components

One commonly used graph problem is finding the connected components of an undirected graph. Given a graph $G = (V,E)$, where V is a set of vertices (of size n) and E is a set of edges (of size m), the connected components of G are the sets of vertices such that all vertices in each set are mutually connected (reachable by some path) and no two vertices in different sets are connected.

Finding connected components is used in many different fields, such as computer vision,[2-5] where pixels in a two- or three-dimensional image are grouped into regions representing objects or faces of objects; spin models in physics,[1, 6, 7] as mentioned above; VLSI circuit design[8-10]; communication networks[11]; program analysis and implementation[12-14]; neural nets; and economics.[15] In short, connected components are useful in almost any situation in which graphs represent data.

In serial computation, connected components can be computed efficiently using a depth-first search. Starting from an initial vertex, edges are traversed from *visited* vertices to *unvisited* vertices, and each of these vertices is labeled with the name of the original vertex of the search. When this search is exhausted, the next unvisited vertex is used to start another search. Since each edge is traversed exactly once and each vertex visited exactly once, the algorithm requires $O(n + m)$ work to label the connected components. This algorithm is very simple and can be implemented in about 15 lines of C code.

Many parallel algorithms have been suggested for solving the connected components problem.[16-28] These tend to be quite different from the serial algorithms. Most are based on repeatedly forming trees out of all the vertices and a subset of the edges, and then contracting the trees. Such algorithms are discussed in detail in Section 6.3.

The connected components problem has a simple serial algorithm and many applications and parallel algorithms that have been designed for it, but there has been little success in getting a fast, general-purpose, connected components algorithm running on parallel machines. There has been some success in special-purpose algorithms that run on certain types of graphs[2, 4–7, 29, 30] (many of which appear in the previously mentioned applications), but these algorithms do not extend to other types of graphs. This is typical of the state of the art in the implementation of parallel graph algorithms.

The purpose of the work described in this chapter was to study various parallel algorithms suggested in the literature for finding connected components and to improve them to get a practical implementation. Our goal was to develop a general-purpose connected components algorithm that works on any graph but achieves running times close to those of special-purpose algorithms designed for particular types of graphs. Because most of the work on parallel algorithms for connected components have derived complexity in terms of asymptotic analysis, aspects of the algorithms that cause constant multiplicative factors are often ignored. We have thoroughly analyzed those aspects of existing algorithms that can be trimmed while still guaranteeing their correctness. By doing this we have made several improvements in constant factors and in the asymptotic performance for particular types of graphs, although we have not made any improvements in the worst-case asymptotic complexity (big-O) of the algorithms.

For the purpose of generality, we decided not to work with algorithms designed for specific communication networks, such as meshes or hypercubes. Of the network-independent algorithms, those that seemed most promising were the Awerbuch–Shiloach[16] algorithm (a variation of the Shiloach–Vishkin[26] algorithm) and the random-mate[18, 25] algorithm. We implemented these and executed them on the Connection Machine CM-2 and the Cray Y-MP (the parallelism allows us to vectorize code fully on the Cray). We then made several improvements. We also implemented a hybrid algorithm that uses features from both algorithms. We ran all the algorithms on four classes of graphs: subgraphs of two- and three-dimensional meshes (these were selected since they appear very frequently in practice), graphs in which each vertex chooses k random neighbors, and fully connected graphs with random subsets of the edges selected.

This chapter analyzes each improvement and describes how well each works for the different types of graphs and as a function of problem size. Our overall conclusion is that our hybrid algorithm or its variant performed best on all our test graphs, outperforming many of the others by a factor of 10 or more. On the Cray, we achieved running times as good or better than those of any previously reported implementations (e.g., see References 7 and 30). We were able to process graphs with five million edges in about a second. Our times on the CM-2 were not as good because of the cost of communication; but they were still as good as previously reported results for a special purpose algorithm.[31]

To implement our algorithms we chose NESL[32] (NESted Language) rather than other data-parallel languages such CM Fortran, C*, or Fortran 90. NESL has two important advantages:

- The data structures in the connected components algorithms, as with other graph algorithms, tend to be very dynamic: the algorithms tend to change dynamically the number of edges on every step. NESL has very good support for such dynamic structures, including automatic sequence allocation and deallocation and automatic load balancing of structures.

- We wanted to run the algorithms on both the CM-2 and the Cray without rewriting any source code.

A disadvantage of NESL is that the code it generates is about two times slower than CM Fortran code (or vectorized Fortran on the Cray). Since we were concerned primarily with relative times, this was not a grave concern. Now that we have determined the best algorithm, it would not be hard to translate to other data-parallel languages.

6.2 NESL

NESL is a strongly typed, applicative (side-effect free) language. It is based on sequences (vectors) as a primitive parallel data type and provides a large set of built-in parallel operations that operate on sequences. In this chapter, sequences will either contain atomic values, as in the sequence

```
[3, -4, -9, 5, 2, 5]
```

or pairs of values, as in the sequence

```
[(2,3), (7,10), (5,-8), (11,2)]
```

and can vary in size dynamically (the size does not have to be specified at compile time).[†]

Parallelism is achieved in NESL through the ability to apply any function in parallel over each element of a sequence. The application of a function over a sequence is specified using a set-like notation similar to *set-formers* in SETL.[33] For example, the expression

```
{negate(a) : a in [3, -4, -9, 5]};
```
$\Rightarrow$ [-3, 4, 9, -5]

negates each elements of the sequence [3, -4, -9, 5]. This construct can be read as "in parallel for each a in the sequence [3, -4, -9, 5], negate a." The symbol $\Rightarrow$ points to the result of the expression. Henceforth we will refer to the notation as the *apply-to-each* construct. The apply-to-each construct also provides the ability to subselect elements of a sequence: the expression

```
{negate(a) : a in [3, -4, -9, 5] | a < 4};
```
$\Rightarrow$ [-3, 4, 9]

can be read as, "in parallel for each a in the sequence [3, -4, -9, 5] such that a is less than 4, negate a." The elements that remain maintain their order relative to each other.

It is also possible to iterate over multiple sequences. The expression

```
{a + b : a in [3, -4, -9, 5]; b in [1, 2, 3, 4]};
```
$\Rightarrow$ [4, -2, -6, 9]

---

† In general, NESL allows the elements of a sequence to be of any type, including structures or other sequences.

adds the two sequences elementwise. The apply-to-each also allows *pattern-matching* to extract one of the elements of each pair in a sequence of pairs:

```
{a : (a,b) in [(2,3), (7,10), (5,-8), (11,2)]};
```
$\Rightarrow$ [2, 7, 5, 11]

NESL supplies two parallel communication instructions:

- seq -> ind returns the values of the sequence seq at the indicated indices ind. This instruction can be thought of as a *parallel read* since we are reading a set of values from seq. Any given index may occur more than once in the sequence of indices, corresponding to a concurrent read of the corresponding value.

- seq <- ind_val, where each element of sequence ind_val is a pair consisting of an index and value, returns the sequence that is like seq except that the given values are placed at the corresponding indices. This can be thought of as a *parallel write*. When an index occurs multiple times, corresponding to a concurrent write, one of the corresponding values is arbitrarily picked.

An example of the read instruction is

```
[8, 17, 14, 9, 11, 22] -> [0, 5, 2, 0];
```
$\Rightarrow$ [8, 22, 14, 8]

where the 0, 5, 2, and 0 are indices. Note that the indices are zero based.
An example of the write instruction is

```
[8, 17, 14, 9, 11, 22] <- [(1,29),(4,64),(1,13),(2,19)];
```
$\Rightarrow$ [8, 13, 19, 9, 64, 22]

Note that the 13 rather than the 29 happened to be written into location 1.

Some other parallel functions are also supplied for manipulating sequences. Table 6.1 lists some of these functions; a full list can be found in the NESL manual.[32]

The let construct is used to bind local variables. For example, in the code

```
function foo(x,y) =
  let v = x * y;
      w = v + x;
  in v/w $
```

the v is bound to the product of x and y, and then w is bound to the sum of v and x. Finally the quotient of v and w is returned. The call foo(2.0,3.0) would return .75.

Comments in NESL are surrounded by percent signs.

6.3 Connected Component Algorithms

This section describes the two basic algorithms used in this chapter. Both are general purpose in the sense that they are applicable to all graphs. The NESL code to implement the algorithms is interspersed with the algorithms' descriptions.

Operation	Description
#a	Return length of sequence a
a[i]	Return element at position i of sequence a
sum(a)	Return sum of sequence a
index(n)	Return sequence of integers 0 to (n - 1)
dist(v,n)	Return sequence of n copies of v
all(flags)	Return true if all flags of sequence flags are true
a ++ b	Append sequences a and b

Table 6.1   Seven of the sequence operations supplied by NESL.

For most examples, we will use the graph in Figure 6.1. In these algorithms, the vertices of a graph are labelled by the integers 0 through $n - 1$. The edges of a graph are represented by a sequence of pairs of endpoints. For the Awerbuch–Shiloach algorithm, each edge is to be given twice, pointing in each direction, as in

[(0,3),(3,0),(0,1),(1,0),(3,4),(4,3),(1,4),(4,1),(4,5),(5,4),(5,8),(8,5)]

For random-mate, each edge need be given only once, pointing in either direction, as in

[(3,0),(1,0),(3,4),(4,1),(4,5),(5,8)]

The algorithms compute a new labeling of each vertex to a connected component. Each component is represented by a single arbitrary member of the component: one of the vertices. Thus, the output of each algorithm is a sequence of the component names for each vertex of the graph, such as [0,0,2,0,0,0,7,7,0] for the example graph.[†]

One common data structure is a *tree*, as defined by a parent relation. Trees are represented by a sequence of integers, where each element contains the index of its parent or itself, if it has no parent. For example, one possible set of trees for the example graph is given in Figure 6.2. These trees are represented by the sequence [0,0,2,0,3,4,7,7,5]. Members of the tree which have no parent are *roots*, for example, 0, 2, and 7. Members which have no children are *leaves*, for example, 1, 8, 6, and 2. A tree of depth one is sometimes called a *star*.

Two common operations on trees in this chapter, as well as in other graph algorithms, are *hooking* and *shortcutting*. Hooking combines sets of trees to form larger trees if there is an edge between the trees. For example, consider the trees represented by [0,1,2,3,4,5,6,7,8], which are all of depth zero because each vertex points to itself. We can then hook these trees with a set of edges. If we use the edges

[(1,0),(3,0),(4,3),(5,4),(8,5),(6,7)]

---

† The position in the sequence corresponds to the vertex number.

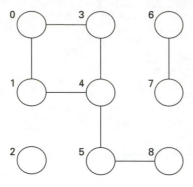

Figure 6.1   An example graph.

the result is the set of trees given in Figure 6.2. Hooking is simply done with the write (<-) instruction, as in

```
[0,1,2,3,4,5,6,7,8] <- [(1,0),(3,0),(4,3),(5,4),(8,5),(6,7)];
⇒ [0,0,2,0,3,4,7,7,5]
```

Note that these edges and their orientation were hand-picked to hook the maximum amount possible with this graph. The idea behind hooking in the various connected component algorithms is to merge subcomponents into larger components.

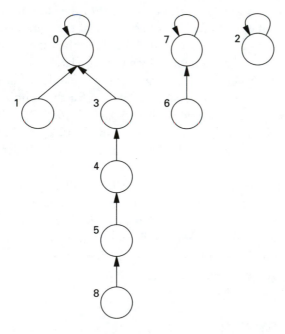

Figure 6.2   An example set of trees.

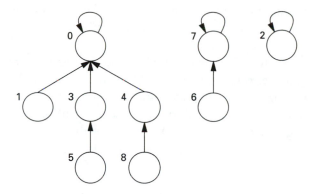

Figure 6.3   Example trees after shortcutting.

Shortcutting partially flattens trees, decreasing their depth by about half. For example, shortcutting the example trees results in Figure 6.3. Shortcutting is simply done with a read (->) instruction, as in:

```
[0,0,2,0,3,4,7,7,5] -> [0,0,2,0,3,4,7,7,5];
⇒ [0,0,2,0,0,3,7,7,4]
```

A tree of depth d is reduced to a star by $\log_2 d$ shortcutting steps.

Following are a few other common functions in these algorithms. Similar to shortcutting, this function maps a parent relation over a sequence of edges, rather than over itself:

```
function parents_edges(ps,es) =
{(pfrom,pto) : pfrom in ps -> es_froms(es);
               pto in ps -> es_tos(es)} $
```

These functions select the sources or targets of sequences of edges, respectively:

```
function es_froms(es) = {from : (from,to) in es} $
function es_tos(es) = {to : (from,to) in es} $
```

Awerbuch–Shiloach

The algorithm of Awerbuch–Shiloach[16] (AS) is based on forming and combining trees of vertices, maintaining the invariant relation that all vertices in a given tree belong to the same connected component. Initially, each vertex is in a separate tree, and the trees are combined to find the maximal such trees. The roots serve as representative elements of the trees, and the algorithm returns the sequence of the roots corresponding to each vertex.

Each iteration of AS hooks and shortcuts trees, and the algorithm terminates when all trees are stars. (The algorithm does not create trees of depth zero.) As both of these operations maintain the specified invariant relation, the final trees correspond to the maximal connected components.

In particular, each iteration uses two different hooking steps. *Conditional* hooking combines two trees so that the larger-numbered root is below the smaller. *Unconditional* hooking only hooks stars onto other trees. When combined, they ensure that no cycles are created in the trees. Also, they hook such that the sum of the heights of all trees is never increased.

Since shortcutting reduces the height of all trees by about half on each iteration, the algorithm requires $O(\log n)$ hooking steps, each of $O(m)$ work. So, the algorithm has a work complexity of $O(m \log n)$ and a step complexity of $O(\log n)$.

In the following code, some of the original comments are also included for comparison. They use the naming scheme of $D(i)$ as the parent of the source vertex of the unnamed edge and $G(j)$ as the grandparent of the edge's target vertex.

```
function shortcut(ps) = ps -> ps $

% ST(i) := TRUE;
  If D(i) \= G(i) then ST(i),ST(G(i)) := FALSE;
  ST(i) := ST(G(i)) %

function starcheck(ps) =
let gps = shortcut(ps);
    sts = {p == gp : p in ps; gp in gps} <-
          {(gp,f) : p in ps; gp in gps | p /= gp};
in sts -> gps $

% If G(i) = D(i) and D(i) > D(j) then D(D(i)) := D(j) %
function cond_hook(ps,es) =
let pes = parents_edges(ps,es);
in ps <- {(pfrom,pto) : (pfrom,pto) in pes;
                        gpfrom in ps -> es_froms(pes)
                | (gpfrom == pfrom) and (pfrom > pto)} $

% If i is in a star and D(i) /= D(j) then D(D(i)) := D(j) %
function uncond_hook(ps,es) =
ps <- {(pfrom,pto) : (pfrom,pto) in parents_edges(ps,es);
                      instar in starcheck(ps) -> es_froms(es)
                | instar and (pfrom /= pto)} $
```

Shortcutting is also done each iteration, and the algorithm loops until only stars remain.

```
function AS_alg1(ps,es,iter) =
let ps1 = cond_hook(ps,es);
    ps2 = uncond_hook(ps1,es);
in if all(starcheck(ps2)) then ps2
   else AS_alg1(shortcut(ps2),es,1+iter) $
```

Before and after the two forms of hooking, the trees always have a form such that a nonleaf vertex is numbered greater than its parent. Neither conditional nor unconditional hooking will create a cycle. For the former, this holds because of the conditions on any edges used in that step. For the latter, if two stars were able to hook to each other, then neither tree could have been affected by the immediately previous conditional hooking (since it creates nonstars because there are no trees of depth zero), but such trees would have been hooked during conditional hooking. Since this is a contradiction, this possibility cannot occur. These arguments are expanded into a full proof in Reference 16.

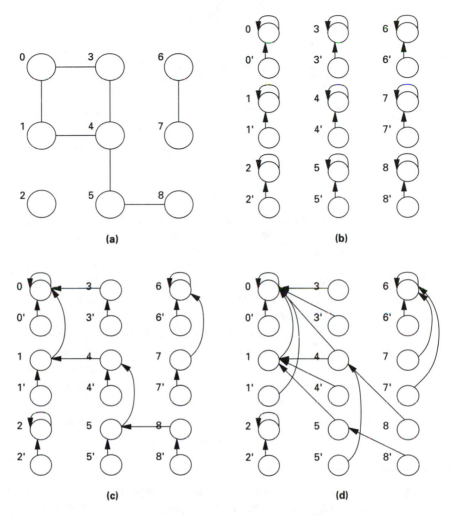

Figure 6.4 Awerbuch–Shiloach algorithm: (*a*) The graph. (*b*) Trees with dummy vertices and edges. (*c*) Trees after conditional hooking. (*d*) Trees after shortcutting.

Figure 6.4 demonstrates a single iteration of the algorithm. In the example, unconditional hooking has no effect.

Initially, the graph is represented such that each vertex is in a separate tree. To ensure that there are no trees of depth zero, an extra n "dummy" vertices and n edges are added. These edges connect the ith vertex with the ith dummy vertex. Doubling the size of the graph in this manner does not affect the complexity of the algorithm.

```
function cc_AS1(es,num_vs) =
let (new_es,newnum_vs) = add_dummy_verts(es,num_vs);
in remove_dummy_verts(AS_alg1(index(newnum_vs),
                        direct_edges(new_es),0)) $
```

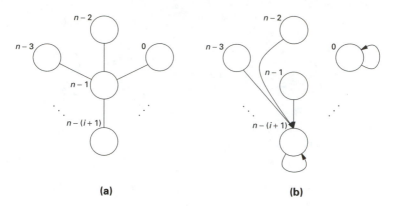

Figure 6.5 (*a*) **Worst case graph for conditional hooking.** (*b*) **Trees after** *i* **iterations of conditional hooking.**

Unconditional hooking is necessary to avoid a worst case of $n - 1$ iterations, as in the graph of Figure 6.5*a*, which would only hook one of the vertices on each iteration. (Figure 6.5*b* ignores dummy vertices and edges.)

This algorithm is a simplification of that of Shiloach–Vishkin (SV).[26] In particular, that algorithm allows a more general class of trees to be hooked during unconditional hooking; in place of the `starcheck` test is a test that determines whether a tree has been used so far in the current iteration. If it hasn't been used previously, it can be used for hooking. The extra data needed to compute this makes the SV algorithm somewhat more complicated and generally slightly slower (once AS is modified to not use dummy vertices).[34]

Random-Mate

The random-mate algorithm (RM) contracts the graph by combining vertices into supervertices. Edge endpoints are renamed using the new supervertices, and any self-edges are removed. The connected components of the new graph are the same as those of the original. The graph is contracted until no edges are left, so the remaining vertices correspond one-to-one to the connected components. Information about the contraction is saved to re-expand the graph, propagating the names of the components to all of the vertices.

This requires $O(\log m)$ iterations, each of $O(m_i)$ work, where m_i is the number of edges in the graph remaining on the ith iteration. If the number of edges decreases geometrically, as the number of vertices does, the total work complexity is $O(m)$, but is $O(m \log n)$ in the worst case. The empirical evidence of Section 6.6 clearly shows this relationship. The step complexity is $O(\log n)$.

This algorithm is based on an adaptation by Reif[25] of the SV algorithm, replacing both kinds of hooking with a single randomized version, called mating. In this step, each vertex is randomly assigned to be a child or parent, with equal probability. Edges from children to parents are selected, with the restriction that only one edge may be selected

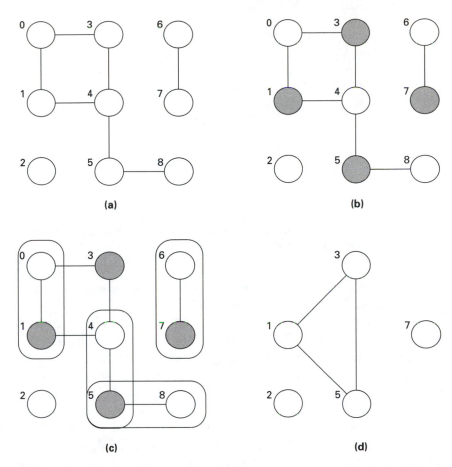

Figure 6.6 Random-mate algorithm: (*a*) The graph. (*b*) Partitioning parents (*shaded*) and children. (*c*) Picking active edges. (*d*) After contracting.

pointing from any given vertex. This restriction is implemented via an implicit concurrent write, which arbitrarily picks a single target for the vertex.

The algorithm combines mating with the graph contraction of Phillips,[24] so that each successive iteration uses a smaller graph. The selected, or *active*, edges are used for this contraction, producing supervertices. The edges are contracted by renaming with the new supervertices and removing self-edges. On average, at least one-fourth of the vertices will be contracted, since half of the vertices are expected to be children and at least half of these will have parents. As the names imply, these edges correspond to the parent relation of the trees in the AS algorithm. After the graph has been fully contracted, the remaining vertices represent the connected components of the original graph, and correspond to the roots of the trees formed in the previous algorithm.

Figure 6.6 graphically represents one iteration of contraction. Next, the graph must be re-expanded using the active edges, to propagate the name of these final supervertices to the vertices of the original graph. For this purpose, the active edges of each iteration

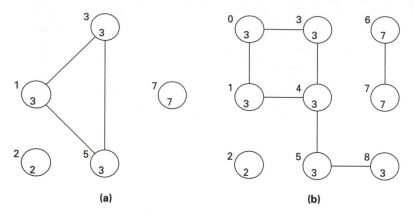

Figure 6.7   **Random-mate algorithm: (*a*) Root names (*within circles*) of contracted graph. (*b*) Propagating root names.**

are placed on the run-time recursion stack. The previous example is continued with the expansion step, as diagrammed by Figure 6.7.

The algorithm is implemented by the NESL code below. As mentioned, the algorithm is recursive, so that the active edges are placed on the stack for use during expansion. The graph is expanded as the recursion stack unwinds, and the supervertex relation returned from recursive calls and the active edges are used to propagate the name of each root to all vertices in its component.

While the vertices are contracted in the sense that some are removed from consideration by using supervertices (compare Figure 6.6 parts *c* and *d*), these vertices are merely renamed. The number of vertices does not decrease as the algorithm recurses; instead, the new sequence of vertices contains duplicates. Reducing the number of vertices is deferred until Section 6.4.

```
function partition(es,step) =
{nthbit(from,step) xor nthbit(to,step) : (from,to) in es} $

function flip_edges(es,flips) =
{(select(flip,to,from),select(flip,from,to)) :
 (from,to) in es; flip in flips} $

function active_edges1(es,step) =
let aes = {e : e in es; active in partition(es,step) | active};
in flip_edges(aes,{nthbit(from,step) : from in es_froms(aes)}) $

function shrink_edges(ps,es) =
{(pfrom,pto) : (pfrom,pto) in parents_edges(ps,es) | pfrom /= pto} $

function reduce_graph1(vs,es,bits,step) =
if zerop(#es) then vs
else let % contraction %
        aes    = active_edges1(es,step);
        new_vs = vs <- aes;
        new_es = shrink_edges(new_vs,es);
```

```
        rs     = reduce_graph1(new_vs,new_es,bits,
                                rem(step+1,bits));
    in   % Compute new roots -- expansion %
        rs <- {(afrom,v) : afrom in es_froms(aes);
                           v in rs -> es_tos(aes)} $
function cc_RM1(es,num_vs) =
if plusp(num_vs)
then reduce_graph1(index(num_vs),es,
                   trunc(log(float(num_vs),2.0)) + 1,0)
else [] int % the empty vector of integers % $
```

6.4 Modifications to Algorithms

In this section, we describe modifications to the previous algorithms. These modifications have two important goals: reducing the graph size and reducing communication costs. Naturally, there are also some optimizations that are algorithm specific and not directly related to these goals.

First, major changes are made to the AS algorithm, greatly reducing the constant factor in its complexity. Next, a modest improvement is given for random-mate. Finally, a hybrid algorithm, incorporating both shortcutting and graph contraction is developed. The effects of these changes on the execution times are discussed in Section 6.6.

AS–Based Modifications

The modifications made in this section are grouped into these three categories of goals: reducing the graph size, reducing communication, and algorithm-specific optimizations. Since some of the modifications are interconnected, subsequent modifications sometimes alter previous ones. In particular, the final algorithm does not incorporate all of the described modifications because of redundancy. A comparison of the effects of these changes in made is Figure 6.16.

Naturally, reducing the size of the graph reduces the amount of computation to be done. In this pursuit, the following optimizations are made:

* Eliminate dummy vertices and edges.

* Contract edges, as in random-mate.

* Do more shortcutting.

The most glaring inefficiency results from the dummy vertices and edges added at the beginning of the algorithm, effectively doubling the size of the graph. These dummies are necessary for the first iteration to ensure that if a tree has been hooked by conditional hooking, then the result is not a star for unconditional hooking. However, specialized versions of hooking and starchecking can be written for that iteration so that the dummy vertices and edges need never be added. The following routines ensure that any vertices with incident edges will be hooked on the first iteration so that unconditional hooking is still guaranteed not to produce cycles.

```
function lonecheck(ps) =
let vs = index(#ps);
in {p == n : p in ps; v in vs} <-
   {(p,f) : p in ps; v in vs | p == v} $

function lone_cond_hook(ps,es) =
ps <- {(pfrom,pto) : (pfrom,pto) in parents_edges(ps,es)
                   | pfrom > pto} $

function lone_uncond_hook(ps,es) =
ps <- {(pfrom,pto) : (pfrom,pto) in parents_edges(ps,es);
                     instar in lonecheck(ps) -> es_froms(es)
                   | instar and (pfrom /= pto)} $
```

The next modification is to adapt the edge contraction of the random-mate algorithm. On each iteration, the edges are replaced by renaming each endpoint with its parent and then eliminating self-edges. A vertex's parent is in the same connected component as the vertex, so if there were a path between two vertices using the old edges, there is still a path between the vertices using the new live edges and the parent relation. Thus, all information necessary for finding the connected components remains. Even though the number of live edges monotonically decreases, the complexity of each iteration is still bounded by the number of vertices because of the shortcutting operations.

To further reduce the depth of the trees, extra shortcutting may be done each iteration. This has two separate benefits. In conjunction with the previous modification of eliminating self-edges, the additional shortcutting produces more self-edges to be removed. Furthermore, having flatter trees allows more hooking to be done on any given iteration and allows the termination condition to be detected earlier. It is generally too expensive to compute the maximum depth of the trees, but the heuristic below gives a reasonable estimate of the maximum number of shortcuts needed, especially for grid-based graphs.

```
function shortcut_n(ps,n) =
if n <= 0 then ps else shortcut_n(shortcut(ps,n - 1)) $

function shortcut_heuristic(num_es) =
if zerop(num_es) then 1
else min(1,trunc(log(float(num_es),10.0))) - 1 $
```

An alternative is to guarantee that the maximal amount of shortcutting is done, which can be done by repeatedly shortcutting until the operation does not further change the trees, as in shortcut_max (below). In practice, however, the improvement resulting from using flatter trees is more than offset by the higher cost incurred by testing whether the shortcut operation modified the graph. (The constant 4 indicates how often to make this test, and is another heuristic.) On the other hand, by guaranteeing that all trees are stars further optimizations could be made, but this discussion is deferred until the subsection "Hybrid Algorithms."

```
function shortcut_max(ps) =
let gps = shortcut_n(ps,4);
in if all({p == gp : p in ps; gp in gps}) then gps
   else shortcut_max(gps) $
```

There is a method of reducing the communication costs in the algorithm. The use of starchecking as a test for termination can be specialized to eliminate much of the communication in this use of the routine. The code `all(starcheck(ps))` can be replaced by a call to

```
function starcheck_all(ps) =
all({p == gp : p in ps; gp in shortcut(ps)}) $
```

There are some additional optimizations that can be made, including

- Reduce the use of unconditional hooking.

- Use a less expensive termination condition.

Unconditional hooking is only necessary in a small percentage of cases. Empirical evidence suggests that a relatively small number of edges are ever used by the step. Only executing the step occasionally (here, every third iteration) improves performance, while still avoiding the need for a linear number of iterations. Also, since the number of live edges is by far the greatest during early iterations, it is best to avoid using the step then. In particular, the use of `lone_uncond_hook` can be omitted on the first iteration.

```
function uncond_hookp(iter) = zerop(rem(1+iter,3)) $
```

Assuming that the previous optimization of contracting the graph is used, the termination condition can be greatly simplified to remove all communication costs of starchecking. If there are no live edges left, it is clear that further iterations of the algorithm only shortcuts, so a special case is made of this to avoid overhead on the last iterations.

After making all of these modifications, the resulting main loop is

```
function AS_alg2(ps,es,iter) =
if zerop(#es) then shortcut_max(ps)
else let ps1 = cond_hook(ps,es);
         ps2 = if uncond_hookp(iter)
               then uncond_hook(ps1,es)
               else ps1;
         ps3 = shortcut_n(ps2,shortcut_heuristic(#es));
         es1 = shrink_edges(ps3,es);
      in AS_alg2(ps3,es1,1+iter) $

function cc_AS2(es,num_vs) =
let ps  = index(num_vs);
    es  = direct_edges(es);
    ps1 = AS_lone_cond_hook(ps,es);
    ps3 = shortcut_n(ps1,shortcut_heuristic(#es));
    es1 = shrink_edges(ps3,es);
in AS_alg2(ps3,es1,0) $
```

RM–Based Modifications

Our one RM optimization is to ensure that each iteration has a nonzero number of active edges, so that the algorithm does not loop through the entire `reduce_graph` routine without the graph changing. The following function simply loops until such a partition is found:

```
function active_edges2(es,bits,step) =
let aes    = {e : e in es; active in partition(es,step) | active};
    newstep = rem(step+1,bits);
in if zerop(#aes) then active_edges2(es,bits,newstep)
    else (flip_edges(aes,{nthbit(afrom,step) : afrom in es_froms(aes)}),
        newstep) $
```

A more general test would require that a "significant" number of active edges be selected in order to use the partition. But then the algorithm sometimes discards many partitions until one is used, and in practice, this did not improve the algorithm. An example of the effects of this change is shown in Figure 6.15.

An unconventional feature of this partitioning is that the mating is not truly random. The "randomness" is generated on the ith iteration by using the $i \bmod (\lfloor \log_2 n \rfloor + 1)$ bit of the (arbitrary) vertex numbers. The code below implements a more conventional version of partitioning. The extra argument flips is a sequence of the same length as that of the vertices, which is allocated only once for efficiency at the beginning of the algorithm. Because of the communication costs involved, the version of the algorithm using this partitioning (RM3) is generally slower in practice, as shown in Figure 6.15. In particular, the two routines produce partitions with similar numbers of active edges, except that the randomized version typically finds larger partitions on very sparse graphs.

```
function partition_rand(es,flips) =
let flips = flips <- {(v,zerop(rand(r))) :
                        r in dist(2,#es * 2);
                        v in es_froms(es) ++ es_tos(es)};
in ({from xor to : (from,to) in parents_edges(flips,es)},flips) $

function active_edges_rand(es,flips) =
let (actives,flips) = partition_rand(es,flips);
    aes            = {e : e in es; active in actives | active};
in if zerop(#aes) then active_edges_rand(es,flips)
    else flip_edges(aes,flips -> es_froms(aes)) $
```

Hybrid Algorithms

There are many ways these algorithms could be combined. One limited approach has already been shown: using the edge contraction of RM to improve the AS algorithm. As we will show, the two algorithms have different strengths, each performing better on some kinds of graphs than on others. Some means of interleaving the algorithms could combine their strengths.

For example, it could make sense to begin with random-mating, to contract many of the vertices and some edges, and then finish using AS. Bounding the maximum number of AS iterations would retain the $O(m)$ best-case work complexity of RM. As will be shown, RM increases the density of the graph in many cases, but the shortcutting of AS works particularly well on more dense graphs. Gazit[18] uses such a combination of a mating algorithm to preprocess sparse graphs into dense graphs, which are then used by an algorithm based on SV.

A more direct approach is to try to combine the graph contraction and shortcutting on each iteration of a hybrid algorithm. This is the approach taken in the following algorithm. Like AS, the algorithm is tree based. But, on each iteration, the trees are completely shortcutted so that only stars are used, which makes one of the preconditions for conditional hooking trivial and also makes unconditional hooking unnecessary. The other precondition for conditional hooking is met by ensuring that the edges are always pointing from the higher-numbered endpoint.

The remainder of the algorithm is more like that of RM. The hooking step is thought of as a renaming, thus creating supervertices. So, like RM the edges are then contracted using the new names. Additionally, the vertices which have just been renamed are removed. Then, the remaining vertices are renamed consecutively from zero. After a recursion on the new graph, an expansion phase is again necessary to undo this renaming and propagate the names of the roots back to all vertices.

```
function flip_up(es) =
flip_edges(es,{from > to : (from,to) in es}) $

% eliminate useless vertices, rename to 0, 1, ...,
  renaming edges accordingly %
function compress(new_vs,old_vs,es) =
let flags = {oldv == newv: oldv in old_vs; newv in new_vs}
    es1   = parents_edges(enumerate(flags),flip_up(es));
in (pack_index(flags),es1) $

function hybrid_alg(vs,es,iter) =
if zerop(#es) or zerop(#vs) then vs
else let % unconditional hooking %
        vs1 = shortcut_max(vs <- es);
        es1 = shrink_edges(vs1,es);
        % contraction %
        (new_vs,new_es) = compress(vs1,vs,es1);
        rs = hybrid_alg(index(#new_vs),new_es,iter+1);
    in % expansion %
      shortcut(vs1 <- {(i,v) : i in new_vs;
                              v in new_vs -> rs}) $

function cc_hybrid(es,num_vs) =
hybrid_alg(index(num_vs),flip_up(es),0) $
```

Figure 6.8 illustrates the contraction steps of one iteration of this hybrid algorithm. The expansion is like that of RM.

The algorithm loops for $O(\log n)$ iterations. Each iteration has a constant number of steps using the nodes, and $O(\log n)$ steps (primarily shortcutting) using the edges. Thus, it requires $O(\log^2 n)$ steps and $O(m \log n)$ work. Since the size of the graph decreases each iteration, it may be possible to prove better complexities.

One variation is to compress from the graph also those supervertices which have no remaining incident edges. Such vertices can be detected by the following function:

```
% return whether each vertex is connected to any other %
function connected(vs,es) =
let is      = index(#vs);
    connects = is <- direct_edges(es);
in {i \= c: i in is; c in connects} -> vs $
```

For some kinds of graphs, particularly grids that are not highly connected, the added reduction in the size of the graph outweighs the communication costs in this detection.

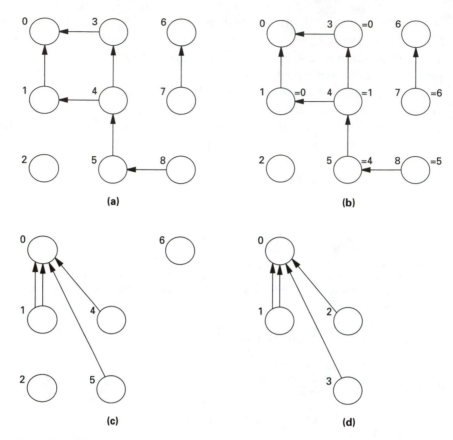

Figure 6.8 Hybrid algorithm: (*a*) The graph. (*b*) After hooking/renaming and shortcutting. (*c*) After shrinking edges. (*d*) After contraction.

6.5 Testing Method

To test the performance and the algorithms, the following classes of graphs were used:

- Subsets of two-dimensional toroidal grids. Each vertex has a subset of the four neighbors of such a grid.

- Subsets of three-dimensional toroidal grids. Each vertex has a subset of the six neighbors of such a grid.

- "Tertiary" graphs. Each vertex has three neighbors picked uniformly at random.

- Subsets of complete graphs. Each vertex is connected to a subset of all other vertices. To some degree, these represent the general case.

Grid-based graphs are commonly used in computer vision and physics. Subsets of complete graphs ("random graphs") represent the most general, and frequently the worst, case. Tertiary graphs are a representative intermediate case.

For the grid-based graphs, two different fractions of edges were used. Graphs having more than two edges per vertex are highly connected, since for the graph to be fully connected each vertex must have at least two edges. Conversely, graphs having fewer than two edges per vertex are not highly connected. So, for two-dimensional grids, using a random subset of more than half of the edges will result in a relatively highly connected graph. The testing here uses subsets containing 30% and 60% of the edges. Similarly, for three-dimensional grids we choose fractions less and greater than one-third: 20% and 40%. For complete graphs, fixed fractional subsets were again used. However, since the number of edges increases quadratically, larger graphs are increasingly connected.

We now define some standard terms of graph theory. These properties of graphs will affect the performance of the algorithms and allow us to explain our results.

The *degree* of vertices in the graph is the number of incident edges at each vertex and is a measure of the connectivity of the graph. Vertices in two-dimensional grids have a degree of four; three-dimensional grids, six; tertiary graphs, at most six; and random graphs, up to n.

An *edge separator decomposition* of a graph is a set of edges which, if removed, will separate the graph and its subgraphs into independent subgraphs of approximately the same size. The size of the separators of a graph is another measure of connectivity. The divide-and-conquer strategy of RM tends to do well on graphs with small separators. Two-dimensional grids have separators of size $O(n)^{1/2}$; three-dimensional grids, $O(n)^{3/2}$; tertiary graphs, $O(n)$; and random graphs, $O(n)$.

The *diameter* of a graph is the length of the longest of the shortest paths between all vertices in the graph. A large diameter indicates that the trees of the algorithms will be deep, so that the effects of shortcutting will be more significant. Two-dimensional grids have diameters of size $O(n^{1/2})$, and three-dimensional grids, $O(n^{3/2})$. Tertiary and random graphs typically have much smaller diameters; for example, the expected size for tertiary graphs is $O(\log n)$.

Recall that the AS-based algorithms assume that each edge is listed twice, pointed in each direction, whereas the RM and hybrid algorithms need only one copy of each edge. So, the AS-based algorithms must use twice as many edges to represent the same graph.

The NESL code was executed[†] on two machines. Unless otherwise specified, data were taken from trials on one-quarter of a 32,000-processor CM-2, that is, 8000 processors with 32 KB of local memory per processor. Some trials were also made using the vector facilities of one processor of a Cray Y-MP.

6.6 Computational Results

The figures of this section compare the performance of the various algorithms. Most plots display the average execution times of several algorithms for graphs ranging in size up to that dictated by the available memory. Execution times are taken as the average over ten trials each, whereas edge and vertex counts are taken from single trials.

---

† NESL is currently compiled to VCODE, which is then interpreted.

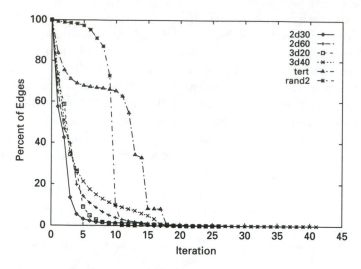

Figure 6.9   **Percent of original edges remaining after each iteration of the optimized RM algorithm (RM2).**

The first set of plots demonstrates how quickly the optimized algorithms contract the graphs. Figures 6.9–6.11 show the percentage of edges that remain after each iteration for each of these algorithms. Figure 6.12 shows the percentage of vertices remaining after each iteration of the hybrid algorithm, the only one to contract the vertices. These plots use the largest graphs allowed in the available memory of the CM-2, although smaller graphs produced similar results.

For the grid-based graphs, the early contraction is very quick, but many iterations are needed to eliminate the remaining edges, particularly for the more-connected graphs. For tertiary and, especially, random graphs, the RM algorithm uses relatively few iterations to terminate, but initially contracts the graph very little. Thus, these few iterations are relatively expensive.

On average, RM contracts between a quarter and a half of the vertices each iteration, depending on the class of graph. As shown by Phillips,[24] planar graphs have at most a constant multiple of more edges than vertices under consideration. And since RM contracts planar graphs into planar graphs, the number of edges decreases at a rate similar to that of the vertices. Figure 6.9 empirically confirms that fact and indicates that the same probably holds for three-dimensional grids.

Again, for random graphs, about the same number of edges are removed as vertices are contracted during the early iterations. But this is a small fraction of the number of edges, since the initial number of edges is proportional to the *square* of the initial number of vertices. Thus, during contraction the graph becomes increasingly dense until it is almost fully connected. At that point, edge contraction becomes very quick, as the number of edges is bounded by the square of the current number of supervertices. For tertiary graphs, a similar phenomenon is seen, except that since the initial number of edges is only a constant multiple of the initial number of vertices, the early iterations

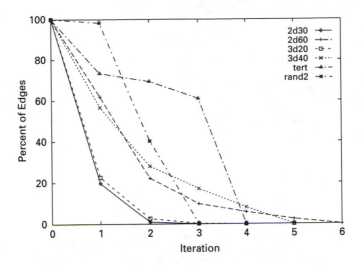

Figure 6.10 Percent of original edges remaining after each iteration of the optimized AS algorithm (AS2).

contract a greater fraction of the edges. As previously noted, a mating algorithm is used by Gazit[18] to transform sparse graphs into dense graphs because of this.

The plots for the optimized-AS and hybrid algorithms are very similar to that of RM, except that many fewer iterations are involved. In particular, both algorithms require only two iterations before most edges of random graphs are removed. Using less shortcutting in the AS algorithm produces results even more similar to that of RM.

RM contracts at least one-fourth of the vertices each iteration. But, the hybrid algorithm generally contracts more vertices by contracting (shortcutting) whole trees and

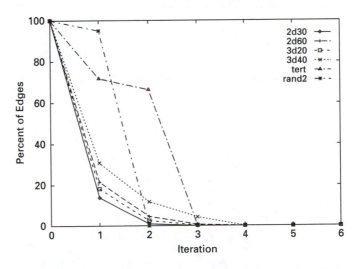

Figure 6.11 Percent of original edges remaining after each iteration of the hybrid algorithm.

6.6 COMPUTATIONAL RESULTS

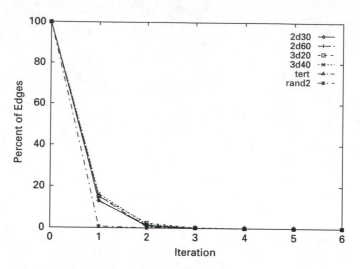

Figure 6.12 **Percent of original vertices remaining after each iteration of the hybrid algorithm.**

removing any resulting singletons. Empirically, the rate of contraction is large—well over 80% on each iteration. The hybrid algorithm's rate of contraction on random graphs is particularly high because the high connectivity of random graphs leads to large trees being contracted.

Figures 6.13 and 6.14 compare the optimized algorithms to each other on the toroidal grids. The former compares the optimized-AS, RM, and hybrid algorithms on two-dimensional grids using 30% of the edges; it also compares the same algorithms using 60% of the edges. The latter compares these algorithms on the three-dimensional grids using 20% and 40% of the graph edges.

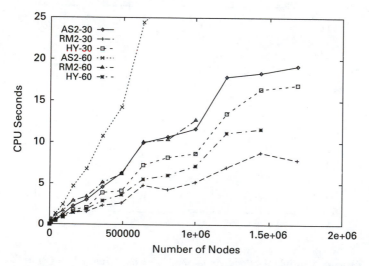

Figure 6.13 **Optimized algorithms on two-dimensional grids: 30% and 60%.**

CONNECTED COMPONENTS ALGORITHMS   Chapter 6

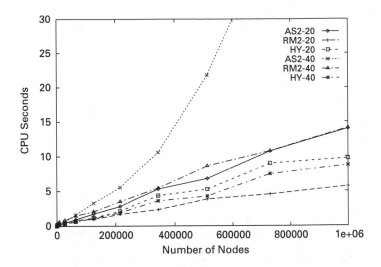

Figure 6.14 Optimized algorithms on three-dimensional grids: 20% and 40%.

These graphs fall into the class of graphs on which RM has an $O(m)$ work complexity. The greater work complexity of AS is evident, especially in the more-connected graphs. However, AS is faster than RM on smaller graphs. The hybrid algorithm is not consistently the best, as RM is faster on the less-connected grids. The "staircase" nature of the plots is due to NESL implementing sequences on the CM-2 by rounding their size up to the next power of two.

Figure 6.15 compares the optimized-AS algorithm to *all* of the RM algorithms on "random" graphs. Here, 2% of the edges of the complete graphs are used. Recall that RM3 is the version that uses pseudo-random partitioning.

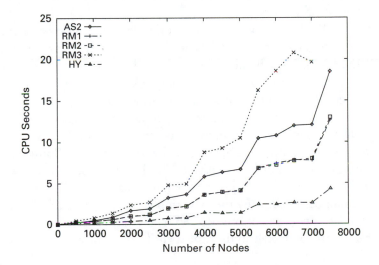

Figure 6.15 Optimized algorithms on random graphs: 2%.

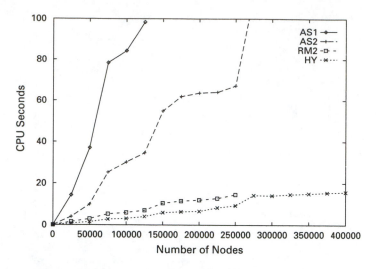

Figure 6.16   **Optimized algorithms on tertiary graphs.**

The RM algorithms do relatively poorly on these graphs. As shown by the first set of plots of this section, RM requires many iterations to remove a significant fraction of the edges. Since the cost of each iteration is proportional to the remaining number of edges, this results in poor performance.

Both versions of AS are compared to the other optimized algorithms using the tertiary graphs in Figure 6.16.

The optimized version of AS is approximately three times faster than the original version. Simply eliminating the dummy vertices and edges halves the time of the original algorithm, with the other modifications accounting for the remaining improvement.[†] But the RM and hybrid algorithms are still about three times faster than even the optimized version of AS on these graphs.

Finally, Figure 6.17 shows timings of the hybrid algorithm on each of these classes of graphs on the Cray. Here, the primary factor in execution time is the degree of connectedness of the graph. More highly connected graphs have fewer connected components and thus allow the graph to contract more quickly.

The hybrid algorithm variation, which also contracts the singleton vertices, lessens the disparity of execution times among graph types, as seen in Figure 6.18. Less highly connected graphs result in significant numbers of singletons, and the variation is up to 80% faster on the graphs tested than the original hybrid algorithm. But for more-highly connected graphs, the communication costs involved in detecting singletons dominate, and the original hybrid algorithm is up to 85% faster than the variation.

Dividing the number of edges by the execution time gives a figure which is comparable to the standard performance metric used in physics. There, the *spin updates* per second consists almost completely of the time spent finding the connected components.

---

† A detailed breakdown of the AS optimizations and the resulting speedups is found in Reference 34.

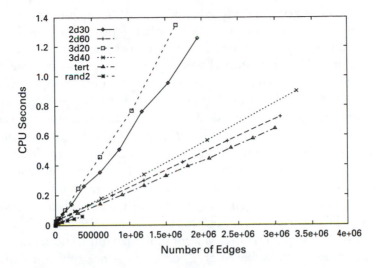

Figure 6.17 Hybrid algorithm on the Cray Y-MP™.

The fastest known algorithm is specialized for two-dimensional meshes and computes 2.5 million spin updates per second on a HITAC S820/80.[30] Figures 6.17 and 6.18 show that the hybrid algorithm computes up to 4.65 million edges per second, and the variant consistently computes between 2.2 and 3.5 million edges per second.

6.7 Conclusions

Our results argue that it is possible to get the same efficiency with a general-purpose graph algorithm that works on all graphs as with special purpose algorithms that work

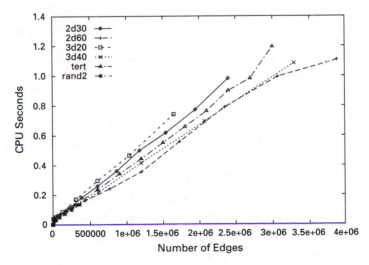

Figure 6.18 Hybrid variant (removing singletons) algorithm on the Cray Y-MP™.

on particular classes of graphs. We specifically showed this for the connected components problem and compared our general-purpose algorithm with an algorithm that works only on submeshes of a regular two-dimensional mesh. We also experimented with our algorithms on various other classes of graphs to see how they are affected by the type of graph. More studies are needed to show this for other graph problems.

The algorithms discussed in this chapter were implemented in a nonstandard language, NESL, rather than a more standard parallel language such as High Performance Fortran, because NESL is well suited for dynamic pointer-based algorithms such as those for finding connected components and other graph problems. We understand that most users would not have the time to learn a new language and environment. We expect, however, that many of the necessary features will become available in more standard languages in the future. Furthermore, all the ideas in the algorithms discussed in this chapter transcend the particular language that is used.

Although it is often stated that PRAM algorithms are not practical, our results argue that by tuning them it is possible to get good performance from theoretically good PRAM algorithms. The types of tuning we used involved removing unnecessary computations, reducing the size of the active data as the algorithm progressed, reducing the amount of communication, and mixing two different algorithms.

Our experimental results show that a hybrid algorithm using features of both the AS and RM algorithms is the best algorithm across all the graphs. It outperforms both RM and the optimized AS by a factor of up to 3, and the unoptimized AS by a factor of about 10.

References

1 R. H. Swendsen and J.-S. Wang. *Physical Review Letters.* **58**, 86, 1987.

2 A. Agrawal, L. Nekludova, and W. Lim. "A Parallel $O(\log N)$ Algorithm for Finding Connected Components in Planar Images," in *Proceedings of the International Conference on Parallel Processing.* Aug. 1987, pp. 783–786.

3 M.-Y. Kao and G. E. Shannon. "Linear-Processor NC Algorithms for Planar Directed Graphs." Technical Report 306, Computer Science Dept., Indiana University, Bloomington, IN, 1990.

4 W. Lim, A. Agrawal, and L. Nekludova. "A Fast Parallel Algorithm for Labeling Connected Components in Image Arrays." Technical Report NA86-2, Thinking Machines Corporation, Cambridge, MA, Dec. 1986.

5 X. D. Yang. "An Improved Algorithm for Labeling Connected Components in a Binary Image." Technical Report 89-981, Department of Computer Science, Cornell University, Ithaca, NY, Mar. 1989.

6 P. D. Coddington and C. F. Baillie. "Parallel Cluster Algorithms," in *LATTICE 90, International Conference on Lattice Field Theory.* Oct. 1990, pp. 17–79.

7 H. G. Evertz. "Vectorized Cluster Search," in *LATTICE 91, International Symposium on Lattice Field Theory. Nuclear Physics B, Proceedings Supplements,* Vol. 26B. May 1992, pp. 620–622.

8   S. Bhawmik, C. J. Lin, K.-T. Cheng, and V. D. Agrawal. "Pascant: A Partial Scan and Test Generation System," in *Proceedings of the IEEE 1991 Custom Integrated Circuits*. May 1991.

9   H. D. Groger. "A New Partition Lemma for Planar Graphs and Its Application to Circuit Complexity," in *Fundamentals of Computation Theory, 8th International Conference, FCT '91 Proceedings*. Sept. 1991, pp. 220–229.

10   H.-C. Shih, P. G. Kovijanic, and R. Razdan. "A Global Feedback Detection Algorithm for VLSI Circuits," in *Proceedings, 1990 IEEE International Conference on Computer Design: VLSI in Computers and Processors*. Sept. 1990, pp. 37–40.

11   B. Awerbuch, A. Baratz, and D. Peleg. "Cost-Sensitive Analysis of Communication Protocols," in *Proceedings of the Ninth Annual ACM Symposium on Principles of Distributed Computing*. Aug. 1990, pp. 177–187.

12   Z. Jovanovic. "Software Pipelining of Loops by Pipelining Strongly Connected Components," in *Proceedings of the International Conference on System Sciences*. Jan. 1991, pp. 351–365.

13   T. J. Marlowe and B. G. Ryder. "An Efficient Hybrid Algorithm for Incremental Data Flow Analysis," in *Conference Record of the Seventeenth Annual ACM Symposium on Principles of Programming Languages*. Jan. 1990, pp. 184–196.

14   P. J. Wright and R. J. Offen. "Optimized Redundant Cell Collection in a Parallel Graph Reduction Machine Using Reference Counts," *Algorithms and Parallel VLSI Architectures*. June 1990, pp. 373–382.

15   M. Houtman and E. Sterken. "The Structure of Macroeconomic Models," in *Dynamic Modelling and Control of National Economies 1989: Selected Papers from the 6th IFAC Symposium*. June 1989, pp. 281–286.

16   B. Awerbuch and Y. Shiloach. "New Connectivity and MSF Algorithms for Ultracomputer and PRAM," in *Proceedings International Conference on Parallel Processing*. 1983, pp. 175–179.

17   S. K. Das, N. Deo, and S. Prasad. "Parallel Graph Algorithms for Hypercube Computers," *Parallel Computing*. **13** (2), 143–158, 1990.

18   H. Gazit. "An Optimal Randomized Parallel Algorithm for Finding Connected Components in a Graph," *SIAM Journal of Computing*. **20** (6), 1991.

19   P. S. Gopalakrishnan, I. V. Ramakrishnan, and L. N. Kanal. "An Efficient Connected Components Algorithm on a Mesh-Connected Computer." Technical Report TR–1467, University of Maryland, College Park, MD, 1987.

20   S. Hambrusch and L. TeWinkel. "A Study of Connected Component Labeling Algorithms on the MPP," in *Proceedings of the Third International Conference on Supercomputing*. May 1988, pp. 477–483.

21   Y. Han and R. A. Wagner. "An Efficient and Fast Parallel-Connected Component Algorithm," *Journal of the Association for Computing Machinery*. **37** (3), 626–642, 1990.

22 D. S. Hirschberg, A. K. Chandra, and D. V. Sarwate. "Computing Connected Components on Parallel Computers," *Communications of the ACM.* **22** (8), 461–464, 1979.

23 P. M. Paradlos and C. S. Rentala. "Computational Aspects of a Parallel Algorithm to Find the Connected Components of a Graph." Technical Report CS–89–01, Department of Computer Science, Pennsylvania State University, University Park, PA, 1989.

24 C. A. Phillips. "Parallel Graph Contraction," in *Proceedings of the ACM Symposium on Parallel Algorithms and Architectures.* June 1989, pp. 148–157.

25 J. H. Reif. "Optimal Parallel Algorithms for Integer Sorting and Graph Connectivity." Technical Report TR–08–85, Harvard University, Cambridge, MA, Mar. 1985.

26 Y. Shiloach and U. Vishkin. "An $O(\log n)$ Parallel Connectivity Algorithm," *Journal of Algorithms.* **3**, 57–67, 1982.

27 U. Vishkin. "An Optimal Parallel Connectivity Algorithm," *Discrete Applied Mathematics.* **9** (2), 235–240, 1985.

28 J. Woo and S. Sahni. "Hypercube Computing: Connected Components." *Journal of Supercomputing.* **3**, 209–234, 1989.

29 T. Hagerup. "Optimal Parallel Algorithms on Planar Graphs," *Information and Computation.* **84** (1), 71–96, 1990.

30 H. Mino. "A Vectorized Algorithm for Cluster Formation in the Swendsen–Wang Dynamics," *Computer Physics Communications.* **66**, 25–30, 1991.

31 R. C. Brower, P. Tamayo, and B. York. "A Parallel Multigrid Algorithm for Percolation Clusters," *Journal of Statistical Physics.* **63** (1/2), 73–88, 1991.

32 G. E. Blelloch. "NESL: A Nested Data-Parallel Language (Version 2.6)." Technical Report CMU-CS-93-129, School of Computer Science, Carnegie Mellon University, Pittsburgh, Apr. 1993.

33 J. T. Schwartz, R. B. K. Dewar, E. Dubinsky, and E. Schonberg. *Programming with Sets: An Introduction to SETL.* Springer-Verlag, New York, 1986.

34 J. Greiner. "A Comparison of Data-Parallel Algorithms for Connected Components." Technical Report CMU-CS-93-191, School of Computer Science, Carnegie Mellon University, Pittsburgh, Aug. 1993.

7

Mathematical Programming and Modeling

STAVROS A. ZENIOS

Contents

This chapter surveys a broad subject area and shows techniques used to solve a variety of application problems on a number of different target machines. Like the graph algorithms discussed in Chapter 6, mathematical programming techniques are abstract, general, and powerful.

7.1 Introduction

Mathematical programming and modeling deals with the representation of complex systems—from engineering, the physical sciences, business and industrial applications—and the optimization of some performance measurement using a computer. The field was "defined" in the 1940s with the development of the simplex algorithm for linear programming,[1] although optimization models had been proposed even before that. The major thrust in this area came with the development of the digital computer. Major developments in computer systems have had a substantial impact on mathematical programming. For example, early computers with limited memory motivated the development of decomposition algorithms for the in-core/out-of-core solution of large-scale problems. Later, the development of the workstation was the catalyst for the proliferation of mathematical programming and modeling in several areas of application. This led to the development of mathematical modeling tools, like high-level algebraic languages.[2] With the PC revolution we have seen the development of a wide range of optimizers, linked with more traditional spreadsheet tools, statistical packages and so on.

This chapter looks at some techniques that have been employed to address the challenges for mathematical programming and modeling, created with the development of advanced architecture computers. The discussion is unavoidably biased from the author's experiences and is limited by the few years of research aimed in this direction; the first volume of research articles on parallel computing for mathematical programming was published in 1988.[3] Nevertheless, this chapter reviews diverse areas of application for mathematical programming where parallel computing is creating interesting opportunities (Section 7.2). It also discusses the problem of planning dynamical systems under uncertainty (Section 7.3) and presents—as a case study—the use of parallel computers in managing portfolios of complex financial instruments (Section 7.4).

While most of the chapters in this book follow a single application through various phases of analysis, implementation, and tuning, this chapter follows a broad subject area—mathematical programming and modeling. It looks at a number of problems in this area and surveys a number of techniques as applied to real problems. Extensive references are provided for readers who wish to follow up on the techniques.

7.2 General Applications of Mathematical Programming and Modeling

Consider the following broadly defined areas of application for mathematical programming:

- Optimization of the performance of engineering systems.

- Estimating optimal (i.e., equilibrium) states of physical systems.

- Optimal scheduling of complex sequences of operations.

- Planning for the efficient performance of large, complex systems.

Each area needs different optimization tools. Looking at these diverse areas we can comment on the challenges faced by different branches of mathematical programming, while keeping in mind the motivating applications.

Optimization of the Performance of Engineering Systems

We refer here to the problem of developing an abstract model that describes the performance of an engineering system. The engineer can change the design parameters of the system and observe its performance by means of the developed model. Optimization tools are then used to fine tune the design parameters until the model reaches a satisfactory—presumably optimal—level of performance. The actual engineering system—once it is built with the fine-tuned design specifications—is expected to operate optimally, as its abstract model did.

The textbook example is the specification of the dimensions of an airplane wing that results in an optimal aerodynamic profile, that is, optimal lift performance. First, a mathematical equation is developed that relates the various dimensions of the wing to the lift power. An optimization algorithm is then used to find the dimension values that result in maximum lift. Of course, as we move from the textbook example to an aircraft manufacturer we realize that complex nonlinear effects—air viscosity, temperature and pressure, effects of the wing boundary as it links with the fuselage, and so on—cannot be ignored. The mathematical equation for lift becomes a complex system of (differential) equations. The numerical solution of these equations presents its own challenges for large-scale computing (see Ortega and Voigt[4] for a recent survey). Furthermore, it has to be embedded within an optimization algorithm.

The computational challenges created by this area of application are in coupling optimization algorithms with numerical procedures for solving differential equations. Research in optimization methods motivated by this broad area of applications has concentrated on the design of unconstrained optimization algorithms, when the function and gradient evaluations are the computational bottlenecks. Most work has concentrated on speeding up the function/gradient evaluation procedures—typically the differential equation solvers (see Wright[5] for a recent discussion). We have also seen some innovative uses of parallelism in the design of the optimization algorithms. Two such examples are the use of *speculative* calculations[6] and the development of multidimensional search procedures.[7]

A speculative calculation is one whose outcome may not be needed. But if multiple processors are available, there is an advantage to executing this calculation so that if its value is required it will be available with no additional computational cost. A search algorithm for a minimization problem, for example, computes the function value along some direction of descent. If the function is sufficiently decreased from its current value, a new direction is computed. The computation of a direction requires first- and second-order derivatives. A speculative algorithm will calculate, for example, first derivatives every time it calculates the function value. If the function has decreased sufficiently and a new direction is needed, the gradient vector is already available. Otherwise, this vector is not used.

Estimating Optimal States of Physical Systems

Quite often, optimization methods are used to determine the equilibrium state of a physical system. A typical example is in the calculation of chemical equilibria:

> Given a set of feed conditions for a [...] multicomponent system at a given temperature and pressure, determine the number and state of phases that exist at equilibrium as well as the composition and quantity of each.[8]

This problem is usually attacked by formulating the Gibbs energy of the system and then invoking an optimization algorithm to compute states of minimum energy, subject to material balance equations. A comprehensive survey of models—and algorithmic approaches—in this general area is given in Seider et al.[9] While the problem is usually easy for simple systems, where only vapor–liquid equilibria exist, complications arise when vapor and multiple liquids are possible, or when chemical reactions are present, and so on. Hence, the energy function might have multiple local minima. Each of them corresponds to a qualitatively different state of equilibrium of the chemical process. To complicate matters further, recent trends in the chemical engineering community emphasize an integrated approach in both process design and flowsheet optimization. Engineers are not just interested in computing the equilibrium state of a process; instead, they want to design a process with the desirable equilibrium state.

The problems arising from this area of application fall under the realm of *global optimization*. Such problems have traditionally been among the most notorious in optimization. This is an area where advanced computer architectures could lead to substantial advances, especially since the presence of multiple local solutions provides a natural way to introduce parallelism. (See the volume by Floudas and Pardalos.[10])

One of the most successful efforts in exploiting parallelism in global optimization is with the use of a stochastic search algorithm.[11] One way to avoid getting "stuck" at one of the local solutions, without moving on to an overall best, is to introduce some randomness in the search direction. Instead of always moving towards a point of lower function value, we may accept, with some nonzero probability, steps that produce an increase in the function value. These steps will lead the algorithm, eventually, to points with even lower function values than the one found in the neighborhood of the current iterate. This approach borrows ideas from the techniques of simulated annealing.[12] Holmer et al.[13] applied these ideas to the calculation of optimal designs of callable bonds, a nontraditional approach to the design of financial products that leads to multiple local solutions.

A second area of application where optimization is used to identify a "desirable" (that is, equilibrium) state is in computerized tomography. This technique has broad applications in medical diagnosis, nondestructive material testing, meteorology, matrix balancing in economics and transportation, seismic data analysis, and so on. See Herman[14] for a textbook treatment of fundamentals, and Schneider and Zenios[15] for some applications. The problem is loosely defined as follows:

> Given a discretization of a physical domain, described by a matrix A, and a measurement vector y of observations made from outside this domain, infer the characteristics x of each discrete cell of the domain.

In the area of X-ray computerized tomography, the physical domain may be a cross section of the human body, y is a vector of attenuations of X rays projected through the body from outside sources and measured by outside detectors, and x are measurements of the X-ray absorption coefficients of each discretized cell of the cross section. The geometry of the discretization and the geometry of the X-ray emissions (parallel, single-source beam, etc.) impose the linear restrictions $Ax = y$. This system may have multiple solutions or, in the presence of noisy or incomplete measurements y, may have no solution at all. Finding a vector x that is the "most" likely given the observation y and some prior knowledge about the cross section leads to entropy optimization problems of the form:

$$\text{Maximize}_{x} \quad \text{ent}(x) \tag{7.1}$$

$$\text{Subject to} \quad Ax = y \tag{7.2}$$

Problems arising from this area of application are usually extremely large due to the desire to get increasingly accurate descriptions of the discretized domain. The number of variables is proportional to the number of cells that we wish to estimate. Entropy optimization problems with millions of variables are not uncommon. Over the last two decades researchers have concentrated on the design of iterative algorithms that do not need to store or manipulate the extremely large A matrix (see, for example, Herman[14] or Censor[16]). More recently we have seen an interest in designing algorithms suitable for parallel computers (see, for example, Herman et al.,[17] Censor,[18] or Zenios and Censor[19]). The next section describes the application of massively parallel computing to a simple instance of model (7.1)–(7.2): *matrix balancing.*

Data-parallel computing for the matrix balancing problem A problem that occurs frequently in economics, urban planning, statistics, demography, and stochastic modeling involves adjusting the entries of a large matrix to satisfy consistency requirements. It is typically posed as follows:

> Given a rectangular matrix A, determine a matrix X that is *close* to A and satisfies a given set of linear restrictions on its entries.

A well-studied instance of this problem—occurring in transportation planning and input–output analysis—requires that A be adjusted so that the row and column totals equal fixed positive values. A related problem occurring in developmental economics requires that the row and column totals (of a square matrix) be equal to each other, but not necessarily to pre-specified values. These problems are known as *balancing* the matrix A. The terms *matrix estimation* or *matrix adjustment* have also been used to describe the same problems.

Model formulation and algorithm One popular mathematical formulation for this problem is the following:

Problem 2.1 Given an $m \times n$ non-negative matrix $A = (a_{ij})$ and positive vectors $u = (u_i) \in \Re^m$ and $v = (v_j) \in \Re^n$, determine the matrix $X = (x_{ij})$ which solves the optimization problem:

$$\underset{x}{\text{Minimize}} \quad \sum_{(i,j) \in E} x_{ij} \left[\ln\left(\frac{x_{ij}}{a_{ij}}\right) - 1 \right] \tag{7.3}$$

$$\text{Subject to} \quad \sum_{(i,j) \in E} x_{ij} = u_i, \quad \text{for } i = 1,2,\ldots,m, \tag{7.4}$$

$$\sum_{(i,j) \in E} x_{ij} = v_j, \quad \text{for } j = 1,2,\ldots,n, \tag{7.5}$$

$$x_{ij} \geq 0, \quad \text{for } (i,j) \in E, \tag{7.6}$$

and so that $a_{ij} = 0 \Rightarrow x_{ij} = 0$.

A simple iterative algorithm that solves the problem is RAS.[15]

Algorithm 2.1 The RAS algorithm.

Input: An $m \times n$ non-negative matrix $A = (a_{ij})$, a positive vector $u = (u_i) \in \Re^m$ and a positive vector $v = (v_j) \in \Re^n$.

Step 0 (Initialization): Set $k = 0$ and $x_{ij}^0 = a_{ij}$, for all $i = 1,2,\ldots,m$, and $j = 1,2,\ldots,n$.

Step 1 (Row Scaling): For $i = 1,2,\ldots,m$, define

$$\rho_i^k = \frac{u_i}{\sum_j x_{ij}^k} \tag{7.7}$$

and update

$$x_{ij}^k \leftarrow x_{ij}^k \rho_i^k, \quad i = 1,2,\ldots,m, \quad \text{and} \quad j = 1,2,\ldots,n. \tag{7.8}$$

Step 2 (Column Scaling): For $j = 1,2,\ldots,n$, define

$$\sigma_j^k = \frac{v_j}{\sum_i x_{ij}^k} \tag{7.9}$$

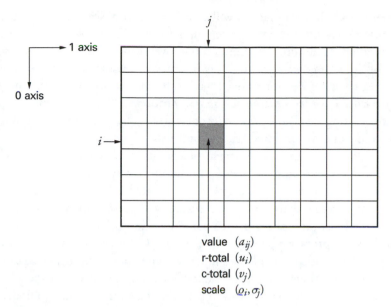

value (a_{ij})
r-total (u_i)
c-total (v_j)
scale (ϱ_i, σ_j)

Figure 7.1   Data-parallel representation of a dense matrix.

and update

$$x_{ij}^{k+1} = x_{ij}^k \sigma_j^k, \quad i = 1, 2, \ldots, m, \text{ and } j = 1, 2, \ldots, n. \tag{7.10}$$

Step 3: Replace $k \leftarrow k + 1$ and return to Step 1.

The RAS algorithm maps naturally to data-parallel computations. In particular, each element of the matrix can be assigned to a distinct processing element. Processing elements that store the data of a row will coordinate to compute a row sum and then proceed with the scaling of the row entries. Multiple rows can be updated concurrently, and the implementation will proceed similarly to update column sums. It is convenient to think of the processing elements as being arranged into a two-dimensional grid, with each element connected to its north, east, west, and south neighbors. Figure 7.1 illustrates the mapping of data onto a two-dimensional grid of processing elements.

Data-parallel implementation for dense problems The data-parallel implementation of RAS for dense problems uses the mapping of data to processors as illustrated in Figure 7.1. Every processor stores the matrix entry a_{ij} and the scaling factor. In addition, both the row total u_i and the column total v_j are stored at the same processor. Hence the $(i,j)^{\text{th}}$ processor stores a_{ij}, u_i, v_j, and the scaling factor.

With this mapping of data to processors, the RAS algorithm is implemented as follows: First, use an add–spread parallel prefix operation along the vertical 0th axis of the processors to spread the partial sum of the matrix entries in each column to some temporary memory location of each processor in the column. Each processor then divides the column total v_j by the partial sum, thereby computing its own value of the scaling factor. All processors in the same row will compute identical scaling factors at this point, but they do so locally with no need for communications. The implementation uses redundant computations to eliminate communication overhead. Finally, each processor uses its local copy of the scaling factor to multiply its entry of the matrix. The same operations are then repeated along the horizontal 1st axis of the processors to do the row scaling.

Data-parallel implementation for sparse problems The representation of sparse problems uses the *segmented parallel prefix* operations. The nonzero entries of the matrix are arranged in a one-dimensional array of processors. The nonzero entries are arranged both row-wise and column-wise. Segment bits are used to denote contiguous segments that contain the data of complete rows and columns. Every nonzero entry of the matrix is, therefore, stored twice: once in a row-wise format that allows row scaling and once in a column-wise format that allows column scaling. This scheme has some redundancy, but allows the efficient use of segmented-scan operations. This scheme for representing sparse matrices was proposed by Blelloch[20]; see also Chapter 6 in this book. Zenios and Lasken[21] proposed independently a similar scheme for representing sparse network problems. The two schemes are equivalent if one associates with a sparse matrix an incidence graph. That is, with each row or column of a matrix associate a node, and with a nonzero entry introduce an arc between the corresponding row node and column node. A comparison of alternative data structures for the representation of network problems is given in Nielsen and Zenios.[22]

Figure 7.2 illustrates the sparse representation of a small matrix. The various data stored at each processor are described below:

1 A field *s-row* of segment bits used to partition the processors into contiguous segments such that processors in the same segment correspond to entries of the same row.

2 A field *a-row* that holds the value of the entry a_{ij}. The matrix entries are allocated row-wise: entries of the same row belong to the same segment.

3 A field *r-total* holds the row total values u_i. All processors in the same row segment hold identical values.

4 A second field of segment bits, *s-col*, partitions the processors into contiguous segments such that processors in the same segment correspond to entries of the same column.

5 A field *a-col* holds the value of the entry a_{ij} in column-wise order. This field provides redundant information, since the nonzero entries have already been stored row-wise in field *a-row*.

6 A field *c-total* holds the column total values v_j. All processors that correspond to the same column (i.e., are in the same column segment) hold identical values.

7 A field *scale* holds the scaling factors for either row or column.

8 Two fields *p-row* and *p-col* hold pointers to map the nonzero entries from the row-wise field *a-row* to the column-wise field *a-col* and vice versa.

With this representation of sparse problems, one iteration of RAS is executed as follows: A segmented add–scan operation on field *a-row* (that is, an add–scan over the

	1	2	3	4	5	
1		a_{12}	a_{13}	a_{14}	a_{15}	u_1
2	a_{21}					u_2
3	a_{31}					u_3
4		a_{42}	a_{43}			u_4
5		a_{52}	a_{53}	a_{54}		u_5
	v_1	v_2	v_3	v_4	v_5	

NEWS address of VP	1	2	3	4	5	6	7	8	9	10	11	12
S-row	1	0	0	0	1	1	1	0	1	0	0	1
A-row	a_{12}	a_{13}	a_{14}	a_{15}	a_{21}	a_{31}	a_{42}	a_{43}	a_{52}	a_{53}	a_{54}	
R-total	u_1	u_1	u_1	u_1	u_2	u_3	u_4	u_4	u_5	u_5	u_5	
P-row	3	6	9	11	1	2	4	7	5	8	10	
P-col	5	6	1	7	9	2	8	10	3	11	4	
C-total	v_1	v_1	v_2	v_2	v_2	v_3	v_3	v_3	v_4	v_4	v_5	
A-col	a_{21}	a_{31}	a_{12}	a_{42}	a_{52}	a_{13}	a_{43}	a_{53}	a_{14}	a_{54}	a_{15}	
S-col	1	0	1	0	0	1	0	0	1	0	1	1

Figure 7.2 Data-parallel representation of a sparse matrix.

row segments) computes the sum of the entries in each row. This partial sum is then used to divide the row total field *r-total*, thus computing the scaling factors. Note that, by the definition of the segmented-scan operator, only the last processor in each segment has the sum of all the entries in the row, and hence only the scaling factor of the last processor is the correct one. A reverse segmented copy–scan is used to copy the correct scaling factor to all processors in the same segment. Finally, each processor multiplies its copy of the matrix value with its local copy of the scaling factor. Before the algorithm can proceed with the column scalings the nonzero entries, just scaled following a row operation, must be copied from the row-wise to the column-wise representation. This is a rearrangement of the contents of the memory field *a-row* according to the sparsity structure of the matrix. The addresses stored in the pointer field *p-row* are used to copy the nonzero entries of the matrix from the row field *a-row* to the column field *a-col*. The algorithm then does a column scaling, which is similar to the row scaling described above.

Test Problems	Error	32K CM-2		Alliant FX/8	Cray X-MP
		(sparse)	(dense)	8 CPUs (sparse)	1 CPU (sparse)
USE537	10^{-6}	0.45	0.18	1.04	0.30
MAKE537	10^{-4}	11.41	6.13	7.50	6.90

Table 7.1 Comparisons of execution times (in seconds) of implementations of RAS on different parallel computers. On the SIMD machine CM-2™ we also compare a sparse with a dense implementation. The Alliant code achieved almost linear speedups. Both the Alliant and the Cray codes were vectorized.

***Computational results on the Connection Machine CM-2*™** Table 7.1 summarizes the computational results obtained using RAS on the Connection Machine CM-2, and compares them against the benchmark implementation of the algorithm on a Cray X-MP™ vector supercomputer and an Alliant FX/8™. See Zenios[23] for details of the experiments.

Optimal Scheduling of Complex Sequences of Operations

Here, we refer to problems where the proper combination—or sequence—of events has to be scheduled to achieve optimal performance of some operation. The classical example is scheduling the tour of a salesman who visits multiple customers and returns to his base in the most cost-effective way. We do not review here the numerous applications of the *traveling salesman problem* (see, for example, Lawrel et al.[24]). Another classical example is scheduling multiple jobs on multiple machines (or assigning jobs to workers) when each machine has different performance profiles and each job needs processing by different machines. Finding a schedule of minimum duration has diverse applications, from the scheduling protocol of a computer system to manufacturing processes to project planning.

Mathematical programming tools motivated by this domain of applications are *combinatorial optimization* problems. Most of these fall in the class of NP, for which it is unlikely that a "good," that is, polynomially bounded, algorithm exists. Given the inherent difficulty of such problems, mathematical programming research has concentrated in two directions:

- Develop theoretical models of the temporal or spatial resources required by broad classes of problems, that is, the complexity theory of parallel computations. See Cook[25] for the foundations and Kindervater and Lenstra[26, 27] for an updated tutorial.

- Develop algorithms for heuristically solving a problem, or for getting approximate solutions quickly.

The development of heuristic algorithms that exploit both the problem structure and novel computer architectures is a very promising area of research that has received very little attention. We surmise that this omission is because, typically, heuristic algorithms are developed by researchers who have a deep insight into the structure of their application. Once an efficient heuristic is developed, the incentive to improve it through parallelism is diminished by the lack of broad applicability. Substantial efforts are being devoted, however, to the problem of exploiting parallelism in the context of branch-and-bound algorithms. The fact that the search space of a branch-and-bound algorithm grows irregularly creates major difficulties in mapping the algorithm to the communication network of parallel machines, or to appropriate memory partitioning of shared-memory machines. In particular the irregular growth of the search space creates load balancing problems (see, for example, Chapter 5). Such problems can be avoided only by shuffling parts of the search space across processors to maintain load balancing. Typically, efforts to parallelize branch-and-bound algorithms result in substantial speed-ups as the algorithm is started, but only moderate speedups as calculations proceed and the search space grows. One needs to find mappings of the search space to the communication network of a parallel machine in such a way that load balancing can be maintained by easy rebalancing of the tree. To quote from Kindervater and Lenstra[27]:

> Parallelism in combinatorial optimization is still in its infancy and holds many promises for further development in the near future.

Planning for the Efficient Performance of Large-Scale Complex Systems

Mathematical programming has been traditionally used for planning large and complex systems. Some examples include air-traffic control management, scheduling power generation and transmission, transportation planning, and manufacturing and distribution scheduling. The modeling of such large-scale systems faces two major challenges that can be resolved with advanced-architecture computers.

First, large-scale systems with many distinct components are usually loosely coupled. Not every component interacts with every other, and when they do the interactions are not easily understood. For example, inclement weather in the Midwest would have an adverse effect on air traffic at East Coast airports. The precise effect is difficult to model. Mathematical programming is, nevertheless, dealing with precise characterizations of the relations between the system parameters (in the form of constraints). A more appropriate framework is to design models that optimize well-defined, localized components of the system, while they use information received from interacting components. The interaction could be quantified by the introduction of *time effects* that indicate the delay until some relevant information is received. This leads to the need for the development of *asynchronous* models of computation. Some interesting developments in asynchronous algorithms for fixed-point and network optimization problems are analyzed in Bertsekas and Tsitsiklis.[28] A prominent example of the use of asynchronous algorithms in modeling a spatially distributed complex system is the routing algorithms used in the Arpanet and Internet communication networks.

The second challenge in modeling large-scale systems is the presence of erroneous or noisy measurements about the system specifications. For example, in planning a power generation system it is usually assumed that the specifications of the power plants and transmission lines are known with absolute certainty. Engineers usually do not subscribe to this notion. Even if we wish to ignore stochastic effects—like equipment outage or seasonal variations in demand—the operating characteristics of the system can only be specified within some range. Assuming perfect knowledge of these data will result in optimal performance of an ideal system that is not quite the same with the real system we are trying to control. Hence, the real system would not necessarily perform optimally. These difficulties can be addressed by the development of *robust optimization* (RO) models, that is, models whose solution remains optimal even when the problem parameters change. The general framework of RO is developed in Mulvey et al.[29] Several interesting applications have already been developed; see Sengupta,[30] Paraskevopoulos et al.,[31] Malcolm and Zenios,[32] and Zenios and Zenios.[33]

Robust optimization for the power capacity expansion problem The power system capacity expansion problem can be described as follows:

Select design capacities over a set of power plants that minimize the capital and operating cost of the system, meet customer demand, and satisfy physical constraints.

Demand for electric power is not constant over time: it changes daily, monthly, or annually. Events like equipment failures add to the complexities of managing such a system. Several authors have proposed stochastic programming formulations.[34–37] A robust optimization formulation for this problem has some desirable properties. First, it introduces a variance minimization term that produces cost structures that are less volatile over time and hence easier to defend in front of administrative and legislative boards. Second, temporary shortages from a given plant configuration are usually met by outsourcing to other utility companies. Hence, introducing a penalty term that will minimize the levels of shortage across different scenarios will ease the arrangements between the collaborating utility companies and reduce interperiod variability.

A single-period power system planning model is given by:

$$\text{Minimize} \quad \sum_{i \in I} c_i x_i + \sum_{j \in J} \theta_j \sum_{i \in I} f_i y_{ij} \tag{7.11}$$

$$\text{Subject to} \quad x_i - \sum_{j \in J} y_{ij} \geq 0, \quad \text{for all } i \in I, \tag{7.12}$$

$$\theta_j \sum_{i \in I} y_{ij} = d_j, \quad \text{for all } j \in J, \tag{7.13}$$

$$x_i \geq 0, \quad y_{ij} \geq 0 \quad \text{for all } i \in I, j \in J. \tag{7.14}$$

P_j and θ_j denote demand and duration for operating mode j; see Figure 7.3. I denotes the set of plant types (e.g., hydro, coal, etc.), and J is the set of operation modes (e.g., base, peak). c_i and f_i are the annualized fixed cost ($/MW) and operating cost ($/MWh), respectively, for plant $i \in I$. Energy demands are given by

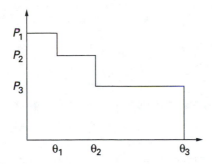

Figure 7.3   Piecewise linear load duration curve.

$$d_j = (P_j - P_{j-1})\theta_j$$

Decision variables x_i denote the total capacity assigned to plant $i \in I$. Variables y_{ij} denote the allocation of capacity to operation mode j from plant i. Their settings are determined after the capacities (x_i) have been constructed, and the demand levels (d_j) observed.

The RO formulation of the power system planning model introduces a set of scenarios $s \in \Omega$ for the uncertain energy demands $\{d\}$. (Scenarios can be introduced for other forms of uncertainty, such as the fraction of plant capacity that will be available under each scenario due to equipment outage,s etc.). The control variables are then scenario dependent and are denoted by y_{ij}^s. The RO model is given by

$$\text{Minimize} \sum_{s \in \Omega} p_s \xi_s + \lambda \sum_{s \in \Omega} p_s \left(\xi_s - \sum_{s' \in \Omega} p_{s'} \xi_{s'} \right)^2 + \omega \sum_{s \in \Omega} p_s \left(\sum_{i \in I} (z_{1i}^s)^2 + \sum_{j \in J} (z_{2j}^s)^2 \right)$$

(7.15)

$$\text{Subject to} \quad x_i - \sum_{j \in J} y_{ij}^s \geq 0, \qquad \text{for all } i \in I \tag{7.16}$$

$$x_i - \sum_{j \in J} y_{ij}^s = z_{1i}^s, \qquad \text{for all } i \in I, \ s \in \Omega \tag{7.17}$$

$$\theta_j \sum_{i \in I} y_{ij}^s - d_j^s + z_{2j}^s = 0, \qquad \text{for all } j \in J, \ s \in \Omega \tag{7.18}$$

$$x_i \geq 0, \quad y_{ij} \geq 0, \qquad \text{for all } i \in I, \ j \in J, \ s \in S \tag{7.19}$$

The function ξ_s is defined by

$$\xi_s = \sum_{i \in I} c_i x_i + \sum_{j \in J} \theta_j \sum_{i \in I} f_i y_{ij}^s$$

Scenario	1	2	3	4	Exp. Cost	Var. of Cost	Excess Capacity
RO model	7824	7464	7579	7446	7578	100	5.6
Stochastic prog.	7560	7320	7620	7380	7470	124	7.3

Table 7.2 Comparison of RO and stochastic programming solutions for the power system capacity expansion problem.

The objective function of this RO formulation has three terms. The first term is the expected cost of the system (in the traditional formulation of stochastic programs). The second term is the variance of the cost, weighted by the goal programming parameter λ. The third term is a function that penalizes the expected value of infeasibilities, weighted by parameter ω. Table 7.2 summarizes comparative statistics between the solution of a stochastic programming formulation of this model, with the RO solution obtained for a particular setting of the parameters. (The parameters were set as $\lambda = 0.01$ and $\omega = 128$. Those values were determined as appropriate given the various tradeoffs between solution and model robustness analyzed in Reference 32. Other parameters may be more appropriate, depending on the goals of the decision makers.) Figure 7.4 illustrates the tradeoffs between the mean and variance of the solution for different values of λ. A detailed description of this model in a high-level algebraic modeling language, with example numerical results, is given in the book by Bisschop and Entriken.[38]

7.3 Planning Under Uncertainty

According to Dantzig, the problem of planning dynamic systems under uncertainty is one of the outstanding open problems in operations research and management science. As the system evolves, new information becomes available and should be incorporated into the planning. It is desirable to hedge against future eventualities by introducing some information about the future in the form of scenarios. The need to introduce uncertainty in optimization models has been felt since the early days of linear programming. Dantzig[39] and Beale[40] independently introduced *stochastic programming models* in the mid 1950s. This line of research led to the development of both theory and algorithms for stochastic programming problems, and a wide variety of applications have been proposed. (Section 7.4 discusses one such application from the domain of financial operations.) However, stochastic programming problems grow in size very quickly. A two-stage model grows in size with the number of scenarios that need to be analyzed. Multistage models experience a combinatorial explosion of scenarios. This "curse of dimensionality"[41] has limited our ability to solve stochastic programming models of meaningful size.

The dynamics of the situation we are modeling are as follows:

A decision maker must make a decision regarding current actions, facing an uncertain future. After these *first-stage* decisions are made, a realization of the uncertain future

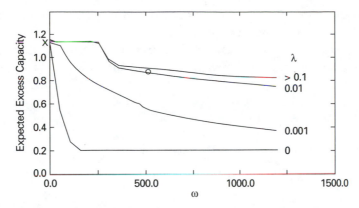

Figure 7.4 **Tradeoff between the mean and variance of the solution in the robust optimization formulation of the power capacity expansion model.**

is observed, and the decision maker determines an optimal *second-stage* decision. The objective is to minimize the total expected cost of the first- and second-stage decisions.

This framework can be readily generalized to more than two stages. The two-stage stochastic programming problem can be formulated as follows (bold letters are used to denote stochastic quantities and the corresponding italic letters designate instances of the stochastic quantities):

$$[\textbf{SLNP}] \qquad \underset{x \in \mathfrak{R}^{n_1}}{\text{Minimize}} \quad c^T x + \mathcal{Q}(x) \tag{7.20}$$

$$\text{Subject to} \quad Ax = b \tag{7.21}$$
$$0 \le x \le u^x \tag{7.22}$$

where

$$\mathcal{Q}(x) = \mathrm{E}\{Q(\textbf{d},\textbf{r},\textbf{B},\textbf{v},\textbf{C} \mid x)\}$$

and

$$Q(d,r,B,v,C \mid x) = \quad \underset{y \in \mathfrak{R}^{n_2}}{\text{Minimize}} \quad d^T y \tag{7.23}$$

$$\text{Subject to} \quad By = r - Cx \tag{7.24}$$
$$0 \le y \le v \tag{7.25}$$

The first-stage decision variables are x, and the cost coefficients of these variables are c. The matrix A and vector b specify constraints on the first-stage decision, and the vector u^x represents upper bounds on the first-stage variables.

The vector y represents the second-stage decisions. The uncertainties of the second-stage scenario are represented by (possibly) stochastic objective coefficients $\textbf{d}$, the (possibly) stochastic constraint matrix $\textbf{B}$, the (possibly) stochastic resource vector, $\textbf{r}$, the vector $\textbf{v}$ of (possibly) stochastic upper bounds on the second-stage variables, and the (possibly) stochastic matrix **C**, which communicates information about the effect of the first-stage decision on the second-stage problem.

For the case where the stochastic quantities **d**, **r**, **B**, **v**, and **C** have a discrete and finite joint distribution, represented by the *scenario set S*, we can write

$$Q(x) = \sum_{s \in S} p^s Q(d^s, r^s, B^s, v^s, C^s | x) \tag{7.26}$$

where the probability of the realization of scenario s is

$$p^s = P\{(\mathbf{d}, \mathbf{r}, \mathbf{B}, \mathbf{v}, \mathbf{C}) = (d^s, r^s, B^s, v^s, C^s)\}, \quad \text{for all } s \in S \tag{7.27}$$

Under the assumption of a finite, discrete event space, it is well known that the stochastic program [SLNP] can be reformulated to the equivalent large-scale deterministic linear program[42]:

[**DLNP**]
$$\underset{x \in \Re^{n1}, y^s \in \Re^{n2}}{\text{Minimize}} \quad c^T x + \sum_{s \in S} p^s (d^s)^T y^s \tag{7.28}$$

$$
\begin{array}{lll}
\text{Subject to} & Ax = b & \text{(7.29)} \\
& C^s x + B^s y^s = r^s & \text{for all } s \in \langle S \rangle \quad \text{(7.30)} \\
& 0 \le x \le u^x & \text{(7.31)} \\
& 0 \le y^s \le v^s & \text{for all } s \in S \quad \text{(7.32)}
\end{array}
$$

The structure of this mathematical program is shown in Figure 7.5. In the same figure we show the structure of the three-stage model, which clearly illustrates the growth rate of this mathematical program as the number of stages and scenarios increases, even modestly. The design of algorithms to curb this curse of dimensionality, or at least solve increasingly large problems, is a field of active research. Parallel processing is naturally playing a key role, since the analysis of scenarios is an "embarrassingly" parallel process. We have seen here three major trends:

1 Use parallel processors as extremely efficient sampling devices and use variance reduction sampling techniques within stochastic programming algorithms. Loosely speaking, importance sampling reduces the dimension of the problem by attempting to identify the most important scenarios. Hence, the size of the problem is reduced to manageable dimensions, while the true solution (i.e., objective value) can be estimated within a confidence interval. This approach has been followed by Dantzig and collaborators in the context of Bender's decomposition.[43, 44]

2 Use parallel processing in the context of decomposition algorithms. The stochastic programming model is decomposed into a series of scenario subproblems that can be solved in parallel. Several decomposition algorithms have recently been investigated for their potential parallelism. In most cases numerical results have been very encouraging, with nearly linear speedups being quite common. See, for example, Wets,[45] Mulvey and Vladimirou,[46] Ariyawansa and Hudson,[47] and Jessup et al.[48]

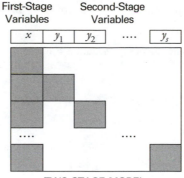

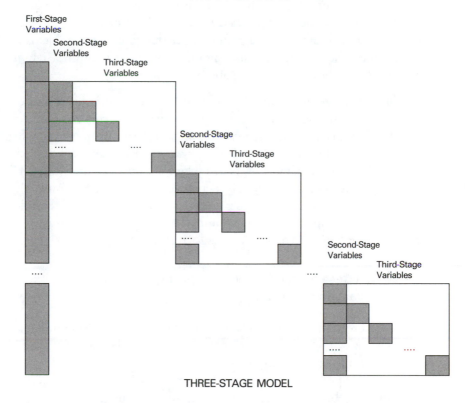

Figure 7.5 **The structure of two-stage and three-stage stochastic programming problems.**

3 Design massively parallel (row-action) algorithms. These decompose the problem by rows of the constraint set and by scenario, and result in a large number of extremely simple subproblems. Those can be solved in parallel, effectively using thousands or millions of processing elements. An important advantage of these algorithms is their scalability and the lack of any synchronization points that would be serial bottlenecks. Nielsen and Zenios[49] have developed such an algorithm and implemented it on a CM-2 with 32K processing elements. The program was used to analyze problems

from asset/liability management with up to 8000 scenarios within minutes of computer time:

Scenarios	Dimensions of Optimization Problem	Time (s)
128	13585×38689	16.2
512	54287×154675	46.3
1024	108559×309281	86.3
2048	217103×618529	163.6
8192	868367×2474017	660

Serial applications of this algorithm do not exist. Hence, it is impossible to gauge the parallel efficiency of the algorithm. Nevertheless, the size of the test problems solved above is one to two orders of magnitude larger than other test problems reported in the literature. These extremely large problems are solved within a few minutes of solution time, as shown in the table above.

We believe that one of the major challenges in this area is the design of *adaptive, scalable* decomposition algorithms, suitable for "universal" architectures like the CM-5. By adaptive we mean algorithms that can decompose the problem in a way that matches its dimensions with the number of available processors. For example, small problems are better solved as monolithic linear programs than by using decompositions. However, if many processors are available it might be better to employ some decomposition. On the other hand, if the number of processors is fewer than the number of scenarios it might be preferable to decompose the problem into as many subproblems as there are processors. Each subproblem will consist of several scenario subproblems.

7.4 A Case Study: Parallel Computing in Mortgage-Backed Financing

This section shows that advances in large-scale mathematical programming and modeling with the use of high performance computers could significantly affect the use of these techniques in real applications. Zenios[50] reviews several applications of management science and operations research that benefitted substantially from advanced-architecture computing. In this section we use, as a case study, models from mortgage-backed financing.

This application combines Monte Carlo simulation with stochastic programming models. This integration was made possible with the use of parallel computing. Early attempts in parallelizing this application on a network of workstations led to *quantitative* improvements in the performance of existing models: we were able to do pricing simulations for complex financial instruments (i.e., mortgage-backed securities) substantially faster than what was possible with top range mainframes. Further work with a massively parallel computer—the Connection Machine CM-2a with 4096 processors—provided the performance we were looking for: we could complete within an hour analysis that would take weeks on a workstation. This led us to re-evaluate potential uses of the pricing model. We can now build optimization models for managing large portfolios of these complex securities. The quantitative improvements realized by the parallel processing technology led to qualitative improvements of the models.[†]

In their simplest form, mortgage-backed securities (MBS) are securities which pass-through the payments (minus a small service fee) that homeowners make on their mortgages to investors. These instruments embody features of both bonds and options. Specifically, the homeowners' right to prepay all or part of their mortgage balance at any time represents a call option. In order for investors to place a price on a MBS, it is necessary to value this call option by accurately simulating anticipated changes in the term structure of interest rates, coupled with the likely prepayment behavior of homeowners. Analysts resort to Monte Carlo simulations to capture the effect of interest rate variations on the cash flow, and thus the value, of these instruments. It should be noted that this is a complex problem since interest rate movements are only one of the factors which influence the likelihood that homeowners will prepay their mortgages. The prepayment of a mortgage is also path dependent: at any point in time the probability of prepayment depends not only on the current interest rates, but also on the previous history of interest rates since the MBS pool was formed.

We have constructed a valuation model for fixed-rate mortgages which captures the primary factors that affect prepayment behavior and values the resulting cash flows. The valuation model integrates the mortgage prepayment model developed at the HERMES Laboratory of the Wharton School[51] with the binomial lattice model of the term structure of interest rates due to Black et al.[52] The flowchart of the valuation model—called MO.S.E.S., for MOrtgage Simulation and Evaluation System—is given in Figure 7.6. The model is iterative, since it needs to be calibrated against current market prices in order to properly identify "cheap" securities. Furthermore, each iteration requires several rounds of simulation (typically 1000) of interest rates, evaluation of the prepayment models, and somewhat elaborate cash-flow calculations pertinent to a mortgage.

How can MO.S.E.S be implemented in parallel? The answer is obvious for some architectures. When the number of processors exceeds the number of required simulations, we can split the workload equally among processors. When all processors complete their pre-assigned load they coordinate to compute average statistics and standard deviations. Typically, we expect the solution time to reduce linearly with the number of available processors. Indeed, on a shared-memory Alliant FX/4 we have observed almost linear speedups when going from one to four processors. The same model was implemented on a heterogeneous network of workstations using a distributed computing environment, *Linda*[53, 54] (see Figure 7.7). The results of the implementation for the valuation of a single security on a different number of workstations were as follows:

[†] This phase of the project is pursued jointly with Blackstone Financial Management and the Federal National Mortgage Association (FNMA) as part of the University/Private Industry collaboration initiative of the Decision, Risk and Management Science program of the National Science Foundation.

Computers	MO.S.E.S. Time (s)
DECstation 5000/200™	38
4 DECstations (linear speedup)	12
7 DECstations (linear speedup)	7
Cray X-MP (1 CPU)	12
Connection Machine CM-2a (4K proc. elements)	1.1

The results with the parallel implementation on the distributed network of worksta-tions and the Cray X-MP vector supercomputer were very encouraging. We were able to complete within several seconds simulations that would typically take minutes. How-ever, our original objective to build a portfolio management system was still not within

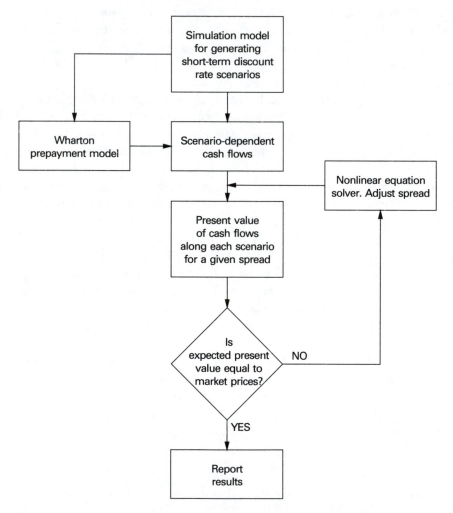

Figure 7.6   Structure of the mortgage valuation model in MO.S.E.S.

reach; pricing a portfolio of 3000 securities would still require several days of computer time (see Figure 7.8). We decided then to explore the use of massively parallel architectures, like the Connection Machine CM-2a. This system has 4096 processing elements—more than the required 1024 simulations. Furthermore, it is a SIMD system that was considered at the time quite inflexible.

It was believed that the structure of the simulations within MO.S.E.S. made them unsuitable for this architecture. The basic problem is the following: Since more processors are available than the required number of simulations it would be necessary to use multiple processors within each simulation. Otherwise, several processors would remain idle, and the performance of the code would fall short of the peak performance of the machine. However, each simulation represents a march forward in time and hence could not be parallelized. Presumably, calculations for period t could not be completed before period $t-1$. We have been able to reformulate the MBS models to use *nested dissection*. Hence, the time-dependent calculations could be executed in $\ln T$ steps, where T is the length of the time horizon (360 months).

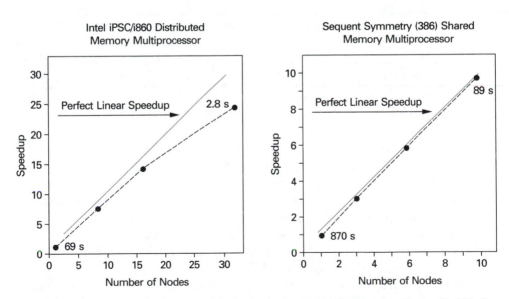

Figure 7.7   **Performance of distributed implementation of MO.S.E.S. using *Networked Linda*.**

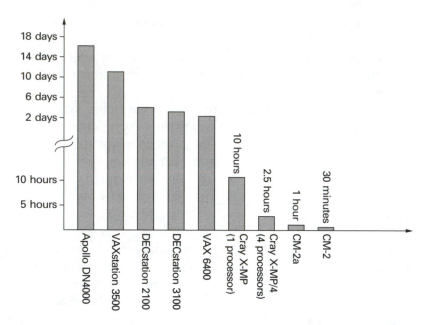

Figure 7.8   Computing time requirements for pricing a portfolio of 3000 mortgage-backed securities.

The overall design was to configure the CM-2a processors into a two-dimensional communications grid of size 1024×512. Hence, we used 2^{19} virtual processors. Each "row" of processors would execute one round of the simulation. The first 360 "columns" were used for the time-dependent calculations, using parallel *scan* primitives of the CM-2a. Consider, for example, the problem of generating interest rate paths from a binomial lattice model of the interest rates. At time period t the interest rate scenario s is given by $r_t^s = r_t^0(k_t)^{\sigma_t}$. Here, $\{r_t^0\}$ and $\{k_t\}$ are vector parameters of the binomial lattice model of Black et al.[52] The *state* of the interest rate path s at period t is indicated by σ_t. For example, an interest rate path that has been going always to an up state after 360 monthly steps will have $\sigma_{360} = 360$. An interest rate path that has been following an up–down/up–down process will have $\sigma_{360} = 180$. To generate sample paths from a binomial lattice we must determine the state of the path σ_t at each time instance t. Then, a virtual processor with coordinates (s,t) in the two-dimensional grid can generate the path by computing $r_t^s = r_t^0(k_t)^{\sigma_t}$. The problem in constructing a continuous path is that the state of the lattice at instance t must be attainable by either an "up" or a "down" step from the state at instance $t-1$. Such a sequence of admissible states is produced as follows: a random bit 0 or 1 is first generated at each virtual processor. A scan–addition on these bits along the time axis generates the state index σ_t for each virtual processor. The state at t differs by at most one from the state at $t-1$, and calculation of the interest rates at every time period can then proceed in parallel for all periods.

For further details of the implementation of this model see Hutchinson and Zenios.[55] The data-parallel implementation executes at approximately 150 Mflops. The pricing of

MATHEMATICAL PROGRAMMING AND MODELING   Chapter 7

the 3000-securities portfolio could be completed within 1 hour. Contrast this with the execution of the code on a Cray X-MP, where 2.5 hours were required for the same calculation. A VAX 6400 would take more than a day to complete this task.

The Connection Machine implementation has made it possible to implement several extensions of the pricing models:

1 Use finite difference approximations of the simulation program to calculate the sensitivity of the mortgage price to small, local changes in the term structure (i.e., the *dollar duration* of the security).

2 Develop a variant of the model to track the price of the security across time.

3 Develop a variant of the model to track the price of the security with changes in the term structure.[56]

Even more important, however, we can now address the problem of managing large portfolios of these securities under uncertainty, using the modeling framework described in the previous section. Extensive validation studies for this model are reported by Holmer and co-workers.[57, 58] These have shown that the multiperiod, multistage models are effective tools in hedging uncertainty in complex financial decision-making problems. They have outperformed significantly simpler models based on single-period portfolio optimization, such as the popular mean–variance approach of Markowitz (see, e.g., Perold[59]) or the mean–absolute deviation models (see, e.g., Konno and Yamazaki[60] or Zenios and Kang[61]). A multiperiod stochastic network formulation is illustrated in Figure 7.9. Nodes along the horizontal axis of the network represent time periods; nodes along the vertical axis represent different investment opportunities. Arcs denote the flow of funds, or investment allocations, across time and among the different investment opportunities.

The stochastic models are, however, extremely large. Not only can the number of time periods and number of securities be several hundreds, but the problem also extends over multiple scenarios. In order to solve such problems one has to design special purpose algorithms and use efficiently a large number of processors. One such approach has been developed by Nielsen and Zenios.[49] The next section describes the mapping of a stochastic network problem to a large number of processors as found, for example, on a Connection Machine CM-2.

Data-Parallel Computing for Stochastic Network Models

To implement a sparse, stochastic network solver we use an extension of the data structures used to represent the graph arising from the sparse matrix balancing problem (see "Data-Parallel Computing for the Matrix Balancing Problem" in Section 7.2). Each network subproblem is stored in a one-dimensional grid of processors of size $(m_1 + m_2) + 2(n_1 + n_2)$. With each arc (i,j) we associate two processors: one at the tail node i and one at the head node j. An additional processor is associated with each node. Processors that correspond to the same node—that is, are assigned to arcs incident to the same node—are grouped together into a contiguous segment. This is the data structure introduced in Zenios and Lasken.[21] In this way the segmented scan operations can be employed for the implementation of the algorithm.

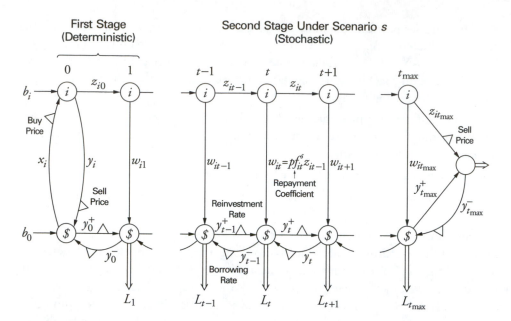

Figure 7.9   Multiperiod stochastic network model for managing a portfolio of mortgage-backed securities under uncertainty.

In order to solve the stochastic network problems we use a two-dimensional grid of processors of size $S \times [(m_1 + m_2) + 2(n_1 + n_2)]$. Each row of this grid is used to represent a single network problem, as outlined above. Since the network topology is identical for all scenarios, the mapping of arcs onto processors and the partitioning of processors into segments will be identical for each row of the grid. Hence, the control of the algorithm is identical for each row of the grid (i.e., for each network problem). Row s will store the data of the network problem for the sth scenario. This configuration is illustrated in Figure 7.10. The algorithm iterates along the row axis until some convergence criterion is satisfied for all the rows. Once the single-scenario networks are solved by iterations along the row axis, the algorithm executes the projection on the non-anticipativity constraints using scan operations along the column axis.

The projection on the non-anticipativity constraints is executed in parallel for all first-stage (replicated) variables. Each first-stage variable (with replications) occupies two columns of the two-dimensional grid representing the stochastic program (Figure 7.10). Each processor holds the scenario probability p^s and the component x_{ij}^s of the current iterate, and computes their product. The products are then added and distributed back to each processor (using the *spread-with-add* parallel prefix) as the projected point $\hat{x}_{ij}$.

7.5 Conclusions

It has often being said that the acid test of a theory is its ability to solve the problems that motivated its development. Mathematical programming has been a fundamental

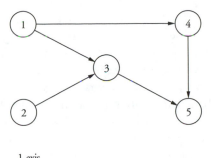

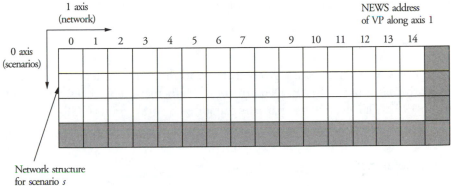

1 axis (network)

0 axis (scenarios)

NEWS address of VP along axis 1

Network structure for scenario s

Data fields in the sth row corresponding to scenario s.

NEWS address of VP along axis 1	0	1	2	3	4	5	6	7	8	9	10	11	12	13	14
Node	1	1	1	2	2	3	3	3	3	4	4	4	5	5	5
Segment bits	1	0	0	1	0	1	0	0	0	1	0	0	1	0	0
Supply/demand	$s_k(1)$	$s_k(1)$	$s_k(1)$	$s_k(2)$	$s_k(2)$	$s_k(3)$	$s_k(3)$	$s_k(3)$	$s_k(3)$	$s_k(4)$	$s_k(4)$	$s_k(4)$	$s_k(5)$	$s_k(5)$	$s_k(5)$
Capacity	∞	$U(1,3)$	$U(1,4)$	∞	$U(2,3)$	∞	$U(1,3)$	$U(2,3)$	$U(3,5)$	∞	$U(1,4)$	$U(4,5)$	∞	$U(3,5)$	$U(4,5)$
Send address in NEWS coordinates along axis 1	0	6	10	3	7	5	1	4	13	9	2	14	12	8	11
Stage bit	0	1	0	0	1	0	1	1	0	0	0	0	0	0	0

Figure 7.10   **Data-parallel representation of a stochastic network problem.**

tool for solving problems from a wide range of applications. However, as one problem is solved, the engineer, manager, or scientist develops further refinements to the application. In this framework, mathematical programming is constantly being challenged to address bigger, more-complex models.

High performance computing promises to provide the computing power required to implement and solve these increasingly complex problems. However, the novelty of the computer architectures that fall in the "high performance" category creates new challenges for the design and implementation of mathematical progamming algorithms. This chapter has shown that these challenges are not insurmountable. They can be addressed successfully and in way that has a major impact on the underlying application.

Several applications have been discussed, and the benefits they gained from research in parallelism have been highlighted. Particularly important are the models for planning under uncertainty and the development of models for *robust optimization*. These models shed new light on a wide range of practical problems, and high performance computing provides the enabling technology for solving them.

Acknowledgments

This chapter is based on a lecture given at the Workshop on Challenges for Computational Mathematics in the 1990s, Department of Mathematical Sciences, Clemson University, in 1992. The research was partially supported by NSF grants CCR-9104042 and SES-91-00216, and AFOSR grant 91-0168.

References

1 G. B. Dantzig. *Linear Programming and Extensions.* Princeton University Press, Princeton, NJ, 1963.

2 J. Bisschop and A. Meeraus. "On the Development of a General Algebraic Modeling System in a Strategic Planning Environment," *Mathematical Programming Study.* **20**, 1–29, 1982.

3 *Parallel Optimization on Novel Computer Architectures.* (R. R. Meyer and S. A. Zenios, Eds.) Annals of Operations Research, Vol. 14. J.C. Baltzer, Basel, Switzerland, 1988.

4 J. M. Ortega and R. G. Voigt. "Solution of Partial Differential Equations On Vector And Parallel Computers," *SIAM Review.* **27**, 159–240, 1985.

5 M. H. Wright. "Optimization and Large-Scale Computation," in *Very Large Scale Computation in the 21st Century.* (J. P. Mesirov, Ed.) SIAM, Philadelphia, 1991, pp. 250–272.

6 R. H. Byrd, R. B. Schnabel, and G. A. Shultz. "Using Parallel Function Evaluations to Improve Hessian Approximations for Unconstrained Optimization," *Annals of Operations Research.* 22, 1990.

7 J. E. Dennis, Jr., and V. Torczon. "Direct Search Methods on Parallel Machines," *SIAM Journal on Optimization.* **1** (4), 448–474, 1991.

8 G. E. Paules IV and C. A. Floudas. "A New Optimization Approach for Phase and Chemical Equilibrium Problems." Technical report, Department of Chemical Engineering, Princeton University, Princeton, NJ, Jan. 1990.

9   W. D. Seider, D. D. Brengel, and S. Widagdo. "Nonlinear Analysis in Process Design," *AIChE Journal.* **37** (1), 1–38, 1991.

10 *Recent Advances in Global Optimization.* (C. A. Floudas and P. M. Pardalos, Eds.) Princeton University Press, Princeton, NJ, 1992.

11 R. H. Byrd, C. L. Dert, A. G. H. Rinnooy Kan, and R. B. Schnabel. "Concurrent Stochastic Methods for Global Optimization," *Mathematical Programming.* **46** (1), 1–30, 1990.

12 S. Kirkpatrick, C. D. Gelatt, and M. P. Vecchi. "Optimization by Simulated Annealing," *Science.* **220**, 671–680, 1983.

13 M. Holmer, D. Yang, and S. A. Zenios. "Designing Callable Bonds Using Simulated Annealing." Report 93–07–02, Operations & Information Management, University of Pennsylvania, Philadelphia, 1993.

14 G. T. Herman. *Image Reconstruction from Projections: The Fundamentals of Computerized Tomography.* Academic Press, New York, 1980.

15 M. H. Schneider and S. A. Zenios. "A Comparative Study of Algorithms for Matrix Balancing," *Operations Research.* **38**, 439–455, 1990.

16 Y. Censor. "Row-Action Methods for Huge and Sparse Systems and Their Applications," *SIAM Review.* **23**, 444–464, 1981.

17 G. T. Herman, D. Odhner, K. Toennies, and S. A. Zenios. "A Parallelized Algorithm for Image Reconstruction from Noisy Projections," in *Large Scale Numerical Optimization.* (T. Coleman and Y. Li, Eds.) SIAM, Philadelphia, 1990, pp. 3–21.

18 Y. Censor. "Parallel Application of Block-Iterative Methods in Medical Imaging and Radiation Therapy," *Mathematical Programming.* **42**, 307–325, 1988.

19 S. A. Zenios and Y. Censor. "Vector and Parallel Computing with Block-Iterative Algorithms for Medical Image Reconstruction," *Applied Numerical Mathematics.* **7** (5), 399–415, 1991.

20 G. E. Blelloch. *Vector Models for Data-Parallel Computing.* MIT Press, Cambridge, MA, 1990.

21 S. A. Zenios and R. A. Lasken. "Nonlinear Network Optimization on a Massively Parallel Connection Machine," *Annals of Operations Research.* **14**, 147–165, 1988.

22 S. Nielsen and S. A. Zenios. "Data Structures for Network Algorithms on Massively Parallel Architectures," *Parallel Computing.* **18**, 1033–1052, 1992.

23 S. A. Zenios. "Incorporating Network Optimization Capabilities into a High-Level Programming Language," *ACM Transactions on Mathematical Software.* **16**, 113–142, 1990.

24 *The Traveling Salesman Problem: A Guided Tour of Combinatorial Optimization.* (E. L. Lawrel, J. K. Lenstra, A. H. G. Rinnooy Kan, and D. B. Shmoys, Eds.) Wiley, Chichester, UK, 1985.

25 S. A. Cook. "Towards a Complexity Theory of Synchronous Parallel Computations," *Enseign. Math.* **27** (2), 99–124, 1981.

26 G. A. P. Kindervater and J. K. Lenstra. "Parallel algorithms," in *Combinatorial Optimization: Annotated Bibliographies.* (M. Oh'Eigeartaigh, J. K. Lenstra, and A. H. G. Rinnooy Kan, Eds.) Wiley, Chichester, UK, 1985, pp. 106–128.

27 G. A. P. Kindervater and J. K. Lenstra. "Parallel Computing in Combinatorial Optimization," in *Annals of Operations Research*, Vol. 14. (R. R. Meyer and S. A. Zenios, Eds.) J. C. Baltzer AG, Basel, Switzerland, 1988, pp. 245–290.

28 D. P. Bertsekas and J. N. Tsitsiklis. *Parallel and Distributed Computation: Numerical Methods.* Prentice Hall, Englewood Cliffs, NJ, 1989.

29 J. M. Mulvey, R. J. Vanderbei, and S. A. Zenios. "Robust Optimization of Large Scale Systems: General Modeling Framework and Computations." Report 91-06-04, Decision Sciences Department, University of Pennsylvania, Philadelphia, 1991.

30 J. K. Sengupta. "Robust Solutions in Stochastic Linear Programming," *Journal of the Operational Research Society.* **42** (10), 857–870, 1991.

31 D. Paraskevopoulos, E. Karakitsos, and B. Rustem. "Robust Capacity Planning Under Uncertainty," *Management Science.* **37** (7), 787–800, 1991.

32 S. Malcolm and S. A. Zenios. "Robust Optimization for Power Capacity Expansion Planning," *Journal of the Operational Research Society.* **45** (9), 1040–1049, 1994.

33 S. A. Zenios and S. A. Zenios. "Robust Optimization for Matrix Balancing from Noisy Data." Report 92-01-02, Decision Sciences Department, University of Pennsylvania, Philadelphia, 1992.

34 F. H. Murphy, S. Sen, and A. L. Soyster. "Electric Utility Capacity Expansion Planning with Uncertain Load Forecasts," *IIE Transactions.* **14** (1), 52–59, 1982.

35 H. D. Sherali, A. L. Soyster, F. H. Murphy, and S. Sen. "Intertemporal Allocation of Capital Cost in Electric Utility Capacity Expansion Planning Under Uncertainty," *Management Science.* **30** (1), 1–19, 1984.

36 G. B. Dantzig et al. "Decomposition Techniques for Multi-Area Generation and Transmission Planning Under Uncertainty." Report el-6484, Electric Power Research Institute, Palo Alto, CA, 1989.

37 A. P. Sanghvi and I. H. Shavel. "Investment Planning for Hydro-Thermal Power System Expansion: Stochastic Programming Employing the Dantzig-Wolfe Decomposition," *IEEE Transactions on Power Systems.* **1** (2), 115–121, 1986.

38 J. Bisschop and R. Entriken. "AIMS: The Modeling System." Paragon Decision Technology, Haarlem, The Netherlands, 1993.

39 G. B. Dantzig. "Linear Programming Under Uncertainty," *Management Science.* **1**, 197–206, 1955.

40 E. M. L. Beale. "On Minimizing a Convex Function Subject to Linear Inequalities," *Journal of the Royal Statistical Society.* **17**, 173–184, 1955.

41 R. E. Bellman. *Dynamic Programming.* Princeton University Press, Princeton, NJ, 1957.

42 R. J. B. Wets. "Stochastic Programs with Fixed Resources: The Equivalent Deterministic Problem," *SIAM Review.* **16**, 309–339, 1974.

43 G. B. Dantzig and P. W. Glynn. "Parallel Processors for Planning Under Uncertainty," *Annals of Operations Research.* **22**, 1–21, 1990.

44 G. Infanger. "Monte Carlo (Importance) Sampling with a Benders Decomposition Algorithm for Stochastic Linear Programs." Report sol-89-13r, Department of Operations Research, Stanford University, Palo Alto, CA, 1990.

45 R. Wets. "On Parallel Processor Design for Solving Stochastic Programs." Report wp-85-67, International Institute for Applied Systems Analysis, Laxenburg, Austria, Oct. 1985.

46 J. M. Mulvey and H. Vladimirou. "Evaluation of a Parallel Hedging Algorithm for Stochastic Network Programming," in *Impact of Recent Computer Advances on Operations Research.* (R. Sharda, B. L. Golden, E. Wasil, O. Balci, and W. Stewart, Eds.) Pergamon, New York, 1989.

47 K. A. Ariyawansa and D. D. Hudson. "Performance of a Benchmark Parallel Implementation of the Van Slyke and Wets Algorithm for Two-Stage Stochastic Programs on the Sequent/Balance," *Concurrency: Practice and Experience.* **3**, 109–128, 1991.

48 L. Jessup, D. Yang, and S. A. Zenios. "Parallel Factorization of Structured Matrices Arising in Stochastic Programming," *SIAM Journal on Optimization.* **4** (4), 833–840, 1994.

49 S. Nielsen and S. A. Zenios. "A Massively Parallel Algorithm for Nonlinear Stochastic Network Problems," *Operations Research.* **41** (2), 319–337, 1993.

50 S. A. Zenios. "Parallel and Super-Computing in the Practice of Management Science," *Interfaces.* **24** (5), 122–140, 1994.

51 P. Kang and S. A. Zenios. "Complete Prepayment Models for Mortgage Backed Securities," *Management Science.* **38** (11), 1665–1685, 1992.

52 F. Black, E. Derman and W. Toy. "A One-Factor Model of Interest Rates and Its Application to Treasury Bond Options," *Financial Analysts Journal.* 33–39, Jan./Feb. 1990.

53 N. Carriero and D. Gelernter. "How to Write Parallel Programs: A Guide to the Perplexed." Technical report, Scientific Computing Associates, New Haven, CT, 1989.

54 L. D. Cagan, N. S. Carriero, and S. A. Zenios. "Pricing Mortgage-Backed Securities with Network Linda," *Financial Analysts Journal.* 55–62, Mar./Apr. 1993.

55 J. M. Hutchinson and S. A. Zenios. "Financial Simulations on a Massively Parallel Connection Machine." *International Journal of Supercomputer Applications.* **5**, 27–45, 1991.

56 S. A. Zenios and R. A. McKendall. "Computing Price Scenarios of Mortgage-Backed Securities Using Massively Parallel Computing," in *Modeling Reality and Personal Modelling.* (R. Flavell, Ed.) Springer–Verlag, Heidelberg, 1993, pp. 374–407.

57 M. Holmer, R. McKendall, C. Vassiadou-Zeniou, and S. A. Zenios. "Dynamic Models for Fixed-Income Portfolio Management Under Uncertainty." Working paper, Decision Sciences Department, University of Pennsylvania, Philadelphia, 1993.

58 B. Golub, M. Holmer, R. McKendall, L. Pohlman, and S. A. Zenios. "Stochastic Programming Models for Money Management," *European Journal of Operational Research.* To be published.

59 A. F. Perold. "Large-Scale Portfolio Optimization," *Management Science.* **30** (10), 1143–1160, 1984.

60 H. Konno and H. Yamazaki. "Mean-Absolute Deviation Portfolio Optimization Model and Its Applications to Tokyo Stock Market," *Management Science.* **37** (5), 519–531, 1991.

61 S. A. Zenios and P. Kang. "Mean-Absolute Deviation Portfolio Optimization for Mortgage Backed Securities," *Annals of Operations Research.* **45**, 443–450, 1994.

8

Scalable Programming in Fortran

SKEF WHOLEY

Contents

Portability of software is important in ensuring that an organization's investment in software continues to be of value as computational platforms and needs evolve. This chapter discusses the idea of scalability, which can be thought of as a kind of portability for a program's performance. The author explains how to write software designed from the start to execute on a wide range of high performance targets. The same techniques are also useful when one needs to port an old "dusty deck" Fortran program to run efficiently on newer platforms.

8.1 What is Scalable Programming?

Scalable programs have been described as those that exhibit linear or near-linear speedup on parallel computers as problem size is increased proportional to the number of processors.[1] The definition of scalability for algorithms and architectures has been refined for parallel computers.[2] These notions can be extended to serial and vector computers. For the purposes of this chapter, a scalable program is one that performs well on a variety of architectures: uniprocessors (such as workstations), vector computers, and parallel computers (including SIMD, MIMD, shared-memory, and distributed-memory machines).

Most programmers are already quite familiar with the rules and benefits of writing *portable* programs. A portable program will run on any computer that correctly implements the language in which the program is written. By avoiding machine-specific or implementation-specific constructs, a programmer may sacrifice some performance or ease of implementation, but since the value of a portable program is so great, these sacrifices are almost always worth the cost. When performance is critical, nonportable constructs can be used with some form of conditional compilation.

In a similar way, and for similar reasons, scalable programs avoid machine-specific constructs and machine-specific optimizations. With an increasing diversity of computer architectures, there is now great value in developing programs that exhibit *portability of performance*, that is, programs that perform reasonably well on different computers. This leads to a practical definition of scalability:

> A scalable program is one whose performance is portable across many different architectures for many different problem sizes.

Compilers play a key role in determining the performance of any program. While it may be possible to imagine a compiler clever enough to transform a nonscalable program into a scalable program, one must acknowledge that few compilers are so ingenious. For a scalable program to run well on a wide variety of machine architectures, it must be able to be compiled well by a wide variety of compilers, spanning a wide range of cleverness.

Thus, an important component of scalable programming is to have realistic expectations of what a compiler can or will do. For this reason, simple expressions of computation are generally more scalable than equivalent but more complicated expressions of the same computation.

On the other hand, one must make *some* assumptions about the minimum level of compiler cleverness available on a *particular* machine. A serial computer may or may not benefit from vectorizing compiler technology, but a vector supercomputer certainly will; a shared-memory parallel computer may or may not benefit from data layout optimizations, while a distributed-memory parallel computer probably will.

Since portability is an important component of scalability, this chapter addresses the specific problem of writing scalable programs in what is probably the most portable of computer languages: Fortran 77. While the concepts discussed in this context are generally applicable to other languages, there may be some which simply are not relevant.

Some of the challenges addressed here arise from limitations of the Fortran 77 language, which have been eliminated in modern dialects like Fortran 90. Fortran 77 is nonetheless of keen interest for several reasons:

- Compilers for modern Fortran dialects are not yet widely available. Fortran 77 is not only more portable than Fortran 90, but Fortran 77 compilers are more mature and, for many users, remain the compilers of choice on many platforms.

- There exists a huge body of work written in Fortran 77 which will remain in active use for some time to come. As Fortran 77 programs are brought to newer computers which support newer dialects, they will not be completely rewritten, but rather will slowly evolve, taking incremental advantage of new language features and, through compilers, new hardware technology.

- To the extent that conversion from Fortran 77 to Fortran 90 can be automated, it is greatly facilitated when programs are written (or incrementally rewritten) in a scalable fashion. Conversion tools like CMAX™,[3] Forge,[4] KAP™,[5] and VAST[6] do their best when given scalable Fortran 77 as input.

The remainder of this chapter is organized as follows: Section 8.2 lists some general rules for writing scalable programs. Section 8.3 analyzes code fragments created with and without the consideration of scalablity rules. Section 8.4 discusses several complete programs which were either constructed using the ideas of scalable programming or were modified to become more scalable. The appendix to this chapter describes a portable facility for dynamic memory allocation in Fortran 77.

8.2 Rules for Scalable Programming

The scalability of a program depends on its use of control structures and data structures. The rules given in this section are guidelines, and in some cases may conflict with other concerns or even with each other. While programmers should follow these rules to the greatest extent possible, there may be good reasons for occasionally breaking them.

Scalable Control Structures

A general rule applicable to both control and data structures is that simple expressions of intent are more scalable than complicated expressions because complexity (very often in the form of "optimization" specific to a particular machine architecture or compiler) can obscure intent, possibly inhibiting a compiler from efficiently mapping the desired computation onto a particular architecture. The more a compiler can determine through analysis, the better job it can do generating efficient object code.

Structured programming Structured programming concepts form the foundation of the rules for using control structures scalably. A very simple view of structured programming is that one shouldn't use GOTO statements. In fact, there are situations when the use of GOTO may be appropriate because it leads to simpler, clearer code. This is especially true in older languages like Fortran 77 which lack constructs for things like abnormal block termination. However, the *indiscriminate* use of GOTO should be avoided. Loops should be written using DO statements whenever possible, and conditional execution should be written with logical IF or block IF statements. In avoiding GOTO in these situations, one produces programs which are not only easier to read and maintain, but are easier for a compiler to analyze.

So, code like this:

```
      IF (F.LT.0) GOTO 200
      I = 0
100 CONTINUE
      IF (I.GT.100) GOTO 200
      A(I) = I*2
      I = I + 1
      GOTO 100
200 CONTINUE
```

should be rewritten like this:

```
      IF (F.GE.0) THEN
          DO 200 I = 1,100
              A(I) = I*2
200       CONTINUE
      END IF
```

Stripmining and loop unrolling A refinement of using DO loops is to use the appropriate number of such loops. Two optimizations frequently done "by hand" at the source level, stripmining and loop unrolling, violate this rule. (Although many compilers now perform these transformations internally, some programmers still apply them at the source level, reducing scalability.)

In stripmining, the depth of loop nesting is increased so that the innermost level of loop has an extent compatible with that of a limited hardware resource, for example, vector registers or cache blocks. To make a program scalable, stripmined loops should be replaced with clearer, equivalent, nonstripmined versions.

So, code like this:

```
C--   Stripmined loop; assumes N is a multiple of 64:
      DO 200 I = 1,N,64
          DO 100 I1 = 0,63
              A(I+I1) = B(I+I1) * C(I+I1) + D(I+I1)
100       CONTINUE
200 CONTINUE
```

should be rewritten like this:

```
      DO 200 I = 1,N
         A(I) = B(I) * C(I) + D(I)
  200 CONTINUE
```

In loop unrolling, the depth of loop nesting is decreased so that some level of loop is eliminated or given fewer iterations. The loop body is replaced by several copies of the original body. This transformation increases the amount of code over which a compiler might perform register allocation, common subexpression elimination, or other optimizations. To make a program scalable, unrolled loops should be "rerolled" by replacing them with clearer, equivalent versions.

So, code like this:

```
C--   Unrolled loop; assumes N is a multiple of 4:
      DO 200 I = 1,N,4
         X = X + A(I) * B(I)
         X = X + A(I+1) * B(I+1)
         X = X + A(I+2) * B(I+2)
         X = X + A(I+3) * B(I+3)
  200 CONTINUE
```

should be rewritten like this:

```
      DO 200 I = 1,N
         X = X + A(I) * B(I)
  200 CONTINUE
```

In some cases, both optimizations are applied to the same loop at the source level, greatly obscuring the nature of the computation. While these transformations may have a place in tuning code when an optimizing compiler is not available, one should recognize that loops so written are unscalable.

So, code like this:

```
C--   Unrolled and stripmined loop; assumes N is a multiple of 64:
      DO 200 I = 1,N,64
         DO 100 I1 = 0,63,4
            X = X + A(I+I1) * B(I+I1)
            X = X + A(I+I1+1) * B(I+I1+1)
            X = X + A(I+I1+2) * B(I+I1+2)
            X = X + A(I+I1+3) * B(I+I1+3)
  100    CONTINUE
  200 CONTINUE
```

should be rewritten like this:

```
      DO 200 I = 1,N
         X = X + A(I) * B(I)
  200 CONTINUE
```

Correspondence between loop nests and array axes Stripmining and loop unrolling are alike in that they destroy a one-to-one correspondence between loop nesting levels and array axes. In scalable programs, this correspondence is fostered and maintained.

By going to an extreme and writing in a "loop data parallel" style, in which each loop nest operates on as many of the data (as many of the array axes, and as much of each array axis) as possible, doing identical or nearly identical operations on each iteration, one can provide a compiler with a clear expression of intent, and in so doing create fertile ground for optimization as well as enable vector and parallel execution.

This principle is likely to find application in grid-style computation where boundary conditions need to be treated differently. Separate interior and boundary loop nests can often be combined into a single loop nest by using mask variables or coefficients set up ahead of time.

So, code like this:

```
      REAL A(N,M), B(N,M)
      ...
      DO 100 J = 1,M
         A(1,J) = 0.0
100   CONTINUE
      DO 101 J = 1,M
         A(N,J) = 1.0
101   CONTINUE
      DO 102 I = 2,N-1
         A(I,1) = 0.0
102   CONTINUE
      DO 103 I = 2,N-1
         A(I,M) = -1.0
103   CONTINUE
      DO 104 J = 2,M-1
         DO 104 I = 2,N-1
            A(I,J) = B(I,J)
104   CONTINUE
```

should be rewritten like this:

```
      REAL A(N,M), B(N,M)
      ...
      DO 100 J = 1,M
         DO 100 I = 1,N
            A(I,J) = MULMASK(I,J) * B(I,J) + ADDMASK(I,J)
100   CONTINUE
```

where MULMASK contains 1.0 at the interior points and is 0.0 elsewhere, while ADDMASK contains 0.0 at the interior points and 0.0, 1.0, and −1.0 along the appropriate edges. Most modern machines can do the multiply–add at a small multiple of memory speed, and looping over the whole array obviates masking on vector and parallel machines.

Machine-specific code   When machine-specific versions of a piece of code are called for, scalable versions should always be retained and made available through some compile time, link time, or run time conditionalization mechanism. It is important that the correctness of any optimized, machine-specific code be easy to verify against the general, scalable version of the same code. There are several options for conditionalizing machine-specific versions of code, including the following three:

(1) The C preprocessor cpp and directives such as #ifdef. For example, if dot product were a highly speed-critical operation,[†] it might be written in this way:

```
#if defined(ABC)
C--    On the ABC machine, use the ABC_DOTP library routine:
       CALL ABC_DOTP(X, A, B, N)
#elif defined(XYZ)
C--    On the XYZ machine, use the XYZ_DOTPROD library function:
       X = XYZ_DOTPROD(A, B, N)
#else
C--    On all other machines, use this loop:
       X = 0.0
       DO 100 I = 1,N
          X = X + A(I) * B(I)
100 CONTINUE
#endif
```

With this approach, code can be conditionalized down to the line level, but recompilation is needed to compare different variants of the same piece of code.

(2) Link-time decision as to which variant of a subprogram to use. With this approach, code is conditionalized at the subprogram level, and subprograms are compiled separately; so relinking is all that is required to produce a different version of a program. For example:

```
       CALL MY_DOTPRODUCT(X, A, B, N)
```

where MY_DOTPRODUCT is defined three ways in three separate files:

```
abc-dotp.f:
       SUBROUTINE MY_DOTPRODUCT(X, A, B, N)
       REAL A(N), B(N)
       CALL ABC_DOTP(X, A, B, N)
       END

xyz-dotp.f:
       SUBROUTINE MY_DOTPRODUCT(X, A, B, N)
       REAL A(N), B(N)
       X = XYZ_DOTPROD(A, B, N)
       END

generic-dotp.f:
       SUBROUTINE MY_DOTPRODUCT(X, A, B, N)
       REAL A(N), B(N)
       X = 0.0
       DO 100 I = 1,N
          X = X + A(I) * B(I)
100 CONTINUE
       END
```

When a vendor supplies optimized subroutine libraries, this is a very effective approach to improving performance while maintaining portability and scalability.

[†] Of course, dot product is a very simple, low-level operation that most compilers on most machines will generate fairly good code for when written plainly. Its appearance here is for illustrative purposes. In practice, code conditionalization would be used for higher-level operations such as equation solvers or sorting routines.

(3) Run-time determination of which variant of code to execute on either the sub-routine or the loop nest level. For example:

```
      X = 0.0
      IF (UNROLL_DOTP) THEN
C--   If loop unrolling is enabled for dot products, use this loop:
      DO 100 I = 1,N,8
          X = X + A(I)   * B(I)   + A(I+1) * B(I+1)
     &             + A(I+2) * B(I+2) + A(I+3) * B(I+3)
     &             + A(I+4) * B(I+4) + A(I+5) * B(I+5)
     &             + A(I+6) * B(I+6) + A(I+7) * B(I+7)
100     CONTINUE
      ELSE
C--   Otherwise use this generic version:
      DO 200 I = 1,N
          X = X + A(I) * B(I)
200     CONTINUE
      ENDIF
```

This approach allows one to select different variants without recompiling or relinking, but may require changing the interface to a program to include new switches to indicate which variants are to be used. The level of conditionalization should be chosen so that switch tests do not appear inside loops or introduce paths of control flow which may be hard for a compiler to analyze or for other programmers to understand.

Scalable Data Structures

Just as one should try to use control structures in a straightforward, clear way, one should use data structures in a simple and direct fashion, avoiding tricks that might obscure the intended nature of the data. Unfortunately, the base data structures available in Fortran 77 very often fall short of cleanly representing complicated data. When Fortran 77 data structures are up to the task, data should be organized in such a way that they are easy to operate on with a clean loop structure as described in the previous subsection.

Literal integer constants as array dimensions Array dimensions often affect performance significantly. For example, on machines with interleaved-memory systems powers of two are generally to be avoided, while on many massively parallel systems powers of two are often desirable. To make switching between systems easier, one should avoid placing literal integer constants in array declaration statements and instead use PARAMETER statements to define axis extents. For large programs, these PARAMETER statements should be placed in a single INCLUDE file.

So, code like this:

```
      REAL A(128,64), B(128,64), ONECOL(128), ONEROW(64)
      ...
      DO 200 J = 1,64
          DO 100 I = 1,128
          ...
100     CONTINUE
200 CONTINUE
```

should be rewritten like this:

```
      PARAMETER (NROWS = 128, NCOLS = 64)
      ...
      REAL A(NROWS,NCOLS), B(NROWS,NCOLS), ONECOL(NROWS), ONEROW(NCOLS)
      ...
      DO 200 J = 1,NCOLS
         DO 100 I = 1,NROWS
            ...
100      CONTINUE
200 CONTINUE
```

Missing or incorrect trailing dimensions Supply as much information as possible, even if it is not strictly required, because some compilers may be able to use it to produce better code. For example, Fortran 77 permits one to omit the extent of the last dimension in the declaration of a dummy array argument, replacing it with *. On linear-memory machines (more on this below) the last dimension is not needed for address calculations, but this robs the compiler of information which might be helpful on other machines. The extent of the last dimension should be passed from the caller as an additional argument.

So, code like this:

```
      REAL A(N1), B(N1)
      CALL FROB_PART(A, B, N2)
      ...
      SUBROUTINE FROB_PART(A, B, L)
      REAL A(*), B(*)
      ...
```

should be rewritten like this:

```
      REAL A(N1), B(N1)
      CALL FROB_PART(A, B, N1, N2)
      ...
      SUBROUTINE FROB_PART(A, B, N, L)
      REAL A(N), B(N)
      ...
```

A more serious problem—because it can affect code correctness—is the practice of lying to the compiler, as was often done in older Fortran dialects. Rather than *, programmers used 1 in the trailing dimension. This practice is still visible today: the Basic Linear Algebra Subprograms (or BLAS)[7, 8] and the much-used code fragments listed in *Numerical Recipes*[9] are littered with trailing dimensions of 1. In these situations, the real extent should be passed and used as above.

The trailing dimension issue is a special case of reliance on sequence association, which is discussed in general later in this section.

Dynamic memory allocation Fortran 77 does not support dynamic memory allocation. This omission forces programmers to step outside the language and resort to either nonstandard constructs or "dirty tricks" to directly manipulate addresses and the areas of memory to which they point. Since dynamic memory allocation is required to implement many real-world applications, anyone hoping to develop a scalable application must, at some point, address this problem. Static allocation—for example, declaring a "big enough" array and just using part of it—will not scale well to many distributed-memory machines because block allocation will leave some processors idle, and it also wastes memory that might be better put to other uses.

Because there is no dynamic memory allocation standard for Fortran 77, some form of conditionalization will be necessary to achieve portability. Dynamic memory allocation calls written in a rigid, idiomatic style will be fairly easy to modify. It is important to provide as much information as possible, even if a particular machine or compiler will not use it. If, for example, an implementation-specific allocation routine takes only an integer representing the number of bytes to allocate (like C's `malloc`), then in using it to allocate an array one should somehow make available in the program text the extents of all array axes as well as some indication of the element type.

So, code like this:

```
C--   Allocate an N x 10 array of integers, assuming a 32-bit wordsize:
      CALL MYALLOC(PTR,N*40)
```

should be rewritten like this:

```
      PARAMETER (IBYTES_PER_INTEGER = 4)
      ...
C--   Allocate an N x 10 array of integers:
      CALL MYALLOC(PTR,N*10*IBYTES_PER_INTEGER)
```

If all allocation calls provide this information in the same format, then conversion to a new dynamic memory scheme can be a simple matter of text manipulation, which can be automated (e.g., with a `sed` script). For example, the above can be easily recast in the CMAX Fortran 77 dynamic memory allocation scheme as

```
C--   Allocate an N x 10 array of integers:
      CALL CMAX_ALLOCATE_2(PTR,CMAX_INTEGER,N,10)
```

The CMAX dynamic memory allocation is fully portable (it does not require any language extensions like `%val` or `pointer`) and easily implementable on a wide variety of machines. It is described at the end of this chapter.

Storage and sequence association Fortran 77 programmers often exploit storage association and sequence association. At their most general, both forms of association rely on a linear-memory model, and because objects so associated are constrained to be allocated contiguously, distribution of data—necessary for parallelism in distributed-memory computers—is curtailed. Thus, storage and sequence association are fundamentally nonscalable.

Storage association is the overlapping of data objects, possibly of different data types and sizes, accomplished via `EQUIVALENCE` or inconsistent `COMMON` declarations.

One reason `EQUIVALENCE` and inconsistent `COMMON` declarations are used is to save memory. Different arrays, used in nonoverlapping parts of the program, are overlapped to save space. To improve scalability, this practice should be avoided. (If memory is truly at a premium, it may be appropriate to use some sort of dynamic memory allocation.)

So, code like this:

```
C--   Overlap small arrays A and B with large array C:
      REAL A(10000), B(10000), C(20000)
      EQUIVALENCE (A(1), C(1)), (B(1), C(10001))
```

should be rewritten like this:

```
C--   Don't overlap arrays:
      REAL A(10000), B(10000), C(20000)
```

and code like this:

```
      SUBROUTINE A
C--   Use BUFSPACE as one big array
      COMMON /BUFSPACE/ BUF_IN(10001)
      ...
      SUBROUTINE B
C--   Carve BUFSPACE into two smaller arrays and one scalar
      COMMON /BUFSPACE/ BUF_OUT1(5000), BUF_OUT2(5000), BUF_OUT3
```

should be rewritten like this:

```
      SUBROUTINE A
C--   Use BUFSPACE1 for BUF_IN
      COMMON /BUFSPACE1/ BUF_IN(10001)
      ...
      SUBROUTINE B
C--   Use BUFSPACE2 for BUF_OUT
      COMMON /BUFSPACE2/ BUF_OUT1(5000), BUF_OUT2(5000), BUF_OUT3
```

Another use of storage association is to subvert the type system. In general, such subversion is not portable and so should be avoided. When absolutely necessary, these nonportable operations should be conditionalized, and implementation-specific intrinsic functions (e.g., for bit manipulation) should be used instead of EQUIVALENCE and inconsistent COMMON declarations. Many Fortran 77 implementations support the MIL-STD-1753 intrinsic functions for bit manipulation.

Sequence association is the reliance on column-major memory order in dimensioning array arguments differently between caller and callee. For example, in the array

```
      REAL X(10,10)
```

element X(1,1) is followed in memory by element X(2,1), element X(10,1) is followed by element X(1,2), and so on.

In one of the most common occurrences of sequence association, multidimensional arrays are passed to subroutines which redeclare them as one dimensional for convenience. Scalable code passes all dimensions and declares dummy arguments consistently with actual arguments.

So, code like this:

```
      REAL A(N,N,N)
      CALL CLEAR_ARRAY(A, N*N*N)
      ...
      SUBROUTINE CLEAR_ARRAY(A, N)
      REAL A(N)
      DO 100 I = 1,N
         A(I) = 0.0
100 CONTINUE
      END
```

should be rewritten like this:

```
      REAL A(N,N,N)
      CALL CLEAR_ARRAY_3D(A, N, N, N)
      ...
      SUBROUTINE CLEAR_ARRAY_3D(A, N1, N2, N3)
      REAL A(N1,N2,N3)
      DO 100 I3 = 1,N3
         DO 100 I2 = 1,N2
            DO 100 I1 = 1,N1
               A(I1,I2,I3) = 0.0
100 CONTINUE
      END
```

A related practice is to do address arithmetic "by hand" at the source level, to build multidimensional data structures out of one-dimensional arrays. This obscures the multidimensional nature of the structure, and is unnecessary with modern compilers which can almost always do a *better* job of optimizing address arithmetic than a programmer operating at the source level.

So, code like this:

```
      DO 200 I3 = 2,N-1
         DO 200 I2 = 2,N-1
            DO 200 I1 = 2,N-1
               A(I1 + (I2-1)*N + (I3-1)*N*N) = I1 + I2 + I3
200 CONTINUE
```

should be rewritten like this:

```
      DO 200 I3 = 2,N-1
         DO 200 I2 = 2,N-1
            DO 200 I1 = 2,N-1
               A(I1,I2,I3) = I1 + I2 + I3
200 CONTINUE
```

Scalable code declares multidimensional data *as* multidimensional data consistently throughout a program.

Summary of Scalability Rules

When writing scalable programs:

- **Don't** use GOTO indiscriminately.
  Do use DO and block IF.

- **Don't** stripmine or unroll loops.
  Do establish a one-to-one correspondence between levels of loop nesting and array axes.

- **Don't** use many small loop nests where one large one will suffice.
  Do write in a "loop data parallel" style, in which each loop nest operates on as many of the data (as many of the array axes, and as much of each array axis) as possible, doing identical or nearly identical operations on each iteration.

- **Don't** apply machine-specific optimizations to the master version of a code.
  Do retain a generic, scalable version of that code which can be selected through some conditionalization mechanism. Also, use vendor-supplied libraries when appropriate.

- **Don't** use literal integer constants in array declarations.
  Do use `PARAMETER` statements to define symbolic names for axis extents, and centralize information in `INCLUDE` files.

- **Don't** bury information in calls to dynamic memory allocation routines.
  Do supply complete information to such routines, and write calls to them in a way that simplifies conversion to other schemes.

- **Don't** exploit storage association or sequence association.
  Do declare data consistently throughout a program, using arrays with the correct number of dimensions.

8.3 Analysis of Scalable Code

This section contains scalable code fragments for several common operations. The fragments presented in this section are accompanied by the performance results from Sun™ and IBM workstations, a Cray Y-MP, and the results of translation using CMAX (a Fortran 77 to Connection Machine Fortran translation tool[10]) and KAP (a Fortran preprocessor which discovers and makes explicit parallelism in a program[6]). The vectorization capabilities of CMAX and KAP are fairly representative of tools available on the market today.

The versions of software used were:

- Sun Fortran 1.4

- IBM AIX™ XL Fortran 02.02.0100.0003

- Cray Fortran CFT77 6.0.0

- CMAX 1.0

- KAP 6.23.

The Sun timings were done on a Sun 4/490; the IBM RS/6000™ timings were done on a model 320H; and the Cray timings were done on one processor of a Y-MP.

Elementwise computation Consider this elementwise array addition:

```
        DO 100 I3 = 1,N3
           DO 100 I2 = 1,N2
              DO 100 I1 = 1,N1
                 A(I1,I2,I3) = B(I1,I2,I3) + C(I1,I2,I3)
100 CONTINUE
```

This *loop order*—the I3 loop outside the I2 loop outside the I1 loop—is chosen for several reasons. On linear-memory machines, contiguous memory locations will be accessed on successive iterations, which enhances cache and paging behavior on uni-processors and does not adversely affect parallelization or vectorization.

This table shows CPU times (in seconds) for executing an elementwise add like the above for all six possible loop orders, with N1 = N2 = N3 = 64:

	Sun		IBM		Cray		Vectorizes	
Loop order	no opt	-O	no opt	-O	no opt	-Zv	CMAX	KAP
1–2–3	1.30	1.23	1.56	0.68	0.0190	0.0019	✓	✓
2–1–3	1.30	1.12	1.56	0.68	0.0180	0.0020	✓	✓
2–3–1	0.67	0.57	1.03	0.68	0.0042	0.0020	✓	✓
3–2–1	0.66	0.54	1.03	0.68	0.0042	0.0019	✓	✓
3–1–2	0.66	0.56	1.56	0.68	0.0180	0.0019	✓	✓
1–3–2	0.72	0.59	1.56	0.68	0.0190	0.0020	✓	✓

The suggested ordering, 3–2–1, is the fastest under all circumstances. With simple dependence-free computation like this, loop ordering does not affect vectorization with either CMAX or KAP.

A compiler for a shared-memory parallel machine can distribute iterations of the outer loop(s) across processors. Because the inner loop(s) access contiguous blocks of memory, there will be little memory contention between parallel tasks.

The clear, simple structure of the loop body makes conversion into parallel code relatively easy. The CMAX converter, for example, will readily turn the above into this parallel array assignment:

```
        A(1:N1,1:N2,1:N3) = B(1:N1,1:N2,1:N3) + C(1:N1,1:N2,1:N3)
```

Now consider this loop nest:

```
        DO 100 I3 = 1,N3
           DO 100 I2 = 1,N2
              DO 100 I1 = 1,N2
                 X = A(I1,I2,I3) + B(I1,I2,I3) + C(I1,I2,I3)
                 C(I1,I2,I3) = X * X
100 CONTINUE
```

The scalar, X, is used as a temporary inside the loop, taking on a new value with each iteration. The presence of the scalar does not prohibit vector or parallel execution because it can be *promoted* to an array, like this:

```
      DO 200 I3 = 1,N3
        DO 200 I2 = 1,N2
          DO 200 I1 = 1,N2
            XTEMP(I1,I2,I3) = A(I1,I2,I3) + B(I1,I2,I3) + C(I1,I2,I3)
            C(I1,I2,I3) = XTEMP(I1,I2,I3) * XTEMP(I1,I2,I3)
  200 CONTINUE
```

While a programmer could make this transformation at the source code level, the previous version of the loop, with the unpromoted scalar, is more scalable because that code is more likely to be compiled efficiently on serial machines, where the value of X can be stored in a register. This avoids a problem that might occur with a compiler which does not do dead-store elimination; for the second version of code, the compiler will issue a memory write for XTEMP(I1,I2,I3), hurting performance. Compilers for vector and parallel machines should be clever enough to promote the scalar automatically.

The table below shows CPU times (in seconds) for executing the above code: N1 = N2 = N3 = 64:

| Version | Sun | | IBM | | Cray | | Vectorizes | |
	no opt	-O	no opt	-O	no opt	-Zv	CMAX	KAP
Array temp	1.20	0.94	1.66	1.04	0.0060	0.0035	✓	✓
Scalar temp	0.84	0.60	1.19	0.71	0.0059	0.0036	✓	✓

The suggested way of writing using a scalar temporary is fastest under all circumstances, except on the Cray, where the two versions perform almost identically. Again, both versions vectorize well.

Array indexing Multidimensional arrays are more structured than one-dimensional arrays, and multidimensional operations upon them can be expressed more clearly and cleanly than upon one-dimensional arrays. When one implements a multidimensional data structure with a one-dimensional array, doing address arithmetic for array indexing "by hand," one sacrifices performance and vectorizability.

This code, in which array indexing is done by hand:

```
      DO 200 I3 = 2,N-1
        DO 200 I2 = 2,N-1
          DO 200 I1 = 2,N-1
            A(I1 + (I2-1)*N + (I3-1)*N*N) = I1 + I2 + I3
  200 CONTINUE
```

should be rewritten like this, to use multidimensional indexing:

```
      DO 200 I3 = 2,N-1
        DO 200 I2 = 2,N-1
          DO 200 I1 = 2,N-1
            A(I1,I2,I3) = I1 + I2 + I3
  200 CONTINUE
```

This table shows CPU times (in seconds) for executing the above code: N = 64:

Version	Sun no opt	Sun -O	IBM no opt	IBM -O	Cray no opt	Cray -Zv	Vectorizes CMAX	Vectorizes KAP
Indexing by hand	0.21	0.12	0.33	0.08	0.011	0.011		✓
Multidim. indexing	0.16	0.12	0.27	0.08	0.011	0.011	✓	✓

Multidimensional indexing is faster and more vectorizable than array indexing by hand.

Reductions In writing reduction operations, such as those provided by the Fortran 90 SUM and MAXVAL intrinsic functions, one should follow the control structure and loop ordering rules for elementwise computation. To sum the elements of a 3-d array, write:

```
      X = 0.0
      DO 100 I3 = 1,N3
         DO 100 I2 = 1,N2
            DO 100 I1 = 1,N1
               X = X + A(I1,I2,I3)
  100 CONTINUE
```

The dependence is limited to one line and is simple enough that idiom recognition in vector or parallel compilers will recognize the operation. When writing for a shared-memory parallel machine, one may be tempted to split X into several variables and compute partial sums in each to avoid memory contention, but this optimization obscures intent, and may not scale well to many processors. If a particular compiler does not recognize the reduction operation, then code conditionalization can be used.

There are several ways MINVAL and MAXVAL could be written in Fortran 77 but, as usual, simpler is better. Because many compilers do not recognize control flow as part of reduction idioms, IF-free code, like this:

```
      X = 0.0
      DO 100 I3 = 1,N3
         DO 100 I2 = 1,N2
            DO 100 I1 = 1,N1
               X = MAX(X, A(I1,I2,I3))
  100 CONTINUE
```

is preferred to:

```
      X = 0.0
      DO 100 I3 = 1,N3
         DO 100 I2 = 1,N2
            DO 100 I1 = 1,N1
               IF (A(I1,I2,I3) .GT. X) X = A(I1,I2,I3)
  100 CONTINUE
```

For N1 = N2 = N3 = 64, for 100 iterations:

Version	Sun no opt	Sun -O	IBM no opt	IBM -O	Cray no opt	Cray -Zv	Vectorizes CMAX	Vectorizes KAP
IF	0.19	0.10	0.37	0.12	0.014	0.0033	✓	✓
MAX	0.37	0.12	0.37	0.12	0.014	0.0033	✓	✓

The loop using MAX is slower than the IF code on the Sun; otherwise, performance seems identical. Both versions vectorize with both KAP and CMAX.

When computing MAXLOC and MINLOC, one must use IF. However, the way one writes still matters. One way of writing MINLOC appears in the Livermore Loops[11] as Kernel 24:

```
1024        M= 1
     DO 24  K= 2,N
         IF( X(K).LT.X(M))  M= K
     24 CONTINUE
```

Here, a scalar variable is not used to hold the running minimum; instead, the array is referenced twice in the test. By holding the running minimum explicitly in a scalar, the number of memory references to the array can be decreased and the code made clearer to both humans and compilers.

So, code like this, which keeps the running maximum implicitly:

```
     DO 100 I = 2,N
         IF (A(I) .GT. A(ILOC)) ILOC = I
     100 CONTINUE
```

should be rewritten like this to keep the running maximum explicitly:

```
     DO 100 I = 1,N
         IF (A(I) .GT. X) THEN
             X = A(I)
             ILOC = I
         END IF
     100 CONTINUE
```

This table shows CPU times (in seconds) for executing the above code: N = 262144:

	Sun		IBM		Cray		Vectorizes	
Version	no opt	-O	no opt	-O	no opt	-Zv	CMAX	KAP
Implicit maximum	0.19	0.13	0.33	0.11	0.074	0.0055		✓
Explicit maximum	0.17	0.09	0.29	0.10	0.066	0.0055	✓	✓

The explicit running maximum code is faster on all machines. With an explicit running maximum, the code is vectorized by both CMAX and KAP; with an implicit running maximum, only KAP can vectorize the code.

Stencils Many programs (e.g., those that do image processing or finite element analysis) compute functions of nearest neighbors of array elements; this general class of operations has been called "stencil computation."

Writing stencils in Fortran 77 is rather straightforward. However, note that this loop nest, with four loops,

```
     DO 200 J = 2,N-1
         DO 200 I = 2,N-1
             A(I,J) = 0.0
             DO 100 J1 = -1,1
                 DO 100 I1 = -1,1
                     A(I,J) = COEFF * B(I+I1,J+J1)
```

```
100        CONTINUE
200 CONTINUE
```

violates the rule of correspondence between array axes and loops; in this case, there are
more levels of loop nesting than there are array axes. Far better is to write out the entire
expression for each element of the destination array so that one array element is computed per iteration of the inner loop:

```
DO 200 J = 2,N-1
    DO 200 I = 2,N-1
        A(I,J) = COEFF * (B(I-1,J-1) + B(I-1,J) + B(I-1,J+1) +
&                          B(I,J-1)   + B(I,J)   + B(I,J+1) +
&                          B(I+1,J-1) + B(I+1,J) + B(I+1,J+1))
200 CONTINUE
```

The second version of the code runs significantly faster on vector and serial computers
and is more easily translated (because of its simpler loop structure) for execution on
parallel computers.

This table shows CPU times (in seconds) for executing the above code: N = 512:

Version	Sun		IBM		Cray		Vectorizes	
	no opt	-O	no opt	-O	no opt	-Zv	CMAX	KAP
4 loops	3.05	2.03	4.24	0.47	0.240	0.025		
2 loops	0.96	0.62	0.86	0.27	0.014	0.014	✓	✓

The 2-loop version is completely vectorized by both CMAX and KAP; the 4-loop version is only partially vectorized by KAP and not at all by CMAX. The 2-loop version
significantly outperforms the 4-loop version on all platforms.

Exception testing Statements executed only under exceptional circumstances (e.g.,
the consequent of an error check) should be moved out of loops, and tests should be
rewritten in a way that permits vectorization.

So, code like this:

```
DO 100 I3 = 1,N
    DO 100 I2 = 1,N
        DO 100 I1 = 1,N
            IF (A(I1,I2,I3) .EQ. 0.0) THEN
                PRINT *, ' Bad element detected.'
                STOP
            ELSE
                C(I1,I2,I3) = B(I1,I2,I3) * A(I1,I2,I3)
            END IF
100 CONTINUE
```

should be rewritten like this:

```
BADELT = .FALSE.
DO 100 I3 = 1,N
    DO 100 I2 = 1,N
        DO 100 I1 = 1,N
            BADELT = BADELT .OR. (A(I1,I2,I3) .EQ. 0.0)
            C(I1,I2,I3) = B(I1,I2,I3) * A(I1,I2,I3)
```

```
100 CONTINUE
    IF (BADELT) THEN
        PRINT *, ' Bad element detected.'
        STOP
    END IF
```

Here, BADELT can be computed using a reduction operation (e.g., Fortran 90's ANY intrinsic). This table shows CPU times (in seconds) for executing the above code, with N = 512:

Version	Sun no opt	Sun -O	IBM no opt	IBM -O	Cray no opt	Cray -Zv	Vectorizes CMAX	Vectorizes KAP
Test in loop	0.80	0.59	1.28	0.68	0.0066	0.0066		
Test out of loop	0.88	0.59	1.33	0.74	0.0100	0.0050	✓	✓

The version with the exception code moved out of the loop vectorizes with both KAP and CMAX. With optimization this version is better on the Cray, presumably because the simplified control structure creates more opportunity for optimization. On the Sun and IBM workstations the suggested code is slightly slower than the other version; optimization nearly eliminates this difference.

Summary Following scalability guidelines leads to programs that not only vectorize well, but often significantly outperform nonscalable code even on serial machines. In the few cases where performance is hurt by following scalability rules, the difference in performance is small.

8.4 Some Case Studies in Scalable Programming

The idea of writing scalable programs in Fortran 77 is relatively new. This section describes three early experiences.

FLO67 This is a computational aerodynamics code developed by Antony Jameson of the Department of Aerospace Engineering, Princeton University. The program simulates three-dimensional airflow past a swept wing and was originally implemented in approximately 5000 lines of Fortran 77 code. As a proof of concept for the idea of scalable programming, the program was rewritten at Thinking Machines Corporation in scalable Fortran 77. The scalable code performs less than 10% worse that the original code on serial machines (Sun 4/490 and IBM RS/6000), and the CMAX translation of this scalable code into CM Fortran performs less than 10% worse than a hand-ported CM Fortran version on a CM-200.[12]

ARPS This atmospheric model from Kelvin Droegemeier at the Center for Analysis and Prediction of Storms, University of Oklahoma, contains over 50,000 lines of modern, well-written Fortran 77.[13] It was implemented by programmers who had a mental model of a parallel machine and avoided making assumptions about the underlying memory model. It took four days to initially port version 3.1 of the ARPS from the IBM RS/6000 to a Connection Machine system.

About 500 lines were changed or added in the initial port, most of which involved manually specifying the distribution of arrays. Ninety-nine percent of the work was done by CMAX, and most of the user's time was devoted to running the application through CMAX and making improvements to the Fortran 77 version based on the efficiency notes.

The tuning of the ARPS for the Connection Machine was done part-time over a period of a few weeks, at the end of which large atmospheric models were being run efficiently on large CM-5 systems. This work was cited by the IEEE in 1993 in their annual Gordon Bell Prize for Significant Achievements in Parallel Processing.[14] We feel the careful engineering of the program is largely responsible for the ease with which it ported. The ARPS was scalable from the start.

X-PLOR This software package for structure determination of biological macromolecules was written by Axel T. Brunger of Yale University.[15] It consists of 70,000 lines of Fortran 77 optimized for vector machines, and it can perform a wide range of the computations needed for X-ray crystallography and nuclear magnetic resonance studies. This program is only slightly larger than the ARPS, but because of its age it presented a much greater challenge to CMAX. After three months of effort, the entire application was successfully passed through CMAX, after which testing and tuning began.

X-PLOR is quite clearly an older, nonscalable program, and is representative of many vector-era programs. As tools improve and the concepts of scalable programming propagate, such ports will become easier in the future.

8.5 Conclusion

This chapter has shown how to construct scalable programs in Fortran 77. Timings and analysis have been presented which show that programs constructed using the techniques and guidelines given perform well across a wide variety of computer architectures and are suitable for translation and execution on vector and parallel computers.

APPENDIX: A Portable Scheme for Dynamic Memory Allocation

CMAX[3, 10] provides a portable facility for allocating dynamic memory. The interface provided by CMAX can be easily re-implemented on a wide variety of machines. The two important features of the design are

- Completely portable use of the facility; no features outside standard Fortran 77 (such as %val or pointer) are required to allocate, manipulate, or deallocate arrays dynamically.

- The interface forces one to fully specify arrays that are to be allocated. In contrast with schemes like Sun Fortran's malloc, which allocate memory in units of bytes, the CMAX scheme requires one to provide the array element type and extents of all array axes. This means that all the information needed to convert that allocation into any other scheme is available.

Calls to allocate and use dynamic memory are kept within the bounds of Fortran 77 by exploiting a trick which essentially relies on sequence association. The "pointer" to allocated memory is returned as an integer offset from the start of a known array. Use of the pointer is accomplished by means of procedure call and array indexing. Because procedure calls in Fortran pass objects by address, indexing into the known array is essentially doing address arithmetic, and the constructed address refers to the dynamically allocated object.

The statement

```
CALL CMAX_ALLOCATE_1(INDEX, CMAX_INTEGER, N)
```

assigns to INDEX the "pointer" to a newly allocated memory region with enough room for N integers. The "pointer" is an integer offset from the beginning of the COMMON array CMAX_MEMORY, and so the allocated memory can be used like this:

```
CALL DO_STUFF(CMAX_MEMORY(INDEX), N)
...
SUBROUTINE DO_STUFF(IARRAY, N)
INTEGER IARRAY(N)
...
```

Strictly speaking, this trick violates some of the rules of scalable data structures; however, the fact that enough information is available for a tool like CMAX to understand the programmer's intent makes up for the non-scalability. Without stepping outside the language, it is not possible to do dynamic array allocation.

The remainder of this section describes the interface.

Header file The cmax.h header file declares the PARAMETERs CMAX_LOGICAL, CMAX_INTEGER, CMAX_REAL, CMAX_COMPLEX, CMAX_DOUBLE, and CMAX_DOUBLE_COMPLEX, which are used to name element types of dynamic arrays.

The header file also declares a COMMON block array CMAX_MEMORY which is used as the base address for allocated memory as described above.

Allocation Arrays of one to seven dimensions (the most required by the Fortran 77 specification) are allocated using calls to one of seven subroutines, CMAX_ALLOCATE_1 to CMAX_ALLOCATE_7. The first argument to each is the index variable to be set; the second argument is the element type (one of the above PARAMETERs); and the third and all subsequent arguments are the extents of the array axes:

```
CALL CMAX_ALLOCATE_1(INDEX1, CMAX_INTEGER, N1)
CALL CMAX_ALLOCATE_2(INDEX2, CMAX_INTEGER, N1, N2)
CALL CMAX_ALLOCATE_3(INDEX3, CMAX_INTEGER, N1, N2, N3)
...
CALL CMAX_ALLOCATE_7(INDEX7, CMAX_INTEGER, N1, N2, ..., N7)
```

Implementation note: The CMAX converter requires that the same index variables be used only for arrays of the same number of dimensions. Index variables may be elements of arrays themselves, in which case all arrays pointed to by an element of the index variable array must be of the same number of dimensions.

Using allocated memory Allocated memory is accessed relative to the base object CMAX_MEMORY:

```
CALL DO_STUFF(CMAX_MEMORY(INDEX), N)
```

Implementation note: The CMAX converter requires that allocated memory be accessed only in called routines. Thus, a loop like the following is prohibited:

```
      DO 100 I = 1,N
          CMAX_MEMORY(INDEX+I-1) = 0.0
  100 CONTINUE
```

Deallocation   Memory is deallocated by passing the index variable to the subroutine CMAX_DEALLOCATE:

```
      CALL CMAX_DEALLOCATE(INDEX1)
      CALL CMAX_DEALLOCATE(INDEX2)
      CALL CMAX_DEALLOCATE(INDEX3)
 ...
      CALL CMAX_DEALLOCATE(INDEX7)
```

Header File

Here is the header file cmax.h:

```
      INTEGER CMAX_MEMORY
      COMMON /CMAX_MEMORY_BLOCK/ CMAX_MEMORY(1) CMF$  LAYOUT CMAX_MEMORY(:SERIAL)

      INTEGER CMAX_LOGICAL
      INTEGER CMAX_INTEGER
      INTEGER CMAX_REAL
      INTEGER CMAX_COMPLEX
      INTEGER CMAX_DOUBLE
      INTEGER CMAX_DOUBLE_COMPLEX

      PARAMETER (CMAX_LOGICAL = 1)
      PARAMETER (CMAX_INTEGER = 2)
      PARAMETER (CMAX_REAL = 3)
      PARAMETER (CMAX_COMPLEX = 4)
      PARAMETER (CMAX_DOUBLE = 5)
      PARAMETER (CMAX_DOUBLE_COMPLEX = 6)
```

CMAX Dynamic Memory Facility

Here is C code for the Sun implementation of the CMAX dynamic memory facility:

```
  extern int cmax_memory_block_;        /* C name of COMMON block */
  void cmax_i_allocate();               /* Forward declaration */

  /* All operands are passed by reference from Fortran to C.
     CMAX_ALLOCATE_1 dereferences the element type and N1; then it
     passes the index address, the element type, and the number of
     elements to CMAX_I_ALLOCATE which does the actual allocation. */

  void cmax_allocate_1_(i, elt_type, n1)
     int *i, *elt_type, *n1;
  { cmax_i_allocate(i, *elt_type, (*n1));
  }

  /* CMAX_ALLOCATE_2 through CMAX_ALLOCATE_7 are similar, but multiply
     the array bounds before calling CMAX_I_ALLOCATE. */

  ...
```

```
/* CMAX_I_ALLOCATE first computes the size (in bytes) of the array by
   multiplying the number of elements (SIZE) by the size of the
   element, then allocates the appropriately sized block using malloc,
   and finally stores the address of this block, as an offset from
   the beginning of CMAX_MEMORY_BLOCK, in the index variable. */

void cmax_i_allocate(p_index, elt_type, size)
    int *p_index, elt_type, size;
{ int i, total_size, temp;
  switch (elt_type) {
      case 1:                   /* cmax_logical */
         total_size = size  * sizeof(int);
         break;
      case 2:                   /* cmax_integer */
         total_size = size  * sizeof(int);
         break;
      case 3:                   /* cmax_real */
         total_size = size  * sizeof(float);
         break;
      case 4:                   /* cmax_complex */
         total_size = size  * sizeof(float) * 2;
         break;
      case 5:                   /* cmax_double */
         total_size = size  * sizeof(float) * 2;
         break;
      case 6:                   /* cmax_double_complex */
         total_size = size  * sizeof(float) * 4;
         break;
      default:
         perror("bad element type");
         break;
  }
  temp = ((int) malloc(total_size));
  *p_index = (temp - ((int) &cmax_memory_block_)) / sizeof(int) + 1;
}

/* CMAX_DEALLOCATE reconstructs the address from the index variable,
   then uses free to free the associated memory. */

void cmax_deallocate_(p_index)
    int *p_index;
{ int temp;
  temp = (*p_index - 1) * 4 + ((int) &cmax_memory_block_);
  free(temp);
}
```

References

1 J. L. Gustafson. "Reevaluating Amdahl's Law," *Communications of the ACM.* **31** (5), 532–533, 1988.

2 D. Nussbaum and A. Agarwal. "Scalability of Parallel Machines," *Communications of the ACM.* **34** (3), 56–61, 1991.

3 "Using the CMAX Converter." Thinking Machines Corporation, Cambridge, MA, 1993.

4 J. Levesque and R. Friedman. "The State of the Art in Automatic Parallelization," *Proceedings of Supercomputing Europe.* Feb. 1993.

5 "KAP User's Guide." Kuck and Associates, Urbana-Champaign, IL, 1988.

6 "VAST-2 User's Guide." Pacific Sierra Research Corporation, Los Angeles, 1986.

7 J. J. Dongarra et al. "An Extended Set of Fortran Basic Linear Algebra Subprograms," *ACM Transactions on Mathematical Software.* **14** (1), 1988.

8 C. L. Lawson et al. "Basic Linear Algebra Subprograms for Fortran Usage," *ACM Transactions on Mathematical Software.* **5** (3), 1979.

9 W. H. Press, B. Flannery, S. Teukolsky, and W. Vetterling. *Numerical Recipes: The Art of Scientific Computing.* Cambridge University Press, New York, 1990.

10 G. W. Sabot and S. Wholey. "CMAX: A Fortran Translator for the Connection Machine System," *Proceedings of 7th International Conference on Supercomputing.* 147–156, 1993.

11 F. H. McMahon. "The Livermore Fortran Kernels: A Computer Test of the Numerical Performance Range." Tech. report no. UCRL-53745, Lawrence Livermore National Laboratory, Livermore, CA, Dec. 1986.

12 S. Wholey, C. Lasser, and G. Bhanot. "FLO67: A Case Study in Scalable Programming," *International Journal of Supercomputer Applications.* **6** (4), 1992.

13 K. Droegemeier, M. Xue, K. Johnson, K. Mills, and M. O'Keefe. "Experiences with the Scalable-Parallel ARPS Cloud/Mesoscale Prediction Model on Massively Parallel and Workstation Cluster Architectures," *Proceedings of the 5th Workshop on the Use of Parallel Processors in Meteorology.* European Center for Medium Range Weather Forecasts, Nov. 1992.

14 G. W. Sabot, S. Wholey, J. Berlin, and P. Oppenheimer. "Parallel Execution of a Fortran 77 Weather Prediction Model," *Proceedings of Supercomputing '93.* 538–545, 1993.

15 A. T. Brunger. *X-PLOR Version 3.0, A System for Crystallography and NMR.* Yale University, New Haven, CT, 1992.

Index

EQUIVALENCE statement 58
Ethernet 68
exception testing 232–233

F77 compiler 80
face-centered field 28, 30–31
factorization 96, 97
fake zones 74, 75
field 28
filtering 41
fineness of grid 17
finite difference 46, 52, 53, 63
flat mesh 22
FLO67 233
Forge 217
Fortran *See* Connection Machine Fortran,
    Fortran 77, Fortran 90, Fortran-D,
    Fortran-P.
Fortran 77
    chaining of operations 101
    code versus data branching 11
    common blocks 28
    data structures 222
    dynamic memory allocation 223, 234
    message passing 84
    scalable programming 77, 217–227,
        233–234
    stencils 231–232
    trailing dimensions 223
    translation to CMF 73, 74, 77–79
Fortran 90 2–4, 7, 57, 98, 230
Fortran-D 2, 83–84
Fortran-P 57, 58, 74–77
forward substitution 75
functional decomposition 63, 68

Gaussian elimination methods 108
Gauss–Seidel iteration 14–15
generalized Schur factorization 97
Germano dynamic closure scheme 51
ghost cells 28, 30–31, 37, 38
global optimization 188
global sum 33, 34
GOTO statements 218

granularity 38, 53, 100, 126
graph
    connected components 157–159
    contraction 172–173, 176
    definition 156
    grid-based 175, 176
    planar 176
    random 176–179
    separator 156
    tertiary 176, 180
grid
    block structured 20
    border points 12
    data representations 5–6
    decomposition 20
    edge values 8
    fineness 17
    increment 68
    interior points 12
    nested 58
    nonuniform 17
    point spacing 47–48
    subdivided 58
    uniform structured 17

Hand optimizations 10
hash function 140
heuristic algorithms 194–195
High Performance Fortran
    block cyclic decomposition 112
    data decomposition 24
    NESL conversion 157
    subset of Fortran 90 2, 84
hooking 161–164, 166
host–node system 62, 84, 143–144, 148,
    149
Householder vectors 101
hydroblock 24, 28
hypercube 21, 22, 34, 149

IBM 3090 105
IBM RS/6000 66, 227, 233
IBM SP1 99
IF statements 218, 230–231